2791

Books by Karl Schriftgiesser

The Lobbyists

*The Art and Business of
Influencing Lawmakers*

KARL SCHRIFTGIESSER

The Lobbyists

The Art and Business of
Influencing Lawmakers

AN ATLANTIC MONTHLY PRESS BOOK

LITTLE, BROWN AND COMPANY · BOSTON

1951

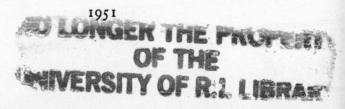

FIRST EDITION

Grateful acknowledgment is made for permission to quote from
the following:

FDR: His Personal Letters, 1928–1945. Edited by Elliott Roosevelt, assisted by Joseph P. Lash. Copyright 1950 by Elliott Roosevelt. Reprinted by permission of the publishers, Duell, Sloan and
Pearce, Inc.

The Control of Atomic Energy. By James R. Newman and
Byron S. Miller. Copyright 1948 by the McGraw-Hill Book
Company, Inc. Reprinted by permission of the publishers, the
McGraw-Hill Book Company, Inc.

The Memoirs of Cordell Hull. The Macmillan Company. Copyright 1948 by Cordell Hull. Reprinted by permission of The
Macmillan Company.

The Public Papers and Addresses of Franklin D. Roosevelt.
Edited by Samuel I. Rosenman. Random House. Copyright 1938
by Franklin Delano Roosevelt. Reprinted by permission of Mr.
Rosenman.

The Pressure Boys. By Kenneth G. Crawford. Julian Messner,
Inc. Copyright 1939 by Julian Messner, Inc. Reprinted by permission of Mr. Crawford.

ATLANTIC–LITTLE, BROWN BOOKS
ARE PUBLISHED BY
LITTLE, BROWN AND COMPANY
IN ASSOCIATION WITH
THE ATLANTIC MONTHLY PRESS

*Published simultaneously
in Canada by McClelland and Stewart Limited*

PRINTED IN THE UNITED STATES OF AMERICA

To the memory of my father
Berthold Schriftgiesser

A lobbyist is anyone who opposes legislation
I want. A patriot is anyone who supports me.

— SENATOR JAMES A. REED OF MISSOURI

We are all ready to be savage in *some* cause.
The difference between a good man and a bad
man is the choice of the cause.

— WILLIAM JAMES

Foreword

THE first amendment to the constitution of the United States secures to the people the unhindered right to petition the government for a redress of grievances. This means that you or I or our worst enemy cannot be restrained from belaboring Congress with demands for the passage or defeat of legislation, whether the demands are reasonable or unreasonable, and whether they are in the interest of the public welfare or for the betterment of private and selfish ends.

Like the other rights secured in the first amendment — freedom of speech, freedom of the press, freedom of worship, and the right of peaceable assembly — the meaning of the right of petition is tempered by the times. The basic meaning of this right does not change, but the interpretation of the meaning does. In the early days of the Republic this right had a very broad meaning indeed, but with the introduction of the first tariff measure it began to change. Private interests, working for private profit, wrapped themselves in the first amendment, sent their emissaries to Congress to act as petitioners by buttonholing susceptible Congressmen in the lobbies of the Capitol, and thus we were given a new word and a new profession.

In this book I attempt to trace the history of lobbying through its development from the simple days of personal persuasion down to the present time and to show how lobbying, which is both good and evil, has become an integral part of the democratic legislative process. It was not until 1946 that Congress took official cognizance of lobbying and, in effect, legalized it by passing the Regulation of Lobbying Act as a part of the Legislative Reorganization Act. Before this happened Congress had allowed lobbies and lobbyists to go about their good and bad activities unhindered and uncounted. From time to time they became so pestiferous pursuing their constitutional ways as to become a veritable menace to orderly legislative procedure. Often they were ignored; sometimes they were scolded. Upon occasion individuals were driven from Washington. Congress, harried, investigated and said harsh things. But nothing was done about them, although several scourging attempts were made, until 1946.

Six years later the act is still on the books. It is an act which does not prevent lobbying. It does not interfere with the right of petition. In one court case at least it has been accepted as constitutional. Its whole purpose is to provide a mechanism whereby the individual who is paid to lobby, or the individual or organization who spends money for lobbying, makes known his identity and the sources of his funds.

I have attempted to tell the story of how this act was so long coming into being, how it was finally passed by Congress, how well it has been obeyed and how badly it has been disobeyed, and what has been learned from the information filed with Congress by those who come under the provisions of the act. I have not tried to "expose" the "pressure boys," but to show the extent of lobbying as it is practiced in Washington and in the hinterland. I have tried to explore both direct and indirect lobbying. And finally I have tried to bring together the vast amount of detailed information gathered by the House Select Committee on Lobbying Activities, which in 1950 investigated "all lobbying activities intended to influence, encourage, promote, or retard legislation" by the Congress of the United States.

This is, I submit, an important story. It affects every citizen. I have tried to be objective, but I admit to one prejudice. I believe that any citizen who petitions the government for a redress of grievances should stand up and say who he is, and what he wants, why he wants it, and who paid his way.

                                                        —K. S.

Contents

APPENDICES

The Lobbyists

The Art and Business of
Influencing Lawmakers

CHAPTER I

The Right of Petition

LOBBYING is as old as legislation and pressure groups are as old as politics. Thanks to our constitutional form of government, both the pressure group and its legislative agent have become, for good or ill, an integral part of our governmental process. This extra-legislative system has its detractors and its defenders. Even if it were wholly undesirable there probably is no way, short of abolishing the first amendment to the constitution, to eliminate lobbying from Washington or from the forty-eight state capitals. It is as necessary to progressive legislation as it is to the preservation of the *status quo*. But for all its moral and legal rights to existence it has long been and will long remain one of the great problems of practical politics, a continuous source of strife and discord within our democracy.

At its highest level, which it attains more often than is perhaps generally realized, lobbying is a positive good. At its common level, if it is not closely watched, it is more often than not detrimental to the welfare of representative government. When it falls to its lowest level, as it has often done in our time, it is morally indefensible and a criminal offense against the people.

Nobody knows who was the first American lobbyist or what interest he represented. He may have been some hanger-on at the House of Burgesses in Virginia or he may have been some crusty fellow importuning the Royal Governor of the Bay Colony as to who had the better right to fish at the mouth of the

Penobscot. The first pressure group in this country to attain immortality was that little gang of painted-up merchants who pushed the British tea into the salt water of Boston Harbor.

When that "brace of Adamses" drove on to Philadelphia to attend the First Continental Congress as representatives of the restless New Englanders, they encountered the same kind of pressure tactics that the congressman is subjected to daily in Washington today. Even before they reached Philadelphia they were met by a group of lobbyists, sent to intercept them in the interests of those rich and powerful merchants — unorganized, but a "pressure group" nevertheless — who would steer the "violent men" away from any dangerous ideas of independence they might be prepared to press.

All through the sessions of the Congress lobbying went on in full force. The hogsheads of Madeira and port that were dispensed and the huge dinners of mutton and pork, duck and turkey, fools and tarts and jellies, that were served by Negro menservants on tables white with linen and bright with English silver, were not offered without a purpose. The merchants, the landowners, the Quakers, the followers of the powerful John Dickinson, used all the wiles of wealth and social prestige to prevent the delegates from the other colonies from insisting upon any drastic action that might endanger the colonial way of life. Thus early was set the pattern for pressure on the American political scene.

When the Revolution was ended the pressures from countless interests increased. The men who were assigned to draft the new constitution were fearfully aware of the dangers that awaited them from persons with ideologies to advance or private purposes to be served. They were so aware of the potentially disastrous effects which outside pressures might have upon their deliberations that they met always behind locked doors. They even refrained from keeping a written record of their proceedings lest word of their intentions leak out and they become beset by a horde of citizens seeking to advance their own interests at the expense of what the delegates believed to be the high purpose of the Constitutional Convention.

The right to lobby was not written into the original document. That was established by the first American Congress when it offered the first amendment to the people for ratification: "Congress shall make no law . . . abridging the freedom of speech or of the press; or the right of the people peaceably to assemble and to petition the government for redress of grievances."

In the days of the great debate over the form of government to be set up in the newly independent nation neither the word "lobby" nor the word "lobbyist" had been invented (except as an architectural term). But James Madison, at least, was well aware of the dangerous potentialities of the pressure group, as his famous *Federalist* (No. 10) makes clear. Substitute the word "lobby" for "faction" in its most widely quoted passage and his warning is seen to have lost little potency over the years:

"By faction," he wrote, "I understand a number of citizens, whether amounting to a majority or a minority of the whole, who are united and actuated by some common impulse of passion, or of interest, adverse to the rights of other citizens, or to the permanent and aggregate interests of the community."

The use of the word "lobby" in describing an agent of a private or corporate interest seeking to influence the duly elected representatives of the people apparently did not creep into the American language until nearly forty years after the constitution was accepted. The first recorded use of the word, according to H. L. Mencken, was in 1829, the year in which Andrew Jackson became President. It originally appeared as "lobby-agent" and was applied to seekers after special privilege at the Capitol in Albany, where Thurlow Weed and others soon made the title well and unfavorably known. Practicing journalists soon shortened the word to "lobbyist" and by 1832 its use was frequent in Washington. From the beginning it was a term of reproach and throughout the nineteenth century it was always so used. Walt Whitman, who grew up in an era which saw lobbying approach its corrupt zenith, cried out against ". . . bawling office-holders . . . kept editors . . . bribers, compromisers, lobbiers, spongers . . . the lousy combings and born freedom-sellers of the earth." Not until 1946, when Congress passed the Federal Regulation of Lobbying Act, was the term given legal, and in comparison with its earlier connotation, respectable sanction.

The history of lobbying in America is, in effect, the history of American legislation. It would be a thankless and probably useless task to try to trace it in all its details, nor could this be done, owing to the secret nature of the profession. But every reader of history knows that hirelings of every interest — railroads, manufacturers, bankers, farmers — have haunted the lobbies of every Congress, sometimes with the most corrupt intent and sometimes to press for the passage of laws which posterity has found good. And we can put our finger on a reasonably accurate date for the beginning of definite pressure tactics upon Congress — the passage of the first Tariff Act in 1789. Alexander Hamilton's Philadelphia Society for the Promotion of National Industry, founded in the early 1800's, can claim credit as the first business lobby formed for the purpose of influencing legislatures on behalf of a powerful faction.

In the 1820's the first of innumerable tariff fights took place. The failure of the Woolen Bill to pass by one vote in 1824 was the signal for a propaganda battle, fully as bitter and fought with almost the same tactics as the great barrage the lobbyists directed against the Holding Company Bill in 1935. Since then the hidden hand of the lobbyist has directed the authorship of all tariff bills that have been enacted by Congress. Prophetic of the public utility lobbyists of our own time were the tactics of the Pennsylvania Society for the Encouragement of Manufactures and the Mechanic Arts in the early nineteenth century. Not content with pressuring congressmen in its behalf, it conducted a campaign to remove the textbooks of Adam Smith and J. B. Say, his French disciple, from the schools and colleges, and even hired a German propagandist and economist, one Friedrich List, to write a substitute for these subversive texts.

A gentleman of imagination and talent, Friedrich List deserves more than passing mention in any dissertation on the history and art of lobbying. He was a stanch protectionist before emigrating to this country, where he found his nationalistic views eagerly received. He became a paid propagandist for what was then called the "American System," and this led one congressman to snap that he himself was nothing but an "importation" — in direct violation of the system he espoused! His greatest contribution to the art of lobbying was his proposal that "the friends of domestic industry should meet annually to prepare the necessary legislation for Congress after discussing the measures and gathering the facts" (in that order). It took seventy years for his idea to take definite form, but his ideal was attained in 1895 when the National Association of Manufacturers, in its time one of the most effective lobbies in the United States, was formed.

As industry developed and the nation expanded, the practice of lobbying increased a hundredfold. Throughout the 1850's special pleaders for special interests, each with his own sure-fire methods, descended by hundreds upon Washington, Albany, and other legislative centers, and these creatures, working for juicy prizes, were as responsible as their employers for making this the era in which, as Professor Roy Franklin Nichols has shown, the American democracy was disrupted.

"The host of contractors, speculators, stockjobbers, and lobby members which haunt the halls of Congress, all desirous *per fas aut nefas* and on any and every pretext to get their arms into the public treasury are sufficient to alarm every friend of his country. Their progress must be arrested." So wrote James Buchanan to Franklin Pierce in 1852.

Industrial pressure groups were coming into an alarming if little recognized existence. The National Association of Cotton Manufacturers was organized in 1854. The United States Brewers Association was soon to complain that "owners of breweries, separately, are unable to exercise a proper influence in the legislature and public administration." The American Medical Association began its long and still active career in influencing public opinion. The Bible Society of America, the American Peace Society, and the Children's Aid Society, to mention only a few, were set up to bring pressure upon legislative and administrative officials through argument, persuasion, organization, and publicity.

If Buchanan was shocked by the goings-on of the "lobby-members" in President Millard Fillmore's Washington, others were to be even more disturbed by the revelations made after Buchanan himself became President.

Several weeks before Buchanan's inauguration certain startling exposures by the *New York Times* were responsible for the eventual expulsion from Congress of one member and the resignation of three others. They had been conducting a highly lucrative lobby racket. The congressmen — and there were undoubtedly others besides those caught at the game — set up a regular scale of prices, in money or land, for their votes. Allied with them were a group of lobbyists whose function it was to let persons interested in legislation know about the scheme. Congressmen would dream up "nuisance bills," or announce themselves as opposed to legitimate proposals. Lobbyists would then get themselves hired, and whoever paid the highest price would get the vote of the corrupt congressmen, either against the "nuisance bill" or in favor of the desired legislation, as the case might be.*

* This practice has lasted down through the years but the consensus of political science investigators is that it has generally been more prevalent in state legislatures than in the Federal Congress. Warren Gamaliel Harding was adept at this game during his younger days in the Ohio State Legislature at Columbus, as I have pointed out in *This Was Normalcy.*

Public exposure did not stop this practice. A startling example of it came to light in the late 1850's when the Bay State Mills of Lawrence, Massachusetts, sent agents to Washington in an effort to modify the duties on wool. The first agent, an honorable businessman, approached congressmen with his pockets bulging with carefully prepared facts and figures. He was laughed out of town. His successor arrived in Washington with his pockets bulging with $70,000 in cold cash. The first thing he did was to hire John W. Wolcott, a professional lobbyist, who in turn hired Thurlow Weed, a vigorous preacher of high protection, and David M. Stone, a writer for the New York *Journal of Commerce*.* The latter two were paid $5,000 and $3,500 respectively

* From my own experience with and observation of the Washington press corps, I should say it was extremely doubtful if such practices are engaged in today. But that the Washington correspondent plays his important part in the over-all technique of pressure politics cannot, I am equally certain, be denied. In his excellent article ("The Press," *Holiday*, vol. 7, no. 2, February, 1950) A. J. Liebling makes the point clear that, with the exception of a few outstanding newspapers like the *New York Times*, the *Christian Science Monitor*, and one or two more, those which maintain Washington bureaus do so "partly for prestige and partly to maintain pressure on the home-region representatives in Congress." Like the Hearst and McCormick representatives (who are "members of a cult rather than reporters in the conventional sense"), whose job is "to furnish two bitter old men, one in San Simeon and the other in Chicago with a projection of an old man's fears and hates," most Washington correspondents find that they, too, must project the political, economic and social predilections of their publishers back home, rather than give an accurate account of how the laws are made and enforced from day to day. Liebling quotes Richard Strout of the *Christian Science Monitor* (which, by the way, prints more news about lobbies and lobbyists than most newspapers) as saying, "The publishers keep talking about a two-party system, but they have made a one-party press," and he gives alarming statistics which show to what a dangerous distance to the right the American press has moved while the American people have consistently moved leftward. There is, he rightly says, less divergence in outlook now than ever before in history. "One consequence is that correspondents spend a considerable portion of their time nagging at the Government instead of covering it. Another is that the most important story in Washington goes uncovered: the story of what intervenes between the expression of popular will at the polls and its enactment into law. I don't know the anatomy of the obstructive body myself, but I'd like to feel that a large force of competent journalists was digging hard to find out. How spontaneously does a 'public outcry' in defense of special privilege break

for "collecting statistics" — or what, in the present parlance of legislative agents, is known as research. Wolcott presumably pocketed the rest of the $70,000. Shortly thereafter the Bay State Mills failed. A select committee of Congress investigated, but lobbying continued unabated and unabashed in that gaudy era.

Rugged exponents of private enterprise, ruthless men like Samuel Colt, Cyrus McCormick, and Edward M. Chaffee, kept their lobby agents busy literally both day and night as they fought with Congress for renewals of their patents on revolvers, reapers and the rubber vulcanizing process. The most brazen, or perhaps the least cautious, of these striving fellows were those employed by Colt. They, and some of their fellow schemers, were exposed to public light when the Letcher Committee released its report in 1855.

Colt was shown to have paid a "contingent fee" of $10,000 to one congressman for which the latter, and presumably other congressmen under his control, refrained from attacking the patent extension bill. Heading Colt's lobby, which had head-quarters in various hotels where wine and food were free and plentiful, was the handsome and florid Alexander Hay. This estimable gentleman knew his way to a congressman's heart. He passed out many handsome and beautifully decorated revolvers which Colt had made up for the purpose but he also kept more attractive bait in the persons of three charming ladies who were professionally known as Spiritualists. According to the record they were, in that day when more than one esoteric cult flour-ished, very active in "moving with the members" of Congress. Also available were other ladies of less spiritual nature, known as "chicks," but whether (or how) they, too, moved with the

out? When Senators from the South join with Republicans to vote against the nominal head of their own party, what does each Southerner get and what does each Republican expect to get? The notion of Congressmen voting to 'get things for their district' is too rudimentary. I should like to know what things the obstructive Congressman wants to get (or preserve) for which people in his district."

members the record saith not. Some of the more resourceful received handsome fees for their patriotic endeavors.

Perhaps the greatest deluge of lobbyists ever to have poured into Washington up to that time came in the wake of the Panic of 1857.

Railroads, manufacturers, bankers and brokers had been ruined by the scores, and thousands of people were unemployed as a result of the October crash of that year, a collapse that, as we now know, had been caused by overproduction at home, overbuying abroad, the overbuilding of railroads, real estate speculations, and a completely unregulated banking system. There seemed to be only one place from which these victims could recoup their losses — the Treasury. And so businessmen, financiers, plungers, speculators and their agents rushed to the capital to beleaguer Congress for help.

"Everywhere," says Professor Nichols, "there was importunity," as what that Pulitzer historian has called some of the greatest lobby efforts in history got under way. They flooded Congress with plans and schemes for the appropriation of public lands; they poured forth bills for the subsidization of railroads, both transcontinental and strictly local; there was a "homestead proposal" to give a farm to every asker; there were proposals to strip the Indians of their remaining lands; practically every state wanted a federally subsidized agricultural college.

The bitterest battle in the corridors and lobbies in this era of unrestrained skulduggery was the one between the "strikers" (a contemporary name for lobbyists) for the Pacific Railroad and the steamship interests. Old rough and ready Commodore Vanderbilt personally took charge of the New York steamship campaign. His prime purpose was to kill the transcontinental railroad bill and to renew his contracts for carrying the mail to California by boat. As so often happens, another group of lobbyists, not often to be found siding with the New York gang, worked by his side — the representatives of Southern interests who were anxious to build up business at Southern ports and who feared the rivalry of the new, free states which the transcontinental railroads would bring into being.

While all this went on, the steamship and railroad lobbyists jostled shoulders with the huge crowd of lesser lobbyists who milled in the corridors demanding funds to widen rivers, deepen harbors, build lighthouses, docks and customhouses, post offices, barracks, hospitals, and subtreasury buildings. The pressures for government-supported "pump-priming" after the Panic of 1857 put into the shade any similar efforts during the early days of the New Deal.

In those wide-open days Washington was filled with a variety of gambling houses whose proprietors worked closely with the lobbyists. When a representative or a senator was unlucky enough to fall into debt, as he frequently did, the managers of the gambling hells had him where he would do them the most good. By threatening exposure, or by demanding payment, they could force the hapless legislator to vote as they wished. The best known of these subdivisions of Congress was Pendleton's. Here Commodore Vanderbilt, on his frequent excursions to Washington, was a regular diner. It hardly seems reasonable to assume that it was mere friendship which caused him to present a team of horses to Pendleton after one of his visits which happened to coincide with a vote on the mail contracts bill.

Not all the legislators were susceptible to the blandishments or the blackmail of the lobbyists. Even in that wild era there were some honest and disturbed men in both houses. Clement C. Clay and Robert Toombs, both Southern Democrats, tried their best to dam the flood of petitions for internal improvements from their key positions on the Senate Commerce Committee. But they found the opposition strong. A coalition of Democrats and Republicans, notoriously susceptible to a variety of private interests, made their way difficult.

In spite of the loud and expensive efforts of the lobbyists the special interests were not always successful. Colt, for example, failed at this time to get his patent renewal and so did McCormick and Chaffee. The Pacific Railroad and the Homestead bills were postponed. The agricultural land grant bill, although successful in the House, was stymied in the Senate. War pension bills, a host of ancient French spoliation claims, and a large number of Indian war damage bills were defeated (thus insuring employment for the lobbyists in the next session). When a bill for the settlement of claims by descendants of Revolutionary War officers came up in the Senate in 1857 it was damned by Senator Clay, who charged that its real authors were a gang of "meddlesome claim agents and lobby members" who, he said, had grown into a "sort of fourth estate in . . . Congress." The sum of the pressures brought against Congress forced that harassed body to appropriate $9,000,-000 more than its immediate predecessor had done and to raise the national debt to a new high level.

About this time a gentleman of wit and culture, who for the next twenty years was to revel in the title "King of the Lobby," arrived in Washington, bringing to the art of lobbying refinements in technique that have hardly been bettered since his day. His polished and painless methods of persuasion have given to Samuel Ward a sort of immortality. When the National Association of Registered Lobbyists is formed its first thought should be to place a statue of this bemustached, immaculately dressed, and twinkling-eyed gentleman just outside the doors of the House and Senate cloakrooms.

Sam Ward was what used to be known as a gentleman of parts. He was as much at home corresponding with Ralph Waldo Emerson as he was passing society chitchat with his cousin Ward McAllister, the inventor of the Four Hundred. His breakfasts of ham boiled in champagne, to which wisps of new-mown hay had been added at the proper intervals to give it flavor, were famous among his friends. He was a great student of the susceptibilities of human nature, which he had studied as a broker in Wall Street, with the philosophers, statesmen and artists of the capitals of Europe, in the California gold fields, and during secret but highly profitable business ventures in Central America. As a lobbyist his motto was, "The way to a man's 'Aye' is through his stomach."

Sam Ward was a Copperhead when he first took his place at table at Chamberlain's fashionable restaurant in Washington. His original intent was to promote peace between the North and the South. But when Hugh McCulloch, the Indiana banker who was to become Lincoln's Secretary of the Treasury, offered him $12,000 a year "plus dinner expenses" to "court, woo, and charm congressmen, especially Democrats prone to oppose the war," he was quick to take the assignment. To those who knew what was going on "inside Washington," however, his real reputation was based on his association with Joe Morrissey, the so-called boss of the lotteries. Morrissey hired him to promote a bill to tax lotteries, a measure he felt he could afford but which would drive his less prosperous rivals out of business.

During the Civil War Sam was in the thick of things, smoothing out a war contract here, hushing up a potential scandal there. After the war he had the big railroad and telegraph combines among his clients. When he was not at his table at Chamberlain's he made his headquarters in the rooms of the Appropriations Committee. He always said he never helped a client who wanted to swindle the government and he denied ever participating in any fraud. But he always worked for the rich and powerful and by his own admission helped many a legislator away from the dictates of his democratic conscience over to the wishes of Sam's demanding and purposeful clients. With his bald head, sweeping mustache and imperial, with diamonds shining in his snowy shirt, with his charming talk and imported wines, he exerted a smiling but corrupt influence in his garish day.

Sam, of course, never lobbied unless he had a fee. Usually when he undertook an assignment he was successful. He was a professional. Henry Adams, who first went to Washington when "old wicked Sam Ward," as he called him, was already becoming a legend, was an amateur. But he was a lobbyist, nevertheless, in his early political days and later upon his return from his years as teacher at Harvard. The breakfasts he served and the dinners he gave were calculated more often than not to sway legislation. But his efforts for civil service reform only made him small fry compared to the railroad lobbyists who were at work for the passage of the Northern Pacific bill. In the Age of Expansion the railroad lobbyists were so active and so effective that Senator J. S. Morrill, a man of rare wit, once rose towards the end of a session and, calling attention to the presence in the outer lobby of the president of the Pennsylvania Railroad, moved the appointment of a committee to wait upon him and learn if there was any further legislation he desired before adjournment!

The railroad "strikers" were not the only lobbyists interested in railroad legislation in the 1870's. The National Grange had been founded in 1867 and it soon became one of the most potent pressure groups, on both a state and national level, that was active at this time. From the start it was interested in any political or economic manifestation affecting the farmer. It sent its delegates to the state legislatures; it demanded that candidates for public office announce their stands on all measures relating to agriculture; but it reserved its greatest strength for lobbying in behalf of measures designed to regulate the railroads. Although it was accused often of being socialistic and subversive of our institutions it was instrumental in several states in forcing legislatures to enact regulatory railroad laws. At the same time it sought improvement of the inland waterways and for this cause it made itself heard, through resolutions and effective agitation, in Washington. In the decade 1870–1880, Congress quadrupled appropriations for river and harbor improvements over any previous decade. To the lobbyists for the Grange should go much of the credit.

Until this decade, lobbying had attracted no vast amount of attention from a morally indignant public although, as we have seen, at least two congressional investigations had revealed widespread corruption among the swarms of agents who continually assailed Congress. In 1874 the Supreme Court, however, found occasion to deliver a stinging rebuke to one form of lobbying which it found reprehensible. For nearly thirty years a gentleman named N. P. Trist had been trying to collect a claim against the United States for services rendered during negotiations on the Treaty of Guadalupe Hidalgo. In pressing his claim he hired a lawyer as his agent, one Linus Child of Boston (and after his death, Child's son), who presumably was responsible for inducing Congress to award him several thousand dollars. When Trist failed to pay Child his 25 per cent fee the latter took it to law and eventually the case reached the Supreme Court.

The evidence clearly showed that the two Childs had tried to influence various members of Congress. No suggestion of bribery was ever made in the trials. It was a clear case of the accepted practice of lobbying for a fee in behalf of a private bill. Said Child's attorneys to the Supreme Court:

We are not here asking the court to open the door to corrupt influence upon Congress, or to give aid to that which is popularly known as "lobbying" and is properly denounced as dishonorable. But we are asking that by giving the sanction of the law to an open and honorable advocacy by counsel of private rights before legislative bodies, the court shall aid in doing away with the employment of agencies which work secretly and dishonorably.

Although this may seem an open and honest defense of a general practice made stronger by the fact that the trial record showed no intimation of any attempt at bribery or any other corrupt practice, the Supreme Court was not convinced. Justice Noah H. Swayne, a Republican and an outstanding constitutional conservative, spoke strongly in his decision:

The agreement . . . was for the sale of the influence and exertion of the lobby agent to bring about the passage of a law for the payment of a private claim, without reference to its merits, by means which, if not corrupt, were illegitimate, and considered in connection with the pecuniary interest of the agent at stake, contrary to the plainest principles of public policy.

If any of the great corporations of the country were to hire adventurers who make market of themselves in this way, to procure the passage of a general law with a view to the promotion of their private interests, the moral sense of every right-minded man would instinctively denounce the employer and employed as steeped in corruption and the employment as infamous. . . .

If the agent is truthful, and conceals nothing, all is well. If he uses nefarious means with success, the spring-head and the stream of legislation are polluted. To legalize the traffic of such service would open a door at which fraud and falsehood would not fail to enter and make themselves felt at every point. It would invite their presence and offer them a premium. If the tempted agent be corrupt himself, and disposed to corrupt others, the transition requires but a single step. He has the means in his hands, with every facility and a strong incentive to use them. . . .

Justice Swayne's fine denunciation of lobbying did little, if anything, to stop the practice of lobbying and the "great corporations" continued "to hire adventurers" for the promotion of their private interests. One year later George Frisbie Hoar, that righteous man from Massachusetts, did succeed, however, in putting a temporary restraint on some lobbyists. As chairman of the Judiciary Committee he forced through the following resolution, which was adopted by the House in May, 1875, and remained in effect throughout the life of the Forty-fourth Congress:

Resolved that all persons or corporations employing counsel or agents to represent their interests in regard to any measure pending at any time before this House or any committee thereof, shall cause the name and authority of such counsel to be filed with the clerk of the House; and no person whose name and authority are not so filed shall appear as counsel or agent before any committee of the House.

The gentleman from Massachusetts explained he offered this resolution because his committee had been considering an important bill in which "an important corporation" had expressed an interest. "Four persons," he said, "coming from different parts of the country, coming from cities and neighborhoods which the different members of the committee come from, have accosted the different members of the committee in regard to that particular measure." Thus back in the 1870's the "grass-roots" method of lobbying, which was to engage the attention of the House Select Committee on Lobbying Activities in 1950, was evidently an accepted practice.

Mr. Charles B. Holstein, the research director for the 1950 Lobby Committee, who unearthed this interesting instance, says that the debate in the House shows that the members were not avid to curb lobbying but that they wanted some method by which they would be able to "recognize the right agents," who could put the case for the bill in authoritative terms.

The 1880's saw a great increase in the activity of lobbyists in Washington and a refinement of their methods. When the Democrats controlled Congress, 1884–1886, great and successful pressures were brought upon its members not to succumb to the lure of tariff reductions. In most instances the pressures were political in nature. Lobbyists made it clear to the Pennsylvania Democrats that they would be severely punished at the polls if they failed to support protection for coal, iron, and steel. The iron manufacturers of Ohio promised reprisals if the Democrats from the state failed to get in line. And in New Jersey the powerful owners of pottery works, then one of New Jersey's largest industries, made themselves heard. Even Southern Democrats were not immune to the open hints of the sugar and coal lobbies.

It was in this general period that minority interests everywhere began to see the value of organization. Many of them, able to prove their strength on the local scene where the votes are cast, found ready allies among members of both houses of Congress.

More and more these gentlemen began to think of themselves as representatives of regional and local interests which more and more they placed above the general welfare. The complex and intricate system of politics by pressure was beginning to take a definite form.

The high-protection lobby, which was in reality a combination of smaller lobbies representing local interests, was not alone in exerting pressure on Congress. What was true of the tariff was true also of all social and economic legislation. Laws relating to land, agriculture, and regulation of monopolies were weighed with reference to local or group interest rather than to public interest.

The system in Congress at that time, whereby the Speaker of the House and two members constituted the all-powerful Committee on Rules, which controlled appointments to all committees and thereby the fate of all legislation, made the lot of the lobbyist easier. It was not necessary for the lobbyist for a special interest to disperse his ammunition. He was able to concentrate upon the committee in charge of whatever legislation he favored or opposed. He could make it clear to its members, all representatives of local communities dependent upon local support for political existence, that he carried weight, not only in the congressman's back yard, but also with the Committee on Rules. Even when moved with the highest motives and the urge for statesmanship, few congressmen dared defy the committee.

A lesson to be learned from this period is that lobbying flourishes most under two political circumstances. One is when the executive is weak. The other is when the parties are decentralized. Both circumstances existed during the administration (1889–1892) of President Harrison. More than one historian has called his four years in office a period of political insolvency. Although the Republican Party controlled both Houses and although the rules of the House had been somewhat liberalized by Thomas B. Reed, the Speaker known as "Czar," there was no leadership in the White House. At the same time neither party was controlled by a vigorous program of action.

In such a situation legislation by lobby was inevitable. Thus the costly pension bill, which milked the country of $60,000,000 a year and which was an outstanding example of a minority group defeating the general interest, was passed. The notorious McKinley Tariff of 1890, which was the net result of myriad lobbies and which annihilated everything President Cleveland had attempted in the way of tariff reform, became law. On almost every front big business received what it sought. With both parties failing to act as a party, pressure groups had a field day putting across special legislation. The only progressive legislation * of the Harrison administration was the passage of the Sherman Antitrust Act, but this was passed to alleviate the public's fears of the growing power of the money groups upon the country. And although ostensibly designed to stop monopoly, it did nothing of the kind.

Thus far we have considered only lobbying before the national Congress, but lobbying had long been a recognized problem in the various states. The first state to give it legal consideration was Georgia, which, in its Constitution of 1877, declared lobbying to be a crime. Two years later California declared improper lobbying to be a felony. In 1890 Massachusetts passed an antilobby act which was to serve as a model for similar legislation in Maryland (1900) and Wisconsin (1905). New York, where lobbying

---

* The 1870's and 1880's saw several minority pressure groups becoming active. For instance, the establishment of the first state Board of Health, in Louisiana in 1867, was the result of minority pressure. This was followed in 1869 by the establishment of a state board in Massachusetts. By 1878 thirteen more such boards had been established, and then a yellow fever epidemic in Memphis, Tennessee, in 1878, brought twelve more into being. Another outstanding example of minority pressure was the passage in 1887 of the Dawes Act, which gave citizenship and land ownership to Indians who renounced their tribal loyalties. The American Red Cross, which belongs in the category of pressure groups, was established in 1881. And in this period such associations as the Society for the Prevention of Cruelty to Children and the National Prison Reform Association were established.

had long been rife and where the term had originated as far back as 1829, followed suit after the Armstrong investigation revealed the lengths to which great insurance corporations would go, in the words of Justice Swayne, to "hire adventurers" for the "promotion of their private interests."

CHAPTER II

The Imperialism of Power

IN 1905 the *New York World* created a furor with its exposures of corrupt practices among the great insurance companies operating under charters issued by the State of New York. The startling but seemingly well-documented newspaper stories met a favorable response from the people, who had been attuned by the words of the muckrakers and the inflammatory speeches of Theodore Roosevelt to suspect that many aspects of big business could stand investigation. Reluctantly Governor Francis W. Higgins, who felt "nothing is to be gained by it," called the Legislature into special session. Without too much ado the gentlemen at Albany appointed a Joint Committee of the Senate and Assembly of the State of New York to Investigate the Affairs of Life Insurance Companies. The ten-volume report of the Armstrong Committee, named after its chairman, Senator William W. Armstrong of Rochester, is one of the most dreadfully fascinating public documents ever published. Its author was Charles Evans Hughes, the conductor of the inquisition which turned out the first important revelations of how far big business had gone in corrupting legislators in every state of the Union, the territories, and in the Congress of the United States to gain its own ends.

We need not concern ourselves here with the unsavory details of the criminal malpractices of the great insurance companies in those magnificently unregulated days, although these details make genuinely rewarding reading. Hughes's great report remains one of the primary sources for historians of *laissez faire*. Our interest, however, lies in its brutally candid account of the lobbyists employed by the insurance companies and how they worked. Thirty years later another investigation, this time by sanction of the United States Congress,* revealed that many of the same methods were still being employed, proving, if nothing else, that lobbying is always with us.

The Armstrong Committee had difficulty in getting witnesses to appear before it. Many of them suddenly decided upon European vacations or sojourns in sanitariums. But it managed to elicit enough information for it to declare:

Nothing disclosed by the investigation deserves more serious attention than the systematic efforts of the large insurance companies to control a large part of the legislation of the State. They have been organized into an offensive and defensive alliance to procure or to prevent the passage of laws affecting not only insurance, but a great variety of important interests to which, through subsidiary companies or the connections of their officers, they have become related. Their operations have extended beyond the State, and the country has been divided into districts so that each company might perform conveniently its share of the work. Enormous sums have been expended in a surreptitious manner. Irregular accounts have been kept to conceal the payments. . . .

The insurance companies, particularly the Equitable Life Assurance Company of the United States, the Mutual Life Insurance Company of New York, the Prudential and the New York life insurance companies, were shown to have spent thousands of dollars to influence legislation. According to the testimony the various companies, presumably in competition with each other, kept mutual and effective watch over all revenue bills coming before Congress which might in any way affect their business. It closely followed every bill that might in any way have a bearing

* The Temporary National Economic Committee on the Concentration of Economic Power in the United States. See especially: *Hearings*, Seventy-sixth Congress, first session. Part 10, Life Insurance. Washington, 1940.

upon insurance companies or their interlocking interests. The well-heeled insurance lobbyists undoubtedly were aware of the fact that the four big companies had quietly contributed more that a quarter of a million dollars to the Republican National Committee in three Presidential campaigns between 1896 and 1904, of which $148,702 had gone toward the election of Theodore Roosevelt and, in the words of George W. Perkins, vice-president of New York Life, for "the maintenance of a proper money standard." As Senator Thomas C. Platt said, in the words of the committee, it was "supposed" that an advantage would be derived by the insurance companies and their allied interests because then Republican legislators "would be ready to respond to an appeal for assistance in case hostile measures were threatened."

Similar tactics were used on the state level "with the idea that they [the insurance companies and their financial allies] would be protected in matters of legislation." The Mutual and Equitable companies were joint operators of the so-called "House of Mirth" in Albany, headquarters for their lobbyists and, presumably, a place of entertainment for the legislators with whom they were in consonance. Mr. Andrew C. Fields, chief legislative agent of the two companies, but on their payroll as head of the Mutual's "supply department," presided over the "House of Mirth." Unfortunately he disappeared when the committee wanted to find out how he could spend the $2,948,762 for printing, stationery, and postage, the ostensible supplies furnished by his department. But in various memoranda found in the companies' files by Mr. Hughes it was adequately established that he followed his written instructions to check on "all banking and insurance matters, taxation schemes, and bills affecting particularly the following interests: safe deposit companies, banks, trust companies, street railways . . . and public places of amusement, etc."

From headquarters in New York City to the "House of Mirth" in Albany there passed a steady stream of instruction. "Memorandum for Mr. F.: Assembly Bill, Introductory 709, introduced by

Mr. Sullivan, should be killed." Lobby agents elsewhere received similar messages and copies of "reading notices" to be inserted, at a dollar a line, as news stories in the newspapers. As far as is known, the insurance companies were the first to put lobbying and propaganda on a solid and professional basis, building up a lobby that for efficiency has seldom been equaled. At least they were the first to be caught at the game. To any suggestion that the maintenance of the lobby was improper the insurance companies retorted that they were "so continuously menaced by . . . improper and ill-advised legislative measures that they have been compelled to maintain a constant watchfulness and to resort to secret means to defeat them."

The committee said this was nonsense and pointed out that "a very large proportion of the voters of the state hold policies of life insurance." These voters, if properly and publicly informed of any legislative matter affecting their interest, could form their own pressure group, see to it that, after "argument and criticism effectively presented," the duly elected representatives voted against it. The committee pointed out that it was the policy holders, after all, who would suffer from unfair legislation, and "the consequences that can be pointed out are almost certain to bring about an early repeal" of any law inimical to the policy holders. "The employment of agents to disburse large sums, and of clandestine methods to defeat legislation is wholly indefensible."

Denouncing the "pernicious activities of corporate agents in matters of legislation," the Armstrong Committee suggested that "the present freedom of lobbying should be restricted." The laws against bribery and corruption, offenses which are difficult to prove, were already sufficiently stringent but they did not "strike at the root of the evil," the committee argued. What was needed, it went on, was a new law "requiring under proper penalties full publicity with regard to moneys expended in connection with matters before the legislature."

Although submitted in 1905 the recommendations of the Armstrong Committee [1] are worth recalling in full today because, as we shall later see, they not only form the basis for the New York State law regulating lobbying and lobbyists, but they have a decided bearing upon all legislation, proposed or on the statute books, written for this purpose.

The Committee therefore recommends . . . that every person retained or employed as counsel or agent to promote or oppose the passage of bills or resolutions by either House or executive approval of such measures shall before entering upon the service file in the office of the Secretary of State a writing stating the name or names of his employer, together with a brief description of the legislative matter with reference to which the service is to be rendered.

The Secretary of State should be required to provide a docket to be known as the "Docket of Legislative Appearances," with appropriate blanks and indices in which the names of counsel and agent may properly be entered.

Fees contingent upon legislative action should be prohibited.

It should also be made the duty of every corporation and association doing business in the State within two months after the adjournment of the Legislature to file with the Secretary of State an itemized statement duly verified showing in detail all expenses paid or incurred in connection with legislation pending at the last session including all disbursements or compensation paid or payable to counsel or agents.

Exception may be made of the duly accredited counsel of municipalities, public boards and public institutions, and also of the ordinary professional services in drafting bills or advising clients as to the construction and effect of proposed or pending legislation where the professional service is not otherwise connected with legislative action.

Violation of the law should be made a misdemeanor, and the failure to file the statements required should subject the offender to appropriate penalties.

These recommendations were excellent — as far as they went. They were based upon the Massachusetts and Wisconsin statutes, which required that lobbyists enter regular appearances and disclose the clients for whom they were working. The Wisconsin statute went much further, making it a misdemeanor for any paid lobbyist to direct or influence a legislator to vote for or against a measure by any means other than appearances before regular committees, by publications and public speeches, or by statements, arguments or briefs delivered to all members of the legislature and filed with the secretary of state. The Armstrong Committee apparently felt this was too drastic a curb upon the constitutional rights of a citizen and so did not recommend such an all-embracing law.

The New York legislature listened to the Armstrong Committee. Undoubtedly it also had read the message which Governor Robert M. La Follette had sent to the Wisconsin legislature, asking for the law which was passed in 1905. At any rate it passed a lobbying law in 1906, following the committee's recommendations almost exactly. It made the penalty for an individual transgressor imprisonment of not more than one year, a fine of not more than $1000, or both.

While the New York legislature was sweeping out its Albany lobbies with a broom that was to prove less efficient than advertised, pressure groups and their lobby agents were extremely busy in Washington, where Theodore Roosevelt was enjoying his first elected term. One of his demands upon Congress was the passage of a law which would bring about government supervision and regulation of the rates charged by the railroads. This produced one of the great political and economic struggles of the first decade of the century, centered around the bitter battle between various interests who stood to benefit from reduced rates and the powerful railroad lobby. The latter had its friends in the Senate, whose plutocratic make-up had only recently been exposed by the crusading novelist, David Graham Phillips, in his articles, "The Treason of the Senate." But the Hepburn Bill passed, although without the amendment which "Bob" La Follette (lately become senator) had introduced in a hope of establishing a basis for computing fair rates that would stand up against a hostile court.

For years two other powerful Washington lobbies had stood off all legislative encroachment on their respective fields of private enterprise. One of them, between 1889 and 1906, had successfully defeated 140 bills designed to enact some kind of an American counterpart to the English Pharmacy Act and bring the great patent medicine and drug manufacturers under some kind of governmental control. Goaded by muckrakers and crusading women's organizations, which were rapidly learning the art of lobbying, President Roosevelt called for the passage of a Pure Food and Drug Act. His own Department of Agriculture, led by Dr. Harvey Wiley and his famous "poison squad," produced effective propaganda against the drug lobby, which wailed that the passage of the bill would put manufacturers out of business. The lobby crumbled against the onslaught of public indignation and the Pure Food and Drug Act was passed. But the drug and patent medicine lobby is still active in Washington today.

Ranged alongside the drug lobby in its fight against the general welfare of the people was the powerful lobby of the canners and packers, whose incredibly intolerable methods of production and manufacture had just been exposed by Upton Sinclair in his novel, *The Jungle*. Again goaded by public indignation, President Roosevelt called for the passage of the Meat Inspection Act. The packers resorted to every known method of lobbying to defeat this bill, but once again they went down to defeat against the pressure of minority groups working in the general interest of the consumer. But pressure groups, working on political spoilsmen and having the good ears of the great defenders of *laissez faire* in the Senate — men like Senator Chauncey M. Depew (who was on the payroll of the insurance companies, by the way), Henry Cabot Lodge, Joseph B. Foraker, Nelson W. Aldrich, Republicans, and Arthur P. Gorman, Democrat — defeated most of Roosevelt's other progressive requests. Income and inheritance taxes, the limitation of arbitrary labor injunctions, regulation of child labor, and the clarification of the Sherman Antitrust Act (which had recently been declared applicable to labor unions by the Supreme Court in the Danbury Hatters' case), fell before as great an assortment of lobbies and lobbyists as had ever flooded Washington up to that time.

Although the evils inherent in pressure groups had now been recognized for some time and lobbies and lobbyists had been exposed and bitterly assailed upon more than one occasion, the whole case against them had never been properly put or philosophically documented.

Such writers as Lincoln Steffens, David Graham Phillips, Ida Tarbell, Ray Stannard Baker and others had unearthed an almost overwhelming assortment of facts. Phillips had revealed the great sham of bipartisanship in the Senate, proving that there was no honest party opposition, that senators of both parties did business together and conducted public debates on the issue solely to deceive the electorate. The others had conclusively described the powerful pressures brought upon the legislators by the vested interests of big business, words that had not lost their sheen in those days. But it remained for a scholar to integrate their findings and to explain the threat to direct democracy which pressure groups exerted.

In 1908 A. F. Bentley published a book entitled *The Process of Government*. It created no great stir, except in certain academic circles, but it was to become a landmark in American political science and a classic of original and penetrating thought.

Bentley's book was the pioneer study of what he called "political misrepresentation." It was based on a theory as old as Plato, who was the first to make the bold suggestion that the real rulers are unseen and unknown to the multitude, but that "always they are there and always they are few." Bentley sought to show how this was true under our supposedly democratic form of government. He sought to show the continuing connivance between the elected representatives and the lobbyists of powerful special interests. He sought to show how organized minorities acting for private interests masqueraded as the majority and persistently defeated the public interest. He thought that government could only be understood when we realized how group pressures functioned within the framework of our governmental system.

Bentley was a profound student who owed a great deal to the work of Thorstein Veblen — even, says Henry Steele Commager, regrettably his style — but perhaps more to the studies and writings of that prophetic if neglected political scientist Lester Ward. It was Ward who once defined the proper function of legislatures as "the scientific control of the social forces by the collective mind of society for its own advantage." In a brilliant analysis of *laissez faire*, written in 1895, Ward had shown that "Nothing is more obvious today than the signal inability of capital and private enterprise to take care of themselves unaided by the state; and while they are incessantly denouncing paternalism — by which they mean the claim of the defenseless laborer and artisan to a share in this lavish state protection — they are all the while besieging legislatures for relief from their own incompetency, and 'pleading the baby act' through a trained body of lawyers and lobbyists." It was Ward who, in the last quarter of the nineteenth century, showed that among the faults of legislation, which he then found limited in scope and imagination and haphazard and unscientific, was the fact that it increasingly reflected the will of special pressure groups rather than the needs of society itself.[2]

Bentley, whose theories in general were those held by such historians and political scientists as James Harvey Robinson, Charles A. Beard, and W. B. Munro, his contemporaries, argued that it is less in the ideas and ideals of men that the causes of social action can be located. Rather, he insisted, the actions spring from the pressures that various groups exert in behalf of those ideas and ideals. To those bred in the old-fashioned ideology of government of, for, and by the people, Bentley's suggestions were little less than heretical — although he was never ostracized or placed upon a list of subversives for having such thoughts. He argued that the theory of "government by the people" was but "a slogan and rallying cry for some particular groups at special stages of their activity." And this led him to assert that democracy must always be considered "in terms of the various group pressures that form its substance." To Bentley, a later scholar has argued,[3] a legislative act is always "the calculable resultant of a struggle between pressure groups, never a decision between opposing conceptions of the national welfare."

There may be reasonable grounds for supposing that Bentley went too far in his sweepingly pragmatic expression of the legislative process. An examination of most of the important national legislation from the Pure Food and Drug Act through, let us say, the Taft-Hartley Labor-Management Relations Act of 1947, however, tends to support his theory. While the New Deal as a whole (and the same goes for the Fair Deal of Mr. Truman) was supported and opposed electorally upon conflicting theories of the national welfare, in the matter of individual legislation the struggle more often than not was between readily definable pressure groups.

The great importance of Bentley's study was in his realization of the fact that under our more or less democratic procedure no one particular group, or even combination of groups, necessarily managed to hold a permanent control over the government. He pointed out that alliances were continually shifting and were, therefore, temporary. They were not the result of a fixed and determinate situation. For this reason, he implied, pressure groups were not inevitably destructive of democracy: by their very nature they did not create an indestructible oligarchy.

Although this viewpoint was not exactly new, at the time of its expression in 1908 it was not nearly so widely held as it is today. Nevertheless, the growing industrialization of the country, with its accompanying struggle for power, and its trend towards bigness, with its accompanying economic imperialism, gave it a validity it had not hitherto had. One by one the varying interests, whether sugar, or coal, or manufacturing in general, were setting up far more elaborate organizations than they had ever before maintained for the purpose of furthering their own specific interests. Sometimes they worked only for their own ends; often they joined with other special groups to press their more general aims upon the national Congress. Most of the big industrial interests, however ruthless with each other they may have been in scrambling for the hog's share of the profits, found common ground in their opposition to labor unions, agriculture, and governmental regulations or controls. They were jointly inventing new techniques of lobbying and their lobbyists were being trained in new methods of propaganda. And they were getting away with murder.

Each lobby, working away in Washington, had but one end: to make government amenable to the measures it advocated; but all of them, working in coalition, were struggling to capture the government itself. By 1924 the big business, industrial and financial pressure groups had all but succeeded in their aims. After 1932 they were momentarily checked.

In the meantime, what of the public? Bentley, of course, had discounted the theory of "government by the people," and it was becoming more difficult all the time to define just who "the people" were, or what "the public" was. Was it really, as Professor R. M. MacIver suggests,[4] nothing more than that "amorphous residuum" that lay outside the contending pressure groups "of business, large and small, of finance, of labor, of agriculture, of the organized professions, of the political bureaucracy itself"? As the twentieth century gained momentum the question became more difficult to answer and we began to lose sight of the national welfare (which, with national unity, is the base on which the logic of democracy rests) to a far greater extent than we realized.

The imperialism of powerful groups — of which the National Association of Manufacturers was then the outstanding example

— was then, as it is now, a constant threat to the general welfare, or more exactly the common interest of all the people. We were beginning to learn, the hard way, that the never ending problem of democracy is how to keep such groups under control and restrain them from placing their narrow interests above the interest of the whole. We failed, however, to do anything drastic towards subjecting the agents of these groups, the lobbyists, to proper regulation, although we learned more about their power of subversion as time went on.

Bentley's book was published the year that saw William Howard Taft elected to keep the Presidential chair warm until after Theodore Roosevelt returned from hunting lions and tigers. Taft was not noted for any overwhelming interest in the general welfare, as against business welfare, but he had at least an interest in progressivism of a sort. During his administration the lobbyists were as active as ever before. One of President Taft's primary objectives was further railroad legislation and congressmen were well aware of the way the railroad lobby and its allies were fighting La Follette in his desperate struggle for a fair rate base. Congress was at the same time concerned with the passage of a Corrupt Practices Act. This had Taft's support, but not his party's, and it was only passed through the efforts of the coalition of insurgents and Democrats. In a way it concerned lobbying, since contributing to the campaign chests of the major parties was, and still is, one of the most potent weapons in the lobbyist's armory. The 1910 act did not attempt to stop such contributions, but to regulate them through adequate publicity as to their sources.

A concerted movement to regulate campaign funds, especially funds channeled secretly to the parties, had been started in 1904 when Perry Belmont, treasurer of the Democratic campaign of that year, organized a society in New York, later known as the National Publicity Law Association, whose main purpose was to bring about legislation prohibiting corporate contributions. This was the issue which Alton B. Parker, the 1904 Democratic presidential candidate, brought up too late and too ineffectually to impress the voters.

The sentiment against secret funds was so great that Taft could not ignore it. Congress accordingly passed the law making mandatory the filing of a statement of campaign receipts and expenditures by both candidates and political parties. The act has since been amended several times and other acts are on the book covering contiguous aspects of political spending. They are of little value in the control of lobbying. Although designed to open up the books of candidates and parties, both Federal and state regulations of this nature have been generally so poorly written that they allow all sorts of evasions. The fact remains that vast sums of money are poured by corporations and lobbying organizations into political funnels, not so much in Washington, but at the grass roots, where the effective lobbyist does his most useful and rewarding work.

CHAPTER III

Masters of Government

THE masters of the government of the United States," said Woodrow Wilson in one of his campaign speeches in 1912, "are the combined capitalists and manufacturers of the United States. It is written over every intimate page of the records of Congress; it is written all through the history of conferences at the White House: that the suggestions of economic policy have come from one source, not many sources. . . .

"Suppose you go to Washington," the Governor of New Jersey continued, "you will always find that while you are politely listened to the men really consulted are the big men who have the biggest stake — the big bankers, the big manufacturers, the big masters of commerce, the heads of railroad corporations, and of steamship corporations. . . .

"Every time it has come to a critical question, these gentlemen have been yielded to and the demands treated as the demands that should be followed as a matter of course. The government of the United States is a foster child of the special interests. It is not allowed to have a will of its own." [1]

With due allowance for the hyperbole of campaign expression it can be said that Mr. Wilson was not too far from the truth. Shortly after his election he made a quiet investigation of the situation in Washington, gathering data with his usual scholarly thoroughness. It came in very handily when the special interests went to work on the first major piece of legislation he submitted to Congress, the Underwood Tariff Bill of 1913.

Written in answer to President Wilson's compelling message to Congress urging a return to tariff for revenue only, the bill was carefully prepared by the Ways and Means Committee, of which Oscar Underwood of Alabama was the chairman and Cordell Hull, representative from Tennessee, a young but vigorous member. It called for 958 reductions, striking specifically against the protection of inflated prices on food, clothing, and the primary necessities of a decent life. The bill was written by a committee in which party unity prevailed and which apparently had determined in advance to abide by the Democratic platform and the demands of the President. Oscar Underwood, the gentleman from Alabama, able, incorruptible, and intensely loyal, had the committee firmly in hand.

Frightened by the menace of a President who had served ample warning and by a Congress prepared to submit to Presidential leadership, the special interests rushed into action. "For a century the people of Washington looked to the drawn-out days when a tariff was in the making as a harvest time," Josephus Daniels later recalled.[2] "People who wished to see that the schedules did not fail to help their particular business were in the habit of moving to Washington. They came with retainers in 1913, as formerly. It was the quadrennial onslaught of the capitol. Hotels were filled, champagne popped, there were dinners galore and a merry time." Thus the old pattern was repeated, as it had been, in one form or another at every session, since the ducks and roasts were set before the "brace of Adamses" at the First Continental Congress.

But this time the milling mob of special pleaders was to be in for a great surprise. Cordell Hull recalls[3] that "we held tariff hearings which passed without special incident except for the tariff lobbyists. For the first time in many years the beneficiaries of high-tariff privilege found themselves confronting an unfriendly committee which would not permit them virtually to write their own rates. This seemed very disconcerting to many of their representatives who appeared before the committee. The lobbyists, as usual, frequented most of the vacant space in the hotels and about the Capitol. Many of them called on all of us who were engaged in preparing the bill. We would receive and hear them courteously, but after that our courses diverged."

The cold and courteous rejection of their special pleas, the adamant refusal of the committee to knuckle under to the representatives of the pressure groups who jammed the hearings, failed to discourage the lobbyists. Rebuffed, they buzzed the more insistently. They realized that the existence of what Oswald Garrison Villard called "the whole log-rolling, favor-swapping, office-buying and generally corrupting protection system" [4] was being realistically threatened for the first time in a century. In their frightened efforts to stave off disaster their activities became an open scandal, and the committee went to Wilson for help against them.

Wilson was in a receptive frame of mind. He believed with Richard T. Ely, the hard-hitting critic of extreme *laissez faire* under whom he had studied at Johns Hopkins, that protectionism was one of the chief reasons why the American government had for decades been a government of special interests. He now saw at first hand proof of Ely's contention that the "temptation to do wrong is absolutely inseparable from protectionism," and that it inevitably forced the protected interests to create lobbies by assessments upon all who profited from the tariffs to exert influence upon Congress without public accounting of any kind.

Even before arriving at the White House Wilson had been doing some research of a very practical nature.* As Daniels puts

---

* Long before he had become an active politician Woodrow Wilson had been aware of the dangers inherent in lobbying. In his doctoral thesis, published as *Congressional Government: A Study in American Politics* (Boston, 1895), and later in *Constitutional Government in the United States* (New York, 1908) Wilson pointed out that the committee system, under which practically all important legislation is written and given its original

it, "In some way they have never yet understood he had a roster of the whole outfit. He knew their whole program, could tell what interests they had come to serve and what members of Congress they had approached and were entertaining. It was a sad day for the hotels and the taxis and the social swim when that queer man in the White House said 'Go.'" His investigation had been so thorough that he "knew their names, their aims, their methods, and their employers."

The Wilsonian purge of the lobbyists, which thrilled the country, was effected by a bristling statement issued to the press on May 26, 1913. "Washington," he said, "has seldom seen so numerous, so industrious, or so insidious a lobby." Thus for the first time in history a President had taken official cognizance of the "invisible government" and in unmistakable terms. He told the lobbyists, who he said were so thick you could not throw a brick without hitting one, to get out of Washington and give Congress a chance to proceed in an orderly way with its great legislative task. So stern was his warning that the capital emptied overnight, except for a few die-hards who, as Cordell Hull said, "became less pestiferous when they discovered just what our policy was and saw they could not influence us."

With this unprecedented Presidential support (and thanks also to the floor leadership of Representative Underwood, who guided debate "like an English finance minister"), the Underwood Tariff Bill passed the House without amendments, an almost unheard-of accomplishment. The frustrated lobbyists now turned to the Senate, presumably less sensitive to pressures and more independent, but where the Democratic majority was precarious and not so well organized. Fearful that a switch of a few votes would open the way to a flood of amendments, President Wilson

---

impetus, was particularly liable to succumb to the lures of the lobbyist. His argument was that while business lobbies could not buy *entire* legislatures they could, and did, keep members of small committees under their bought control.

made full use of the prestige of his office in an effort to bolster party morale, using many of the same tactics as the lobbyists. He sent letters to wavering senators and grabbed the spotlight of publicity through public statements. In spite of all this and the revival of the Democratic caucus as a means of keeping in control the recalcitrants, who were led by the "sugar Democrats" from Louisiana, the party line did not hold. Amendments were added. But the bill passed. In conference the lobbyists once again ran up against Senator La Follette, who managed to keep out several notorious "jokers" which the special interests tried to insert.

The great tariff fight of 1913 held an important lesson for those willing to learn. For once the pressure groups, used to working in the past in the secrecy of committee meetings, were forced into the open. For once they were confronted with a unified party, proving the contention of Bentley and others that party discipline under a strong and centralized leadership is likely to work far more for the benefit of democracy than an "independent" Congress upon which the lobbyists can play at will.*

President Wilson's warning to the lobbyists to get out of Washington and let the legislature function met with both approval and complaint. Voicing the official attitude of the interests whose toes had been stepped upon, the *New York Times* accused Wilson of having "mistaken for lobbying" the "usual" and "legitimate" efforts of industry to present its case. But this sentiment was not that of the general public. Approving telegrams and letters by

* Wilson's and Underwood's victory was temporary. Prosecution of the war took up the administration's energies in the second Wilson term. When the Republicans took office in 1920 the tariff lobbyists were once again welcome in Washington. They had their way with the Fordney-McCumber tariff in 1922. In that period of nationalistic astigmatism Congress, beset by pressure groups, ignored the economic law that a creditor nation must accept more imports. This mistake was furthered in 1930, under President Hoover, when the Hawley-Smoot Act brought protective tariffs to the highest point ever reached in United States history. See: *This Was Normalcy*, by Karl Schriftgiesser. Boston, 1948. Pp. 92–94, 128, 159, 255, 268–269, 276.

the score poured in on the White House. There is no evidence that they sprang from any organized source. As a later historian has said, they "revealed a social anger not to be deceived by pious rationalization." [5]

In the midst of the excitement caused by the Presidential ukase the *New York World*, the newspaper closest to the Wilson administration and the one whose exposures had previously brought about the insurance investigation in New York, got wind of the activities of a lobbyist for the National Association of Manufacturers. The story which Martin M. Mulhall told on the front page of that newspaper was of such an inflammatory nature and involved the integrity of so many public officials and members of Congress that it could not be ignored. Speaker Champ Clark moved swiftly to appoint a select committee, headed by Representative Finis J. Garrett, the majority leader. In the meantime the Senate Judiciary Committee ordered a subcommittee, headed by Senator A. B. Cummins, the insurgent Republican from Iowa, to go to work.

Each investigation was conducted with thoroughness, but it was the Garrett Committee that during four months of intensive labor turned out sixty volumes of testimony which "laid bare an almost incredible history of intrigue, intimidation, bribery and solicitation by the NAM's high-pressure lobbyists in the capital." [6] That this organization had for years contributed to the disruption of democracy, not only through the unethical practices of its Washington representative but through the violence of its strong-arm antilabor activities, was proved beyond a shadow of a doubt.

Mulhall was shown to be in a class by himself, the lobbyist extraordinary. He had his own private office in the Capitol. He had on his NAM payroll the chief page of the House who, for $50 a month, kept him informed of what was going on in the cloakrooms. Even more important was his close association with Representative James T. McDermott, a Democrat from Chicago, and Representative John Dwight, the minority leader, who fed him advance information on proposed and pending legislation. This Mulhall passed on to his boss, James A. Emery, for many years the NAM's chief legislative strategist. Through these valuable contacts Mulhall was able even to dictate the appointment of representatives friendly to the NAM to committees where they would be the most useful.

The NAM's lobbying network was far flung. The association itself and the National Council for Industrial Defense, its union-smashing subsidiary, "took an active interest and vigorous part in Congressional campaigns . . . for the re-election of members whose views were in harmony with their legislative program . . . and resorted to questionable and disreputable means to bring about the defeat of members who had not approved their policies." In these campaigns both organizations had spent "large sums of money . . . and extended their activities into various districts throughout the country, where methods employed were secretive, reprehensible, and deserve the severest condemnation by the House." [7]

In the course of the hearings Representative William J. McDonald, a Progressive from Michigan and the spark plug of the investigation, asked Philip J. Bird, the general manager of the NAM, a pertinent question that summed up not only the activities of lobbyist Mulhall but the association's attitude towards them.

"Now, I want to ask you in all fairness," he said, "whether, if you believe in all those multifarious activities of Colonel Mulhall, the buying of members of labor unions, the using of these employees of the Government, these efforts to obtain hearings before committees of Congress and efforts to prevent them, efforts to keep Members away from Congress and keep them in Congress, efforts to change votes, and all these activities in election districts — I ask you honestly if you justify these proceedings as in line with the legitimate work of your organization?"

"Yes, sir," said Mr. Bird. And a little later he went on, "I think, sir, that these investigations . . . will be a great enlightening incident to manufacturers of this country. I believe that it will impress upon them, more than anything else that has been done, the necessity of manufacturers standing together to preserve rights that they hope to enjoy in this country of ours, and therefore I say that these investigations must eventually — not immediately but eventually — be of a great deal of good to us, because it will convince manufacturers of conditions of which we have been unable to convince them single-handed . . . I consider this exposé — if it is called an exposé — a sunlight ray from heaven." [8]

The Garrett Committee piled up an overwhelming mass of data on the NAM's lobbying, on its violent union-busting activities, and on its incessant labors in behalf of juggling tariffs. The last named, of course, is what had touched off the scandal. The committee proved that the National Tariff Commission Association, another NAM subsidiary, had engaged former Representative James E. Watson, who later became Republican senator from Indiana, to lobby in its behalf before the Republican-dominated Congress in 1909 when the question of a Tariff Commission was being considered. Watson said to the committee: "I had charge of the organization and campaign for a tariff in the House and Senate, and I had various members of Congress coming to me to report about how their delegations stood."

Watson was also used to help Mulhall influence the appointment of members of important committees. On one occasion he had tried to get Speaker Cannon to appoint an NAM stooge to the Committee on Rivers and Harbors, but "Uncle Joe" did not do so.

The majority report of the committee was not so vehement in the condemnation of the NAM lobbyists as the evidence seemed to warrant. None of the association's officers or employees was punished, on the grounds that the House had power only to punish its own members. Six of the seven congressmen who apparently had been "reached" by the NAM or its agents were absolved of wrongdoing while the seventh, the unfortunate McDermott, ob-

viously involved in Mulhall's machinations, was "strongly cen-
sored" and allowed to resign.

The general attitude of the select committee toward the powerful National Association of Manufacturers, which had wielded
such great pressure upon Congress, is best summed up in this
quotation from its final report:

> The correspondence between officials and employees of the associa-
> tion . . . shows it to have been an organization having purposes and
> aspirations along industrial, commercial, political, educational, legis-
> lative, and other lines, so vast and far-reaching as to excite at once
> admiration and fear — admiration for the genius that conceived them
> and fear for the ultimate effects which the successful accomplishment
> of all these ambitions might have in a Government such as ours.[9]

The Garrett investigation received widespread attention
throughout the country and its unfavorable repercussions were
such, even among manufacturers, that one of the NAM's historians had to admit they "stimulated for a while desertions from
the ranks."

Out of the investigations came a bill, the first of its kind ever
introduced in Congress, which would have made mandatory the
registration with the Clerk of the House of all agents and lobbyists operating in Washington on behalf of individuals, associations, or corporations. The House report which accompanied this
bill contained a broad, and probably unconstitutional definition
of lobbying, which it defined as the "activities of a person or a
body of persons seeking to influence Congress in any way whatsoever." [10] The bill passed the House, perhaps because of its sense
of guilt for having let six of its tarred members off scot-free. The
bill died in the Senate. Not for thirty-three years was a Lobby
Registration Act to become the law of the land.

While Congress was investigating the subversion of the legislative process by the National Association of Manufacturers another lobby as industrious and insidious, if not so numerous, as
that which had aroused President Wilson's ire was nesting down

in the national capital. Guided by some of the most brilliant if distorted minds the profession of lobbying has ever employed, the prohibitionists were scurrying in and out of the Capitol cloakrooms on their errands of disaster.

The story of prohibition, which has become the classic story of pressure politics in the United States, began in the Age of Jackson. In 1833 what had been a scattered local manifestation emerged as a national force when delegates from twenty-one state societies formed the United States Temperance Union. Originally it was educational in its nature, content to exert its influence upon the individual, but by the 1840's the inherent American maxim of "there ought to be a law" was being repeated more often. Neal Dow, an astute Maine politician, showed the way to get a law when, in 1851, he persuaded the Maine legislature to dry up that state. Within a decade twenty other states had followed the Down East example. With the end of the Civil War came a decline in prohibitory activity, blamable on the "moral laxity" of the times. But in 1874 the Woman's Christian Temperance Union was founded in Cleveland and from this stemmed, in the 1890's, the Anti-Saloon League.

Under the driving force of this increasingly rich and powerful organization the nineteenth-century ideals of individual responsibility and temperance were abandoned. They were replaced by a return to the "medieval idea of sumptuary legislation governing private conduct by fiat of law." [11] Fifteen years after the founding of the Anti-Saloon League, "like a tidal wave the temperance hosts were sweeping saloons out of the rural districts from coast to coast. As [Bishop James] Cannon [Jr.] expressed it, 'the walls of Jericho were falling down before the armies of the Lord.' " [12] The Lord's dry command hitherto had issued no communiqué to the effect that its ultimate war aim was national prohibition, but in 1911 it met in Washington to map the strategy that was ultimately to bring about the unconditional surrender of the American Congress.

Its plan of attack was to secure a Federal law forbidding the transportation of liquor into states where its sale was illegal. Several attempts to get Congress to enact such a law were abortive, but in 1913 the Webb-Kenyon Act was passed. This was the first great triumph of the prohibition lobby, led by the resourceful Wayne B. Wheeler and his able ally from the South, Bishop Cannon. They had learned how to work in the legislative lobbies back in the states, where, starting at the lowest levels, they had browbeaten and threatened their way to statewide victories.

When President Taft, doubting the constitutionality of the act, vetoed it, Congress passed it over his veto. It was immediately attacked in the courts but Wheeler, that man of overwhelming zeal, who privately agreed with the President, devoted four years to doing battle with the distinguished attorneys who represented the liquor interests and finally, in 1917, the act was upheld by the Supreme Court. Meanwhile the prohibition lobby, rich and tireless, labored in every state and in Washington for an amendment to the constitution that would end forever the dreadful traffic in intoxicating liquors.

A spokesman for the United States Brewers Association, one of the oldest lobbies in Washington and until the passage of the Webb-Kenyon Act one of the most successful, called attention to what he described as "an impressive fact" — namely, that Congress had passed the bill with more than a two-thirds majority "in the face of the united effort of all the branches of the alcoholic liquor traffic." Thus the nation was once again afforded an example of the clash of interests engaged in a merciless war to capture the government itself, which was, according to Bentley, the ultimate end of all pressure groups.

From Washington the Anti-Saloon League, following the classic pattern, turned to the grass roots. Its first real chance to show its power came with the election in 1916. When the votes were counted it was apparent that the league had advanced an important step. Congress, although still predominantly Democratic, had a larger percentage of "dry" members than heretofore. This was not by chance. Wayne B. Wheeler told why. "We laid down such a barrage as candidates for Congress had never seen before, and such as they will, in all likelihood, not see again for years to come." [13]

As the war psychology grew and congressional attention was turned to such matters as the Selective Service Act and the creation of a War Labor Board the astute master minds of the prohibition lobby made effective use of the national state of mind. In the closing session of the Sixty-fourth Congress Wayne B. Wheeler induced Senators Wesley Jones of Washington and William King of Utah to introduce resolutions calling for the investigation of two German brewers' associations suspected of disloyalty. This clever move of tying temperance to patriotism, at a time when the American people were keyed up to a pitch of exaltation, was a stroke of genius. The eighteenth amendment was submitted to the people quickly thereafter and within a little more than a year had been ratified by enough states to become the law of the land.

The imposition of prohibition upon the United States was almost entirely the work of a lobby. Unscrupulous and determined, willing to use any and every known method of propaganda and lobbying, a minority pressure group had managed to capture the government. For many years to come few members of Congress could get elected without submitting to the demands of this lobby. In the end, after years of bloody strife and lawlessness such as the wildest frontier days had not seen, the same methods that the prohibitionists had used were turned against them and the eighteenth amendment was repealed.

Back in 1911 a leading strategist of the Anti-Saloon League presented to the annual convention a short text on how to win. The choosing of issues, he said, the introduction of bills, and lobbying before legislatures, were all of great importance. But "back of all such endeavor there must be a nation-wide movement of public opinion, voicing itself in a way that will be heard by every congressman. Petitions are important if presented in sufficient volume; personal communications to members are still more effective; personal interviews are best of all, where the citizen can come face to face with his member and make known his wishes for legislation as a true American sovereign." [14]

This has become a commonplace, but the prohibitionists were the first organized minority to show the way to make use of this technique on a national scale. Since then we have learned that what seems like "a nation-wide movement of public opinion" is far too often nothing more than the synthetic creation of lobbyists and propagandists for special interests working against the national welfare for the sometimes open, but more often hidden, purpose of their employers.

CHAPTER IV

The Concentration of Power

THE function of the lobbyist, it has been said by an experienced observer of the Washington scene, is to burn the bridges behind the voter and what he voted for.[1] The voter, not knowing just what he had voted for in 1920 except that amorphous thing called Normalcy, paid little heed to the agents of the pressure groups when the Sixty-seventh Congress settled down to work in April, 1921. President Harding, who had come to the White House partly through the machinations of Harry Micajah Daugherty, one of the busiest lobbyists ever to beset the Ohio legislature, ignored their presence. Congress accepted them as part of the system.

In the years that followed Harding's scandalous arrival and departure big business, as the Republican Party was to learn to its sorrow, had its way. As Calvin Coolidge was about to say, the business of America was business; its agents, infesting the lobbies of the Capitol, were allowed to go unmolested. In the twelve years of Harding-Coolidge-Hoover prosperity the tariff lobbyists and others engaged in furthering private enterprise and fostering the American Way had their fruitful innings. A few days after Calvin Coolidge was inaugurated, Senator Kenneth B. McKellar, a Democrat from Tennessee, painted a picture for his colleagues that had long since become familiar.

There are lobbyists from the sugar interests, for the steel interests, for the fertilizer interests, for the cotton manufacturers' interests, for prohibition and for anti-prohibition, for postal employees, for labor organizations, for railroads, for civil service employees, for the equal rights of women, for the bonus, for those opposed to the bonus, for the shipping interests, for Henry Ford's acquisition of Muscle Shoals, for the water-power trust, for the oil interests, for the disabled service man, for the manufacturers, for the Army, for the Navy, for national aid to education, and many other interests. Washington is honey-combed with lobbyists. The hotels are full of them.[2]

While practically all the lobbyists on McKellar's list escaped censure, one of the youngest lobbies in the group was rapidly becoming one of the strongest and it was to get in the hair of all three Presidents of the Era of Normalcy. By 1925 the veterans' lobby, which had come into being almost before the armistice was signed, was no longer in the amateur division. Controlled by the politically minded leaders of the American Legion, its influence over Congress had become so extensive that more than one observer remarked that its capture of Congress was complete. In 1927 the Legion's own "legislative committee" boasted, "The Legion alone was responsible for the enactment into law of many . . . measures, having drawn the legislation, obtained its introduction, aided its progress in committee by testimony and legislative effort, and finally prevailed upon the House and Senate to take favorable action in time for approval by the President."

Many people who were not opposed in principle to the payment of a bonus to the veterans of the World War, looked with genuine alarm upon the American Legion's rapidly growing influence upon American life as a whole. Its propaganda, militaristic and fantastically un-American tradition and constitutional fiat, was spread far and wide, in newspapers, in the schools and colleges. It made far more noise than the number of its members warranted and congressional ears were peculiarly sensitive to its eagle screams.

The story of how the American Legion became so powerful began almost as soon as the Legion had been started by young

Theodore Roosevelt, Jr., Bennett Clark, and others, in Paris shortly before the end of the war. In order to obtain a charter from Congress, Luke Lea, the man who later was widely publicized for his attempt to "kidnap" Kaiser Wilhelm II, and Thomas W. Miller, who later became Alien Property Custodian, set up a Washington office. At the first national convention of the Legion they were authorized to remain as the Legion's national legislative committee. They were joined by John Thomas Taylor, a Washington lawyer, whose genius at lobbying has been one of the phenomena of official Washington for many years.[3]

To Taylor fell the task of building up the Legion lobby until it became the most tightly knit in Washington since the heyday of Wayne B. Wheeler and the Anti-Saloon League. An aggressive and skillful gentleman, Taylor once boasted, informally, that he "personally had written between 1500 and 2000 bills" during his first ten years as head of the lobby. A large number of these bills became law. It was Taylor who perfected the lobbying technique first practiced by the prohibitionists. Marcus Duffield has described vividly the five-point process of how to get a law on the statute books, a process now widely employed by pressure groups of high or low degree.

When the necessity of legislation is decided upon by the inner circle, according to the Taylor process, a member of a local post of the Legion is assigned to introduce it as a resolution. This gives it a grass-roots origin. Once it is passed by the post it is forwarded to the annual department convention, where it receives further endorsement before it is sent on to the national convention, with delegates assigned to push it through the resolutions committee. Once it is approved and endorsed by the committee it is sent to the floor for approval by the membership. Having reached this stage it automatically becomes a part of the American Legion's official legislative program for the ensuing year.

Up to this point the proposed law has been the product of the Legion's own theoretically democratic process. Now it is turned over to the legislative experts of the Washington lobby, who write it from their long experience in drafting bills. Its introduction into Congress is "a formality," for the lobby has had its key men "in all branches of the government." "Whatever the proper committee of the House of Representatives or the Senate, there will be found either a Legionnaire or a sympathizer who will not only introduce the bill but see it through committee if possible and right onto the floor of Congress." [4]

The Legion knows just about what will happen to every bill it writes and introduces. In its Washington lobby headquarters it keeps a record of the voting habits of every member. It also maintains what it calls its "status book," in the "prosaic pages" of which "is many a thrilling account of a bill carefully drawn up, introduced, steered through a committee, nursed along despite seemingly impossible obstacles, and then triumphantly rushed through Congress in the last hours of a session over the corpses of a dozen luckless measures by dint of maneuvers of politics known only to a seasoned lobbyist."

The American Legion's legislative committee once laid before the annual convention of the Legion its attitude towards legislation. It is worth quoting here for it is an attitude held, but not always satisfactorily expressed, by all pressure groups:

"It must be recognized," said these emissaries of King Legion, "that Congress does not lead in settling questions of public, political, or economic policy. . . . *Legislation is literally made outside the halls of Congress by groups of persons* interested in legislation, mainly with economic motives, and *the deliberative process within Congress constitutes a sort of formal ratification.*" [5]

Writing about the "embattled veterans," Roger Burlingame vividly described how their chief lobbyist, John Thomas Taylor, could walk through the halls of the Capitol "like a commander," receiving at his will the attention of congressmen of both parties. Any congressman who dared say no to him would be deluged with a flood of messages from the ex-soldiers in his district within

twenty-four hours.[6] There being more than 10,000 posts of the
Legion throughout the country, the pressure from "back home"
that the Legion can command is overwhelming. The Legion
forced through a bonus bill when Harding was President only to
have him exercise the veto power on it. The House passed it over
his veto and in the Senate it was barely sustained. The Legion
lobby was victorious in the election year of 1924 when it passed
the bill over President Coolidge's veto, despite the actions of a
vigorous and well-heeled antibonus lobby which received its support and directions from Wall Street.

By 1927 the Washington lobbyists — the Legion and others —
had again become so bold that the Senate expressed its alarm. A
committee was set up to inquire into their activities and, if the
situation warranted it, to recommend legislation for their regulation. The able Senator Thaddeus H. Caraway was placed in
charge and he conducted the public hearings, which, however,
failed to set afire the indignation of a complacent public still well
pleased with the Coolidgean way of life. They led, nevertheless,
to the second attempt by Congress to regulate lobbyists.

Senator Caraway was seriously concerned with the constitutional implications involved in the writing of any law which
might seem to be in possible conflict with the first amendment.
As he told the Senate during debate on the bill he was not at all
sure how such a law would fare at the hands of the reactionary
Supreme Court. This timidity kept him from writing a strong
regulatory bill and he confessed that it did not cover everyone
he wanted to get at. It did, however, make an attempt at defining
lobbies and lobbyists, an exercise in legislative semantics that was
still worrying the lawmakers even after the passage of the lobby
title in the Legislative Reorganization Act of 1946, nineteen years
later.

Lobbying, as defined in 1927, was ". . . any effort in influencing Congress upon any matter coming before it, whether it
be by distributing literature, appearing before committees of Con-

gress, or seeking to interview members of either the House of Representatives or the Senate." A lobbyist was ". . . one who shall engage, for pay, to attempt to influence legislation, or to prevent legislation by the national Congress." [7]

It can be seen from these quotations that the bill was not carefully drawn. Especially weakening was its complete omission of any apparatus that would get behind the lobbyist and reveal the true source of his income. But it was a step in the right direction, as the editorial writers said. It passed the Senate without a dissenting vote but it died a quiet death in the pigeonhole of a House committee.

In his report Senator Caraway touched upon a situation that had hitherto been neglected by lobby probers, but which had long been an annoyance and which, in light of the so-called "five percenter" investigations in 1949, now sounds familiar. He pointed out that there were between 300 and 400 "alleged associations" listed in the District of Columbia telephone book, of which he estimated 90 per cent were "fake associations." These were, he charged, "engaged in obtaining money from those who live away from Washington under the belief that they are promoting some theory of government in which they are interested, or protecting or advancing the interests of some business in which they are engaged." He estimated that $95 out of every $100 "go into the pockets of these fake associations." Needless to say, Senator Caraway's "exposure" of the "fakers" attracted more attention than the serious situation created by the real lobbyists who were engaged in the disruption of the democracy on behalf of the special interests for whom they worked hard and earnestly.[8]

While Senator Caraway was engaged in his unsuccessful campaign to put a halter on the lobbyists, President Coolidge was moving in his cautious way to advance the cause of world peace. At Geneva representatives of his administration as well as of other great powers were vainly trying to agree to a reduction in naval armaments which would carry further the agreements that had been reached at the Washington Conference of 1921. But after weeks of argument and discussion the conference broke up in failure. American newspapers tried to explain to a dispirited people that Great Britain was to blame for the unexpected fiasco. They should have looked closer at home.

Two years later, while President Hoover was preparing the way for another disarmament conference at London, a gentleman named William B. Shearer, who described himself as an "American, Christian, Protestant and Nationalist," and whose name was familiar to most of the correspondents who had cabled the bad news from Geneva, broke into the news. In the New York courts he filed a suit to recover $257,655 which he claimed was owed him by the New York Shipbuilding Company for services as naval expert, propagandist, and lobbyist at Geneva and in Washington. Thus the way was paved for the exposure of one of the most subversive lobbies ever brought to light by congressional investigation.

Like the rest of the nation President Hoover was shocked by the intimations of chicanery emanating from Shearer's suit. Publicly condemning the propaganda which had been spread for the purpose of creating "international distrust and hate" he demanded an explanation from the shipbuilders, ordered the Attorney General to look into the matter, and suggested to the Senate that it get "to the very bottom" of the scandal.

With what can only be called reluctance a subcommittee of the Senate Committee on Naval Affairs stumbled through a lengthy investigation that revealed "one of the most unsavory stories in the long history of American scandals." [9] Although the inquisitors were none too keen in their questioning and failed to follow through on several startling leads, they managed to spread upon the record — 700 pages of it — an amazing account of Shearer's crude lobbying. It was definitely proved that he had been sent to Geneva by the shipbuilding interests and had done everything in his power to defeat the purpose of the conference. Afterwards he had been appointed a sort of lobbyist general for those interested in bigger naval appropriations and for those interested in subsidies for the merchant marine.

Among his chores as lobbyist and propagandist — sometimes the dividing line is invisible — was preparing articles for the Republican Presidential campaign of 1928, in which he tarred peace advocates as traitors and tried to besmirch the reputation of former Secretary of State Charles Evans Hughes. He wrote speeches for such pressure groups as the Daughters of the American Revolution and the American Legion, who were suckers for anything that sounded belligerently patriotic. He worked for William Randolph Hearst at $2000 a month, writing big-navy propaganda. His contacts with the Navy Department were shown to be extensive. Among the shipbuilders whose testimony revealed the extent of his activities were Charles M. Schwab, E. G. Grace, and C. L. Bardo, president of the New York Shipbuilding Company and, a few years later, President of the National Association of Manufacturers.

After Geneva, Shearer devoted his energies to lobbying in Washington for passage of the Merchant Marine Bill enacted during the Coolidge administration. He was shown to be an expensive operator. According to a letter from Mr. Bardo it cost the shipbuilding interests $150,000 to put this measure through Congress. Of this large sum $30,000 went for publicity and advertising, $26,000 for the "service of experts," and $23,000 for Washington hotel expenses. This heavy expenditure, in Mr. Bardo's words, was "carried on in the interests of the shipper, shipbuilder, shipowner, and suppliers of materials used in ship construction." Among the beneficiaries of the legislation called upon to pay the bill were General Electric, Bath Iron Works, Worthington Pump and Machinery, and the American Brown Boveri Electric Corporation.

Not all of Shearer's activities were brought out in this inquiry.

Much pertinent data remained hidden until unearthed in 1935 by Senator Nye and the Munitions Investigation Committee which he headed. Then it was shown that the shipbuilding lobbyist claimed credit, not unjustly, for the appropriations for building eight 10,000-ton cruisers authorized by the Sixty-ninth Congress; and it was further shown that he had much to do with the introduction of the $740,000,000, 71-ship building program brought before the Seventieth Congress. For his services during the year 1928 he acknowledged receipt of $25,000 from the Bethlehem Shipbuilding Company. At the same time other lobbyists for the shipbuilding interests claimed credit for the passage of the cruiser bill, the second deficiency bill, and other measures. That Washington was swarming with lobbyists, working closely with high officials of the army as well as the navy, not only during the Era of Normalcy but as late as 1935, became a well documented fact in the record of the Nye committee.[10]

One result of the Shearer investigation and the Senate debate over the London Treaty was the unmasking of an organization which had long appeared before the public as a great patriotic society but which was one of the most potent pressure groups then in existence. The Navy League, largely founded and supported by munitions and supply interests, had been able for many years to dictate headlines and intimidate private citizens without its true nature as a propaganda outfit for big-navy interests being revealed. But the truth was made manifest when it assumed the lead in fighting ratification of the treaty. It was clearly proved to be the mouthpiece for shipbuilders and navy yards, munitions and aircraft manufacturers, and for a clique within the navy which worked with these interests. Senator Arthur Capper told the Senate: "The country should be grateful to President Hoover for having torn off its mask and shown it to us as the greedy commercial organization it is — seeking to make excessive profits from the Government for steel and shipbuilding companies under the plea of superpatriotism." The Navy League's standing as an effective lobby was pretty well demolished, but as late as 1941 the Temporary National Economic Committee found it still to be of sufficient importance to warrant several pages of attention in its monograph, *Economic Power and Political Pressures*.[11]

At the same time that all this was happening the great privately owned electric power industry was engaged in one of the most widespread propaganda campaigns of which we have a record. During the 1920's Senator George Norris and others began the long drive that led eventually to the establishment of the Tennessee Valley Authority, which the historian Henry Steele Commager has said is "in many ways the most remarkable achievement of the first half of the century." [12] It brought into being one of the most expensive lobbies in history, the National Electric Light Association, which, under the title of the Edison Electric Institute, still watches carefully over the legislative destinies of the industry.

In 1926 Senator Norris introduced a resolution for an investigation by the Federal Trade Commission of public utility practices. Two years later that body submitted its report. It was, however, so inadequate, so lacking in definiteness, and so obviously the result of inconclusive questioning, as to be practically useless. Senator Thomas Walsh of Montana thereupon introduced another resolution calling for a Senate investigation of utility financing. This met with the vigorous opposition of the utilities. Senator Walsh himself described to the Senate the pressure that was brought to bear upon the committee that held hearings on the resolution:

"The first group appearing in opposition to the inquiry was the National Electric Light Association, composed of 893 electric operating companies, 324 manufacturing companies, 263 associate companies, and 93 foreign companies; the American Electric Railway Association, composed of 337 operating companies, 35 associate companies, 423 manufacturing companies; the American Gas

Association, composed of 469 operating companies, 25 holding companies, 350 manufacturing companies, and 17 associate companies."

This formidable array was "marshaled by Mr. George B. Cortelyou," the Montana Democrat continued, "and it is well known that these great organizations, through their representatives, assembled here in the city of Washington before Congress convened last December, set up spacious and luxurious quarters here, and called to their aid experts in various lines, including experts in securing legislation from Congress and in defeating legislation before Congress."

Then followed the line that is becoming increasingly familiar to readers of this book: "There was assembled here the most formidable lobby ever brought together in this city."

Senator Walsh estimated that the lobby represented capital to the amount of nearly 10 billion dollars. Joined with the electric, electric railway, and gas lobbies was the lobby of the investment bankers, who suavely told the committee that "they caused investigation into public utility securities and, therefore, there was no necessity for any by the . . . Senate or by any governmental authority at all."

"Then," Senator Walsh continued, "we had the American Manufacturers Association * appearing by one James A. Emery, the employer and co-worker of the infamous Mulhall, whose villainies were exposed by a committee of the Senate in 1913." [13]

As has happened before, the concentration of power to defeat the legislation had an adverse effect; it had all the appearance of ganging up on Congress. Realizing that the resolution stood a good chance of passing, the lobbies changed their tactics and sought to have the investigation carried out by the Federal Trade Commission, which, in the light of the earlier 1928 report, they obviously felt would be more tractable. Senator George offered

---

* Senator Walsh obviously meant the National Association of Manufacturers.

an amendment to this effect. The resolution with the amendment was approved on February 15, 1928. The Commission went to work the next month and carried on its investigation for more than a year and a half. Its report was no whitewash.

Early in the 1920's the electric power utilities had awakened to the growing threat of governmental regulation and control of power that might eventually lead to public ownership of this most vital facet of the national economy. They thereupon launched a nation-wide propaganda campaign to educate the American public about the dangers to the American Way of Life that would come if the utilities were ever allowed to slip from private enterprise to public control. The National Electric Light Association was the foremost of a well integrated group of organizations that, operating under the Joint Committee of National Utility Associations, spent over $1,000,000 annually to propagate its viewpoint. Said the Federal Trade Commission:

"To such an extent has the utility program taken into consideration 'every public contract' that no campaign approaching it in magnitude has ever been conducted except possibly by governments in war time." [14]

It cost a vast amount of money to carry on this campaign, but this did not matter to the utilities because, as the Commission quoted M. H. Aylesworth, director of the National Electric Light Association, as saying, "the public pays." Including more than $25,000,000 for advertising in 1923 alone!

The utilities flooded every possible outlet of public information. Newspapers, magazines, lecture platforms, forums, service organizations, civic societies, schools and colleges, Sunday schools, pulpits — everything was used except skywriting, said the director of publicity for the NELA — were made the object of the utility propagandists in this all-out effort to block effective governmental regulation and forestall public ownership or operation.

The impressively successful extent of the public utility propaganda all over the country was such that many a schoolboy of

that period still remembers that it was considered all but subversive even to intimate in a history or civics class that the utilities were not the greatest benefactors of mankind since history's
dawn.

Thus, at the grass roots, the utilities sought to make the way
easier for the lobbyists in Washington and in the state capitols.
And at the same time they paved the way for the great and bitter
battle between themselves and the New Deal — a battle which was
to lead at last to the law regulating lobbyists and lobbies enacted
in 1946.

CHAPTER V

Senator Black Investigates

LOBBYISTS fare the worst, we have seen, when there is bold leadership in the White House and party discipline in Congress. There is no question that both Presidential leadership and party discipline existed to an extraordinary extent in the early days of the New Deal. At no time, of course, has Washington been entirely free from paid agents of all the interests and this was as true during this period as at any other. The passage of the National Industrial Recovery Act toward the end of the famous One Hundred Days filled the hotels to the very ceilings with businessmen and their agents as they sought, in the maelstrom that was Washington in those days, to get the best possible consideration for their own enterprises under the codes that were being written through the provisions of this emergency measure. Many of the trade organizations which today have offices in Washington came into being at this hectic time, but lobbying was at a low ebb while Congress was still under the spell of Roosevelt and while the Brain Trust was still charting a course of recovery. But long before the end of President Roosevelt's first term, party lines began to crumble and the big pressure groups once again were sending their emissaries scrambling up the slopes of Capitol Hill.

By the beginning of 1935 Congress had already resumed its role of an independent and recalcitrant body and was lending its ear not only to the mellifluous voice from Pennsylvania Avenue but to the tough talk from the "pressure boys." This significant year not only saw the New Deal thrown on the defensive and forced to exert all its strength and wiles to save itself from destruction but it saw an alignment of the common people definitely on the side of the New Deal. President Roosevelt did not have to wait until the 1936 election to know where he stood, for 1935 was the year which witnessed the introduction of the public opinion polls. These mystic criteria had thirteen years to go before they were to be discredited as a gauge of popular beliefs. In 1935 they showed a preponderant majority of all classes supporting the President and the greater part of his program. Arrayed against him was only the large-income group, those whom he had called money-changers and threatened to drive from the temple.

In this critical year close observers of the political scene noted signs of defection. Northern Democrats occasionally deserted party leaders, but this was not so disturbing as was the growing affiliation of a loose bloc of Southern conservative Democrats with reactionary Republicans. Both these groups were more amenable to the politics of pressure and patronage than to an abiding belief in the need for strong party leadership and national party principles. They were willing and eager to take their directives from the more powerful interests "back home" and they opened the way for the great assault upon the New Deal that was soon to come in all its fury. But in general party leadership still prevailed (strangely enough, this was almost exclusively managed by Southerners like Hugo Black, James F. Byrnes, Alben W. Barkley, Harry S. Truman, Claude Pepper, Fred M. Vinson, and Harley M. Kilgore) and it was potent enough to beat back the angry drives against the New Deal line by the various blocs of malcontents under the influence of the bankers, utility magnates, and assorted businessmen whose hatred of "that man in the White House" and all his works was growing day by day.

The first effective attacks from pressure groups had come in 1934. There is no question that the lobby of the big commercial farmers defeated the program devised by Rexford G. Tugwell to improve the lot of the sharecroppers and tenant farmers. And that same year Northern Democrats, including every senator from New England to Ohio, responded to the lobbies of the insurance companies and the bankers to oppose the Frazier-Lemke Farm Bankruptcy Act with its provision for a five-year moratorium on mortgage foreclosures. Responding to pressures from home, however, Southern and Western Congressmen banded together to make it law. The inflationary Silver Purchase Act was another victory for Western pressure groups.

In 1935 the American Legion demonstrated that it had not lost the right to boast of being the perfect lobby, when it forced through its $2,200,000,000 Soldiers' Bonus Act over President Roosevelt's veto, by the huge vote in the House of 318 to 90.

This year also saw the beginning of a shifting lobby fight that still continues and that will probably go on until the question is finally settled. Both Presidents Coolidge and Hoover had lent their support to the vast international improvement known as the St. Lawrence Seaway and Power Development. A treaty for its accomplishment had been negotiated before President Roosevelt took office. Farmers in the Mississippi Valley wanted it, for it meant cheaper freight rates. To everyone within its reach it meant lower electric power costs when the international rapids were harnessed — a project potentially as productive as TVA. Its benefits to the interior of Canada would be tremendous. Its helpful influence would stretch from New England into the entire American heartland. It would bring the sea into the Middle West, move Europe's markets that much nearer the great agricultural centers of the Western world.

Because these very benefits threatened their established superiority, the utility companies, the railroads, and the eastern shipping interests fought bitterly. In Congress party lines disappeared before the pressure of these three powerful lobbies. Despite the fact that the treaty had had Republican Presidential support, Republican senators from the East joined Democrats from the South, including the notorious Huey Long (whose passion to share the wealth never interfered with his subservience to the New Orleans shipping interests) until all the senators from the Atlantic sea-board states were lined up for the defeat of the treaty. President Roosevelt threw his support behind it and his floor leaders strug-gled valiantly to hold the party line. They did manage to main-tain a majority, but the treaty was rejected because of the two-thirds rule. Thus special interests, definitely in the minority, thwarted the will of a majority of the people.*

Among the New Deal measures which the power lobby fought unsuccessfully, with the aid of other lobbies opposed in principle to the establishment of any regulatory bodies, was the Federal Communications Commission. But the greatest defeat of the lob-bies came about with the passage of the Securities and Exchange Act. This measure was one of the bases of the New Deal struc-ture, a reform that had been long overdue. Clear in the minds of everyone was the stock market crash of 1929. Wall Street had done nothing in the interim to show an inward desire to regulate its affairs in consonance with the needs or wishes of the common community. Although millions of Americans had never invested as much as a dime in stocks or bonds, the traditional belief that the affairs of Wall Street affected the life of almost every Ameri-can was prevalent, and not without reason. The American public had learned the bitter lesson that politics are not far removed from economics. They knew that banks and stock exchanges bore

* There are in Washington today several well-established and registered lobbyists whose main concern is the St. Lawrence Seaway and Power De-velopment, interest in which was revived in President Truman's 1950 message on the state of the Union. Representation is about equally divided pro and con. But, of course, many lobbyists whose major interests lie elsewhere, representatives of shipping, railroad, mining, and electric power interests particularly, work against it whenever the occasion arises, as it did in the 80th Congress when the Senate, following no party lines, eliminated the issue by voting to recommit a St. Lawrence Seaway bill, 57 to 30. Mining interests fought it — until the discovery of the Labrador ore deposits, when they began to shift!

a great part of the responsibility for the state of affairs in which the people found themselves. They were firmly resolved to follow the New Deal all the way in its brave attempt to bring these understandable economic factors under some measure of control. Nor did the proposed law seek unreasonable power in providing for setting up an agency that would regulate the stock exchanges, compel full and truthful information for investors, restrain the more reckless practices of gamblers, brokers, promoters, corporation managers, and investors themselves.

The financial interests, screaming against bureaucracy, launched an unbridled attack against the proposed SEC. The majority of the nation's newspapers sided with them. The amount of money which was spent to defeat this measure has never been estimated, but it was obviously a staggering sum. The newspaper and radio propaganda against the bill alone was tremendous. Every known method of exerting pressure on Congress was used. The longer the battle raged the more apparent was it that the anti-SEC lobby was gaining success in its drive to intimidate Congress. The bill became stalled and seemed destined for defeat, or at least for such emasculation as to make it useless, when President Roosevelt returned from a vacation spent fishing in Southern waters. With the pointed remark that he would have to use the same "tough guy" tactics he had learned while battling the "barracuda and the shark" he rallied his scattered forces and saved the day. Thoroughly backed by the public (although a reading of the newspapers would not reveal this) and using all the power of Presidential pressure, Roosevelt forced the bill through.

That he had the public's approval was made clear by the returns of the 1934 election, which demonstrated that the people were behind his administration and program for greater economic controls. In spite of the Democratic — or should it more properly be called Roosevelt — landslide in 1934, Congress was soon rent by new party divisions. The pressure groups took new heart. The old-line lobbies, particularly the National Association of Manufacturers, went to work with all the resources at their command to defeat the passage of the Social Security Act of 1935. But many a minority pressure group, including the increasingly efficient labor lobby, countered with arguments in its favor. At the same time a wide variety of "crackpot" organizations, such as those of Doctor Townsend and Father Coughlin, then promoting his Union for Social Justice, and of Huey Long, leader of the Share-Our-Wealth Society, descended upon Washington to promote their various schemes, leading President Roosevelt to warn that "organizations promoting fantastic schemes have aroused hopes which cannot possibly be fulfilled." * The Social Security Act, with all its imperfections, was enacted, and helped deflate the Townsend-Coughlin-Long schemes.†

The passage of social security legislation, which the NAM propagandists continued for several years to attack as bureaucratic and sought to prove unconstitutional, and of the 1935 Revenue Act, which increased taxes on inherited estates, the bigger incomes, excess profits, and large corporate incomes, while decreasing taxes on smaller business incomes, were marked by violent opposition from the established lobbies. Strangely enough the Wagner National Labor Relations Act was steered through Congress with a minimum amount of opposition from such or-

---

* The frightening nature of these organizations, which together claimed a membership of close to 20,000,000, helped arouse Congress to a need for social security legislation, although none of them supported the administration bill. President Roosevelt took cognizance of them again when, shortly before the enactment of the social security law, he transmitted his request in June, 1935, for a revision of the tax laws to revoke former Secretary of the Treasury Mellon's system of favoritism to the upper-income groups, a system which had allowed J. P. Morgan and his partners to escape payment of income taxes in 1932. "Social unrest and a deepening sense of unfairness are dangers to our national life which we must minimize by rigorous methods," he said. Congress responded by enacting the far from rigorous Revenue Act of 1935 in spite of bitter press and lobby attacks upon it as an un-American, soak-the-rich measure.

† While Congress was debating the Social Security Bill, efforts were made to secure adoption of a national health insurance program. The lobby for organized medicine, led by the American Medical Association, raised such a furor that the proposal was dropped. See Beards, *op. cit.*, p. 290.

ganizations as the National Association of Manufacturers,* although after its passage the NAM was not to cease striking at it until it put over the Taft-Hartley Act, one of the few outstanding legislative victories in its long history as a lobby.

Although, after the One Hundred Days, practically every measure sponsored by the administration met with the opposition of from one to one hundred lobbies, none created the excitement or filled the American press with as many hysterical words as did the historic battle for the passage of the Holding Company Act. So unrestrained was the fight on both sides that those who lived through it still have the uneasy feeling that blood flowed through the streets of Washington in those days.

The Public Utility Holding Company Bill, known as the Wheeler-Rayburn Bill, was a reform measure stemming from the unbridled actions of the utility magnates, Samuel Insull and the rest, back in the dreadful days of Normalcy. It was aimed at toppling those supercolossal paper structures in the electric utility field, the fantastic nature of which had been clearly demonstrated through long and thorough investigation by the Federal Trade Commission. "Congressional investigations had laid bare many of the questionable methods employed by financiers in promoting these corporate leviathans and had disseminated the suspicion that their sponsors had often been imprudent and in some cases deceptive, if not clearly dishonest." [1] The Democratic Party, in its 1932 platform, had pledged itself to regulate them. So well had it been proved that the industry cried for regulation by the Federal government that it seemed hardly likely Congress would seriously listen to any arguments against the proposed measure. Yet this is exactly what happened. One of the most brazen lobbies in the history of the country — and, for once, this term is not exaggerated

---

* The Wagner Act was one of 31 major legislative proposals enacted into law between 1933 and 1941 which was opposed by the National Association of Manufacturers. The NAM supported only 7 of a total of 38. See "NAM: Spokesman for Industry?" by Alfred S. Cleveland, *Harvard Business Review*, vol. xxvi, no. 3, May, 1948, pp. 353 ff.

— descended upon Washington, and found ready allies among the political opponents of the New Deal in Congress and the press, who saw in this well-financed lobby a further weapon against the Roosevelt administration.

The key to the Public Utility Holding Company Bill, the issue on which it was the most violently attacked, was the so-called "death sentence," the provision which called for the breaking up of these unsound structures. The conflict over the "death sentence" lasted throughout the greater part of the first session of the Seventy-fourth Congress. From the beginning public utility interests, headed by the Committee of Public Utility Executives, which included most of the big companies except Associated Gas & Electric (which, in the person of the notorious Howard C. Hopson, maintained its own lobby), and the Edison Electric Institute, spent thousands of dollars to defeat the measure. Their propaganda found ready publication in a large segment of the national press. The voice of support was drowned by the indignant roars of opposition.

With his usual excellent sense of timing President Roosevelt stepped into the affray with a special message to Congress on March 12, in which he denounced the utility holding companies as "private empires within the nation" and denounced their efforts to check Congress as lobbying:

I have been watching with great interest the fight being waged against public utility holding-company legislation. I have watched the use of investors' money to make the investor believe that the efforts of government are designed to defraud him. I have seen much of the propaganda prepared against such legislation — even down to mimeographed sheets of instruction for propaganda to exploit the most far-fetched and fallacious fears. I have seen enough to be as unimpressed by it as I was by similar efforts to stir up the country against the Security and Exchange Bill last spring.

So much has been said through chain letters and by word of mouth that misrepresents the intent and purpose of a new law that it is important that the people of the country understand once and for all the actual facts of the case. . . . It is time to make an effort to reverse that process of the concentration of power which has made most American citizens, once traditionally independent owners of their own businesses, helplessly dependent upon the favor of the very few, who, by devices such as holding companies, have taken for themselves unwarranted economic power. I am against private socialism of concentrated private power as thoroughly as I am against governmental socialism. The one is equally as dangerous as the other; and destruction of private socialism is utterly essential to avoid governmental socialism.[2]

Congressional supporters of the Wheeler-Rayburn Bill were quick to take the hint implicit in the message. While they made no outright denial of the right of the public utilities to "seek the ear of the legislator" they demanded an investigation which would reveal the lengths to which the power lobby had gone. The result of this demand was the creation of a Senate committee to explore the matter. Senator Hugo Black was named as its chairman.

One of the most able senators the upper house had known in many years, with a mind like a whiplash, with the zeal of a crusader, and with an intense belief in economic justice, Senator Black was the ideal man for the task. His investigation was a model of thorough and courageous application; it bravely used all the power of congressional edict to get at the heart of the matter it was assigned to investigate. It spared no one, was adamant in the use of subpoena, and utterly defiant of all the pressure of wealth and power brought against it. The Hearst press, raging mad, called it the "Blackguard Committee" and called upon high heaven and the constitution to stop its iniquitous invasion of the rights of private individuals. The rest of the press, equally angry but more restrained in language, referred to it not as an investigation but as an inquisition. Senator Black was unmoved.

Under Senator Black's relentless examination it was learned that the organized lobby against the Wheeler-Rayburn Bill was masterminded by Philip Henry Gadsden, chairman of the Committee of Public Utility Executives, who admitted having spent $151,865 up to the time of the start of the investigation. The

Edison Electric Institute was shown to have been an active and big spender. One of its employees, Burnham Carter of the publicity firm of Ivy Lee & T. J. Ross, was paid at the rate of $5000 a month. His contribution was to bring to Washington friends of various congressmen who "turned on the heat" in no uncertain terms. The Associated Gas & Electric Company was revealed as the spender of thousands of dollars for advertising in the Hearst chain of newspapers. Hopson's firm hired several "big shot" lawyers to help direct its campaign, among them Pat Hurley, who had been President Hoover's Secretary of War, and Bruce Kremer, a friend of Homer Cummings, the New Deal Attorney General. Joseph Tumulty, who had been President Wilson's secretary, admitted to receiving $33,500 from four large power companies, of which $12,500 came from Commonwealth & Southern, the utility for which Wendell Willkie was the articulate spokesman.*

---

* Tumulty testified that during 1934 and 1935 he got, in addition to his utility fees, $10,000 from the Bureau of Raw Materials, $1250 from Arthur O'Brien, $25,000 from Lehman Brothers, $10,000 from National Distillers Products, $12,500 from Manuel Quezon, $2000 from the United States Rubber Company, and, for three years' services, $15,000 from the New York law firm that represented Lloyd's of London.

"One of the most engaging and certainly one of the most sentimental of the Washington lobbyists," Kenneth Crawford wrote, "Tumulty is a holdover from an older, now declining school. Knowing all who amount to anything in Washington, liking them and receiving affection in return, he gets results as a special pleader before Administration agencies, many of which are well stocked with employees he has recommended. He also may have some influence with individual members of Congress in an over-the-brandy sort of way. He seldom appears before a Congressional committee." Kenneth G. Crawford, The Pressure Boys. New York, 1939. Pp. 61–62.

"Not being willing to lobby," Tumulty wrote after the Black investigation in a pamphlet entitled Statement, "and being ashamed to tarnish old friendships to eke out a fee, I give to clients, rich and poor alike, the only thing a free soul possesses — the modest ability that gives to an honorable professional engagement the brain and vision one has. That I gave freely, honorably, unstintedly, and cleanly, to those who sought my counsel and cooperation in the matter of the Wheeler bill." Crawford, op. cit., quoted p. 62.

For an official summary of the Black Committee findings see Congressional Record, vol. lxix, pp. 10229–10254.

The Black Committee concerned itself mostly, however, with the Associated Gas & Electric Company. Among the embarrassing discoveries was the fact that Basil O'Connor, former partner of President Roosevelt, was a member of its legal staff. Mr. O'Connor was the brother of John O'Connor, a representative from New York City and chairman of the powerful House Rules Committee. The latter professed loyalty to the aims of the proposed holding company legislation, but it was well known in the inner circles of the New Deal that he was doing all in his power to obstruct its passage without compromising his position as a leading New Dealer. It was because of this that President Roosevelt "purged" him from the Democratic Party in the 1938 elections when he told the New York voters that O'Connor was "the most effective obstructionist" on Capitol Hill.

Conclusive of the Presidential charge of lobbying though all this was, it did not set off fireworks half as sparkling as those ignited by Elmer Danielson, a Western Union messenger boy from Warren, Pennsylvania. It was this nineteen-year-old "Mercury" who told how he had been sent out to solicit telegrams in opposition to the Wheeler-Rayburn Bill, at three cents a telegram, which were then sent free to Representative D. J. Driscoll in Washington. When Driscoll received some 816 in two days he became suspicious and "tipped off" the Black Committee. From Elmer the investigators worked forward until they proved that thousands of telegrams were sent to Washington — sometimes at the rate of 4000 an hour — signed with names taken at random and without authority from telephone books and directories. Although many of the telegrams were destroyed before the committee could seize them, the committee was able to prove the great flood of protest, supposedly spontaneous from a citizenry suddenly aroused to the socialistic dangers of the New Deal, was in reality a wholly false and malicious propaganda drive by the utilities.

Another hysterical outburst of protest arose when President

Roosevelt allowed the records of personal incomes to be opened
by the committee. This invasion of private rights, however,
showed that between them the Associated Gas & Electric system
and the Committee of Public Utility Executives had spent almost
$1,000,000 to defeat the Holding Company Bill.

By concentrating on the affairs of the billion-dollar utility empire that had been built up by Howard C. Hopson during the
1920's, until it represented $1,000,000,000 of capital with gross
annual earnings of $100,000,000 and embraced more than 300
operating and other units in half the states of the union, the Black
Committee and the Senate Banking Committee, of which Fer-
dinand Pecora was chief counsel, made the passage of the Holding Company Act inevitable. Hopson, by his defiance and arro-
gance, became a symbol of what President Roosevelt, in his
second inaugural, called "princes of privilege" and "economic
Tories." His refusal to appear before the committee until there
had been a long and comic-opera chase by committee deputies
through Washington cocktail rooms filled the newspapers with
lurid stories. But when he was finally cornered and practically
dragged before his questioners the information elicited from him
shocked the nation and threw popular support behind the New
Deal program of reform in banking, investment, stock market,
and public utility practices.*

While Senator Black was proceeding with his investigation,
the House Rules Committee, under Representative O'Connor's
chairmanship, decided also to look into the matter of lobbying.
The House investigation was, to put it mildly, a fraud. It concentrated its fire upon the "administration lobbying" † to get the

---

* Hopson, whose personal fortune once was estimated at $47,000,000, saw
his billion-dollar pyramid collapse in the depression of the 1930's, and was
sent to jail in the early 1940's on charges of defrauding stockholders of
$20,000,000.

† In 1950 there was much talk in Congress about the necessity of investigating "administration lobbying" during the investigation of lobbying
authorized by the House. The matter, however, was not deeply probed.

bill passed. Its investigation was perverted into a whitewash of the utilities, but this did not stand up against the revelations made by Senator Black. Nevertheless the House did its best to sabotage the Holding Company Bill and succeeded in denaturing it to such an extent that the act as finally passed was a compromise between the House and Senate bills. Although the final bill proved less effective than its original sponsors in the New Deal had hoped, it nevertheless was a tremendous administration victory and it was historically important because for the first time it authorized the regulation of public utilities through the Federal Power Commission and the newly created Securities and Exchange Commission.

Out of this great commotion, it was hoped by persons genuinely interested in the process of government that there would at last emerge an act which in some effective manner would curb the activities of lobbyists who, as the matter of fraudulent telegrams had definitely proved, went far beyond the right of petition secured in the first amendment. And for a time it appeared that success was in sight.

Senator Black introduced a bill in the Senate which would require lobbyists to register and reveal the sources of their income. It was a good measure, soundly drafted, undoubtedly the best that had ever been offered Congress. It broadly defined lobbying as "any effort to influence the action of Congress upon any matter coming before it, whether it be by distributing literature, appearing before committees of Congress, or interviewing or seeking to interview individual members of either the House of Representatives or the Senate." This improved bill, like that of Senator Caraway's bill in 1927, passed the Senate, but in the House it was a different matter.

Representative O'Connor, aided by such reactionaries as Howard Smith of Virginia and Eugene Cox of Georgia, had made a farce of his investigation from the start. His committee had turned most of its fire against Tom Corcoran, one of the drafters of the Wheeler-Rayburn Act, and other New Dealers, and had in various ways protected Hopson from Black. Now this same clique proceeded to sabotage the Black antilobbying bill by introducing to the House such stringent amendments that it was unacceptable.

During this period Senator Black said over the radio: "Contrary to tradition, against the public morals, and hostile to good government, the lobby has reached such a position of power that it threatens government itself. Its size, its power, its capacity for evil; its greed, trickery, deception and fraud condemn it to the death it deserves."

He spoke too soon. The antilobby bill was killed in conference, after having passed both houses.

Senator Black did not confine himself to the utility lobby. His committee laid bare the lobbying activities, both before Congress and various administrative agencies, of air transport operators, shipowners, operators, and others involved in air and ocean mail contracts.

Although his antilobby bill died he had a measure of success. Congress wrote into the Public Utility Holding Company Act several stringent restrictions. It not only forbade public utilities to contribute to party campaign funds but it made it unlawful for any person "employed or retained by any registered holding company . . . to present, advocate, or oppose any matter affecting any registered holding company . . . before Congress or any member of a committee thereof, or before the Securities and Exchange Commission or Federal Power Commission . . . unless such person file . . . a statement of the subject matter in respect of which such person is retained or employed, the nature and character of such retainer or employment, and the amount of compensation received or to be received, directly or indirectly, in connection therewith." It also required that such agents file financial statements "within ten days of each calendar month during such retainer and employment." Encouraged by the passage of this law Congress later passed a statute similarly regulating the lobbies of shipbuilders and operators through registration with the Maritime Commission.

Black's committee also had the pleasure of exploring the rich background of the Liberty League, revealing the pressure groups which backed this anti-New Deal organization.

In 1938 another law was passed which, as Professor Belle Zeller has pointed out, lends weight to the legality of requiring special agents to register with the government. This was the Foreign Agents Registration Act, which required every agent of a foreign principal to file a detailed statement of the nature of his activity with the State Department and to label all propaganda as such and deposit file copies with the Library of Congress.

Congress, however, did not respond to further demands to put some sort of bridle * upon the lobbyists, although their activities continued to increase. Their connection with the concentration of economic power, which had become a question of increasing importance during President Roosevelt's second term, was dealt with by the Temporary National Economic Committee which was set up by Congress at the President's request in 1938. Among the "evidence" gathered by this committee was an excellent monograph [3] by Donald C. Blaisdell, an economic expert engaged by the committee. Mr. Blaisdell made several recommendations for a lobby registration act in his monograph, which was published in 1941, shortly before the TNEC ceased to function, but they fell on deaf ears.

Nor was Congress in a mood to listen when, in 1944, President

* Unless the amendment of the Criminal Code in 1940 can be considered as such. In this year Title 18, Sec. 241a, was revised to forbid anyone to endeavor ". . . corruptly or by threats of force, or by any threatening letter or communication . . . to influence, intimidate, or impede any witness . . . in connection with any inquiry or investigation being had by either House, or any committee of either House, or by any joint committee of Congress . . . or by such methods to attempt to interfere with the proper administration of law or proceedings of inquiry." See: *American Political Science Review*, vol. xii; no. 2, April, 1948, "The Federal Regulation of Lobbying Act," by Belle Zeller, pp. 239 ff.

Roosevelt sent out a message in which he specifically called for lobby regulation. Among other things he said, "There are the pests who swarm through the lobbies of Congress and the cocktail bars of Washington, representing special groups as opposed to the basic interests of the nation as a whole." He made his suggestion after we had been in the war for three years and it is little wonder that Congress felt it had more important matters to consider. But there were in Congress some who listened and took note and bided their time. Chief among them was Robert M. La Follette, Jr., whose father had done in Wisconsin in 1905 what the national Congress had consistently failed to accomplish.

CHAPTER VI

Regulation at Long Last

THE need to overhaul Congress had been recognized for many years. Shortly before President Roosevelt's death in the early spring of 1945 Congress itself became convinced that the time was ripe for a serious self-examination. Amid widespread approval of press and public a Joint Committee on the Organization of Congress was created and, as many editorial writers expressed it, soon went to work on the difficult but necessary process of "streamlining" the supreme legislative body of the United States.

The chairman was Senator Robert M. La Follette, Jr., whose investigation in 1939 of "violations of the right of free speech and assembly and interference with the right of labor to organize and bargain collectively" was one of the most brilliantly conducted of all Senate investigations. He was widely respected in Congress as one of its most talented parliamentarians. His vice-chairman, Representative A. S. Mike Monroney of Oklahoma, had a good reputation as a political thinker along liberal lines.

Much was expected of this committee and several worthwhile reforms were incorporated in the Legislative Reorganization Act that became law in 1946, although it was justly criticized for failing to reform the House Rules Committee, for failing to put a curb on the filibuster, and for leaving untouched the vitiating seniority rule for committees. It did, however, write and get enacted the first Federal law compelling the registration with the House and Senate of all lobbyists appearing before those bodies.

There were many factors favoring such a law in 1945 and 1946. For one thing, President Truman had come to the White House almost directly from the Senate. Before his election to the Vice-Presidency in 1944 he had distinguished himself as chairman of the effective Senate War Investigating Committee. With the exception of Warren Gamaliel Harding, he was the first twentieth-century President to come to the office of chief executive from the ranks of Congress. Both as senator and as a congressional watchdog he was well aware of the existence of pressure groups and their methods of compulsion. He was to become more articulate on this subject than any of his predecessors, especially during the Eightieth Congress and the 1948 campaign, when the obvious existence of powerful and arrogant lobbies fed him with excellent political ammunition. He was to go farther than most of his predecessors in exposing their activities, especially as his relations with Congress worsened in the months following his brief and nearly disastrous effort to walk the middle road.

As the head of the War Investigating Committee,[1] where he had examined the machinations of most of the great industries supplying the Arsenal of Democracy and where his probing finger had touched several war frauds, he had, among other things, cleared up a nasty mess involving wartime "five and ten per-centers" and their infamous activities as "peddlers of influence." Probably few senators knew more intimately the lengths to which private interests would go to get lucrative war contracts than this stubborn man who didn't want to be President. He came to the highest office with his eyes open.

Less than a year after becoming President, he paused in the course of his prepared address to tell a Jackson Day Dinner audience that "my friends in Congress have got to make up their minds whether they're for veterans' rights or whether they are going to bow to the real estate lobby." These words, which were prophetic, followed by a few days Speaker Rayburn's declaration that "this town, for the past six months, has been seething with lobbyists out to kill rural electrification and public-owned power in general" and Senator James E. Murray's declaration that the "small ruling clique in the American Medical Association" was out to defeat the Administration plan for Federal health insurance.

On March 12, 1946, Democratic Representative Adolph J. Sabath of Illinois, chairman of the House Rules Committee, offered a resolution proposing the establishment of a special committee to investigate "any and all groups which have or are engaged in present propaganda campaigns or lobby to defeat legislative measures for the relief of the acute housing shortage . . . abolish or weaken price control; and all groups which have been or are engaged in the power lobby." Another resolution of a similar nature had earlier been introduced by Representative Margaret Chase Smith, a Maine Republican and later Senator. Sabath's resolution was revised by the Rules Committee. It would have had that body conduct the investigation — and it added the lobbying activities of Federal agencies and employees. But neither the Smith nor the Sabath resolution passed the House.

Senator La Follette's committee was fortunate in having engaged the services of Dr. George B. Galloway as research director. Dr. Galloway, later the author of *Congress at the Crossroads*, had only recently been the head of the Committee on Congress for the American Political Science Association and had, in a special report for 1945, recommended that "all groups, representatives of which appear before Congress, should register and make full disclosure of their membership, finances," and other data.[2]

The La Follette-Monroney committee, created, as it said in its report, in response to a "widespread congressional and public belief that a grave constitutional crisis exists in which the fate of representative government itself is at stake," held thirty-nine public hearings between March 13 and July 29, 1945. One hundred and two witnesses, including congressmen, officials from the executive branch, and representatives of 24 private organizations (some of which were later to come under the lobby provisions of the act), gave their ideas as to how to strengthen Congress and enable it to do a better job. There were no sessions especially devoted to lobbying, it is interesting to note, and no witnesses were called to testify solely on this problem. In fact the legislative history of the Reorganization Act does not indicate that the investigators singled lobbying out for particular study, being content to accept such animadversions on lobbying as fell from the lips of witnesses in the course of general discussion. However, the committee in its report revealed that it had heard "many complaints" of attempts by "organized pressure groups" to influence the decisions of Congress on legislation pending before it or in committees.[3]

The phrase "pressure group" had moved from the academic circles of its origin to that of general usage. Left-wing writers (many of them representing minority pressure groups) had made effective use of it throughout the New Deal era. Minority pressure groups had long since taken over the methods first used by the National Association of Manufacturers and the insurance companies and later perfected in the extreme by the power lobby. The increasing political awareness of large segments of society, the vital part played in politics by such organizations as the Political Action Committee of the Congress of Industrial Organizations, and the growth of regulatory administrative agencies upon which labor and consumer groups often found it necessary to "exert pressure," had helped to instruct the popular mind in the most effective ways of persuading Congress and its agents to listen to its pleas.*

* Modern lobbying techniques, ranging from grass-roots pressure to the flooding of Congress with petitions and telegrams, were used to good purpose in promoting the United Nations, the Bretton Woods agreement, and the passage in 1946 of the Atomic Energy Act. I describe and discuss the great lobby battle over the Atomic Energy Act, one of the most stirring episodes in lobby history, in which big business and its military allies were forced to face their own weapons, in a later chapter.

In 1946 the manufacturers' lobby, the real estate lobby, and the power lobby were engaged in what as careful a student as Dr. Zeller has described as "an unprecedented amount of lobbying" in all-out battles to defeat the Administration program for continuance of price controls, for veterans' housing, and for the extension of public power projects along the lines of TVA. The time was propitious for bringing these and all other lobbies under some form of control. Whether or not the tactic of not over-publicizing this purpose was deliberate on the part of the La Follette-Monroney committee, it was intelligent, for an open battle — the political atmosphere being supercharged as it was — might well have led to the measure's defeat. This would not have been too difficult at the hands of congressmen who, while giving lip service to "some kind of regulation," were submissive to the very pressure groups the committee was determined to bring under at least a modicum of control.

The La Follette-Monroney Legislative Reorganization Bill was presented to Congress on May 15, 1946, accompanied by a carefully prepared report which revealed the committee's sensitivity towards possible criticism of its lobby provisions on constitutional grounds. The potential unconstitutionality of the measure was the problem that caused the most discussion in the rather casual debate that preceded enactment.*

Anticipating this, the committee wrote:

We fully recognize the right of any citizen to petition the government for the redress of grievances or freely to express opinions to individual members [of Congress] or to committees on legislation or on current political issues. However, mass means of communication and the art of public relations have so increased the pressures on Congress as to distort and confuse the normal expressions of public

---

* In its final form the lobby provisions became Title III of the Legislative Reorganization Act of 1946 (Public Law 601, Seventy-ninth Congress, Chapter 753, second session) with the official short title, "Federal Regulation of Lobbying Act." For the sake of clarity it will be referred to hereafter as the Lobby Act.

opinion. A pure and representative expression of public sentiment is welcome and helpful in considering legislation, but professionally inspired efforts to put pressure upon Congress cannot be conducive to well considered legislation.[4]

Elsewhere it spoke of its "hesitation" over making any recommendation that might "stifle" the "free expression of the will of the people" but it obviously was convinced that the "registration of organized groups and their agents who seek to influence legislation" was well within the prerogatives of Congress and not in conflict with the first amendment.[5] Having cleared to its own satisfaction the matter of the constitutional right to enact lobby legislation, the committee proceeded to persuade Congress to accept the bill which it had prepared. The entire Reorganization Bill, as Representative Monroney put it, was one which represented "no views and no individual authorship" and dealt with "no ideologies or anything except the functional reorganization of Congress."

Senator La Follette's introductory remarks are still pertinent:

In the last analysis, Congress is the center of political gravity under our form of government because it reflects and expresses the popular will in the making of national policy. Too often, however, the true attitude of public opinion is distorted and obscured by the pressures of special-interest groups. Beset by swarms of lobbyists seeking to protect this or that small segment of the economy or to advance this or that narrow interest, legislators find it difficult to discover the real majority will and to legislate in the public interest.

As government control of economic life and its use as an instrument of popular welfare have increased, the activities of these powerful groups have multiplied. As the lawmaking, money-raising, and appropriating agency in the Federal Government, the acts of Congress affect the vital interests of these organized groups, many of which maintain legislative agents on or near Capitol Hill. These agents seek to transform the aims and programs of their groups into public policy by having them embodied in general legislation, by changing the tax laws to suit their own purposes, by using their influence to reduce or eliminate the appropriations for agencies they dislike and to increase the appro-

priations for agencies they favor, and by pressing for the ratification
or rejection of treaties, Presidential nominations, and constitutional
amendments.

A pressure-group economy gives rise to government by whirlpools
of special-interest groups in which the national welfare is often neglected. The pulling and hauling of powerful pressure groups create
delays and distortions which imperil national safety in wartime and
threaten paralysis and bankruptcy in time of peace.* The public welfare suffers in the warfare of private groups, and Congress becomes an
arena for the rationalization of group and class interests.[6]

Because the "legislative intent" is an important factor in future
interpretations of almost all controversial measures, the following
three points by the authors of the Lobby Act, setting forth those
to whom the act would apply, are worth noting:

First. Those who do not visit the Capitol but initiate propaganda
from all over the country in the form of letters and telegrams, many
of which have been based upon misinformation as to facts. This class
of persons and organizations will be required . . . not to cease or
curtail their activities in any respect, but merely to disclose the
sources of their collections and the methods in which they are dis-
bursed.

Second. The second class of lobbyists are those who are employed
to come to the Capitol under the false impression that they exert
some powerful influence over Members of Congress. These individuals
spend their time in Washington presumably exerting some mysterious
influence with respect to the legislation in which their employers are
interested, but carefully conceal from Members of Congress whom
they happen to contact the purpose of their presence. The title in no
wise prohibits or curtails their activities. It merely requires that they

---

* "There are about 4000 national organizations in the United States with
memberships totaling at least 80,000,000," Senator Paul Douglas wrote early
in 1950. "Each one is actually or potentially a pressure group. Many of
them — it seems to me, most of them — come to Washington seeking something. Their motives are not bad. Often the ends they advocate are plainly
good. But if every group is given all it wants, even all it needs, Uncle Sam
will go broke; and the referee in bankruptcy is likely to be a dictator!"
"Big Grab at Washington," by U. S. Senator Paul H. Douglas (with James C.
Derieux), *Collier's,* February 11, 1950, vol. 125, no. 6, p. 20.

shall register and disclose the sources and purposes of their employment and the amount of their compensation.

Third. There is a third class of entirely honest and respectable representatives of business, professional, and philanthropic organizations who come to Washington openly and frankly to express their views for or against legislation, many of whom serve a useful purpose in expressing the views and interpretations of their employers with respect to legislation which concerns them. They will likewise be required to register and state their compensation and the sources of their employment.[7]

The bill accompanying this report, an integral part of the Legislative Reorganization Bill, was not debated very fully in either the House or the Senate. In both houses the members were seemingly more interested in other aspects of the measure, particularly in certain proposed restrictions of patronage, the raising of legislative salaries, and the limitation of various committees. But both houses did give Title III a going over, and it met a measure of opposition. Democratic Senator Elmer Thomas of Oklahoma, who was against the entire reorganization bill, made an abortive attempt to have its various parts referred to a number of committees for "study and report." Senator Brien McMahon of Connecticut thought it should be clarified so that there would be no question but that the Congress of Industrial Organizations, the Political Action Committee, the National Association of Manufacturers, the Chamber of Commerce, "together with 500 or more others," would be compelled to register under the act.

Senator John L. McClellan of Arkansas, who had all the appearance of a gentleman who doth protest too much, was the bill's most outspoken critic. He questioned whether it was clear enough in its definition of who should come under its provisions — a question that has been raised, but for different reasons than the senator's, by several organizations and individuals since the act's passage. "Would each individual representing the Grange or . . . the other farm organizations be compelled to register before coming to Washington to confer with me?" he wanted to know, and

he went on with righteous indignation to deny that "the propaganda and the pressure type of mail" had any influence on him
for he, and he thought this was true of all other senators, was
"smart enough to smell them out." But he did think that the "professional propagandists who are always trying to agitate the people," whom he did not further identify, should be made known to
the public and to Congress.

In the course of his criticism Senator McClellan, without quite
knowing it, perhaps, touched upon one of the major weaknesses
of Congress: what Harold J. Laski has called "the inherent ero-
sion of principle" that accompanies the tendency of our supposedly national representatives to represent minorities rather
than majorities and, under our system of geographical representation, particularly minorities purely local in origin.[8] Senator
McClellan, ever jealous of the interests of his own state but (like
the majority of his colleagues) often myopic when it came to fit-
ting these interests into the pattern of national welfare, was quite
distressed because he feared that the act would hamper representatives of Arkansas interests who might come to Washington
to confer with him. He didn't want his friends in the Chamber
of Commerce or the Grange to be called lobbyists! It escaped
him that it might be of legitimate interest and value for his colleagues, and for citizens from beyond the boundaries of Arkansas,
to have a way of discovering the wellsprings of his statesmanship.

"I should not be willing," he said, ". . . to prevent the president of the Farm Bureau or the president of the CIO or the
president of the AFL or others who fill positions similar to that
in my state, from coming to Washington and conferring with
their Congressional delegations unless they agreed to register and
to report as professional lobbyists. . . . I think it is probably an
abridgment of the civil rights of our citizens, when and if the law
does go that far." He wanted an exception written into the bill
that would exempt the "honest and respectable" representatives

from registering "when he contacts the representation of his own state in Congress."

Senator Wallace H. White, Jr., of Maine seemed to have a clearer conception of the purpose of the bill when he declared: "It is everlastingly true that, unless members of the House and the Senate are able to know who is appealing to them, they never are able properly to evaluate what is said to them or what is written. It is absolutely essential, if we are to give the proper weight to what comes to our ears and desks, that we shall know who are the people and what is the interest of the people who are making their representations to us." *

In the House, whose members are presumably more susceptible to pressure tactics than senators, the debate was even more desultory. Republican Representative Jessie Sumner of Illinois objected to the lobby title on constitutional grounds, likening registration of lobbyists to the registration of enemy agents and calling it, rather incongruously, another step towards totalitarianism, while Representative Charles W. Vursell, also a Republican member from Illinois, pointed out that "with the centralization of government which has grown up in the past number of years, it is almost necessary for organizations like the Grange and the Farm Bureau to have their representatives here practically all the time to keep them apprised as to legislation affecting millions of farmers throughout the nation."

The entire Reorganization Bill passed the House with the lobby title substantially as presented by the committee. Amendments to other provisions of the bill, however, sent it back for further consideration in the Senate. In the meantime several organizations engaged in lobbying had become alarmed at the act. Among them were the National Association of Manufacturers and the Committee for Constitutional Government, whose counsel had prepared

---

* For the debate on the Lobby Act of 1946 in the Senate and the House see index of *Congressional Record*, vol. 92, Parts 5 and 8, Seventy-ninth Congress, Second session. All quotations not otherwise credited are from the *Record*.

memoranda for the purpose of showing that the proposed act was a restrictive measure. Senator Albert W. Hawkes of New Jersey, long recognized as a leading mouthpiece for Eastern manufacturing interests, revealed that "some of the finest organizations in the United States" were "concerned lest the provisions of the reorganization plan against lobbying might be construed to the Chamber of Commerce of the United States, which was organized at the request of the President of the United States to assemble information and make it available for members of his cabinet and the various governmental agencies." * Senator La Follette told him that if the Chamber of Commerce engaged in lobbying it would come under the act; and Senator White told him that the "Chamber of Commerce stands on the same footing with every other institution in the United States."

Having met with the approval of both Houses of Congress and been signed by President Truman, the Federal Regulation of Lobbying Act (Title III of the Legislative Reorganization Act of 1946) became the law of the land on August 2, 1946. Strangely enough the historic event received but slight attention in the national press. Such comment as there was seemed to agree with the opinion of the conservative Raymond Moley that the act was not objectionable but afforded "reasonable regulation" that was long overdue.[9]

* The United States Chamber of Commerce was organized as a wholly unofficial body in 1913 at the suggestion of President Taft.

The Lobbyists Register

THE Regulation of Lobbying Act was the first recognition by Congress of the tremendous part played in our political life by the pressure groups that had grown up with such tremendous strides since the Civil War. As we have seen, there was no attempt or intention on the part of Congress to restrict the activities of these groups. Nothing in the act says what a pressure group or a lobbyist may or may not do, or may or may not say, before Congress, or any committee of Congress, or in the presence of any congressman. The lobbyist for the National Association of Rabbit Fur Raisers is still at liberty to corner Representative McCaracul in the corridors of Capitol Hill and urge him to vote a heavy tariff on South African skunk, to ply him with Manhattans at the Carlton cocktail room, to furnish him with statistics for a slashing speech that will be heard by six confreres but will roll with onomatopoeia through the pages of the *Congressional Record*. All the lobbyist has to do is to admit his profession, name his employers, define the terms of his employment, and submit his expense account. Surely an honorable man, engaged in legitimate practice, should not object to this mild procedure. Nor should any organization interested in national legislation object to an honest accounting of the sources of its funds and membership, which is all the law requires.

But a great many pressure groups and a great many professional lobbyists did object strenuously to the Lobby Act. During the first year it was on the statute books it was more honored in the breach than rigorously adhered to. For one thing, the act was not clearly written, although a close examination does not show it to be as confusing as some of its enemies would pretend.

The act * does not offer a succinct definition of a lobby or of a lobbyist. But it places under its regulation any "individual, partnership, committee, association, corporation, and any other organization or group of persons" (Sec. 302[c]) who "by himself, or through any agent or employee or other persons in any manner whatsoever, directly or indirectly, solicits, collects, or receives money or any other thing of value to be used principally to aid, or the principal purpose of which person [individually or collectively, as above designated] is to aid, in the . . . passage or defeat of any legislation by the Congress of the United States." (Sec. 307)

Any persons coming under this definition, with certain exceptions, shall "before doing anything in furtherance of such object, register with the Clerk of the House of Representatives and the Secretary of the Senate. . . ." (Sec. 308[a]) The registrations, to be made under oath, must contain the following information: ". . . the name and address of the person by whom he is employed, and in whose interest he appears or works, the duration of such employment, how much he is paid and is to receive, by whom he is paid or is to be paid, how much he is to be paid for expenses, and what expenses are to be included." (Sec. 308[a])

Under these provisions both lobby organizations and individuals acting as lobbyists are required to register. Having done so, the lobbyist must also file with the House and with the Senate detailed and sworn quarterly reports giving the following information: all money received or spent by him during the quarter for lobbying activity; to whom it was paid; the purposes for which it was paid; "the names of any papers, periodicals, magazines, or other publications in which he has caused to be published

* See Appendix A.

any articles or editorials"; and the "proposed legislation he is employed to support or oppose." (Sec. 308[a])

There are certain exceptions to the foregoing. It is not required that "any person who merely appears before a committee of the Congress . . . in support or opposition to legislation" shall register. Nor need "any individual who owns, publishes, or is employed by" any newspaper or other regularly published periodical "which in the ordinary course of business publishes news items, editorials, or other comments, or paid advertisements, which directly or indirectly urge the passage or defeat of legislation," provided that the publisher or employee "engages in no further or other activities in connection with the passage or defeat of such legislation, other than to appear before a committee of the Congress. . . ." (Sec. 308[a]) The act also excludes persons who are members of a political committee as defined by the Corrupt Practices Act, and duly organized state and local committees of a political party. And it further excludes "any public official acting in his official capacity" (Sec. 308[a]), another clause which has caused some confusion.

Besides the above registration and filing requirements, the act calls for the quarterly accounting by any person (in this instance meaning an organization, corporation, or similar association) which shall receive or spend any money for the *principal purpose* of aiding or influencing directly or indirectly the passage or defeat of legislation. This calls for the listing by name and address of all contributors of $500 or more; the total sum of all contributions made during the calendar year; and the name and address of each person to whom an expenditure of $10 or more has been made; and the total sum of all expenditures, as well as the purpose for which such expenditure has been made. (Sec. 305[a])

Recognizing that the essential value of such information lies in the publicity which it receives and in the availability of the information to all citizens as well as to interested members of Congress, the act calls for the quarterly publication of all registrations in the *Congressional Record*. Persons to whom the act applies who fail to register are liable to a fine of not more than $5000, imprisonment for not more than a year, or both. This violation is in the nature of a misdemeanor. However, any person found guilty of violation is prohibited for a three-year period "from attempting to influence, directly or indirectly, the passage or defeat of any proposed legislation, or from appearing before a committee of the Congress in support of or opposition to proposed legislation," at the risk of a maximum penalty of $10,000 fine and five years' imprisonment for such felonious action.

At first glance it would appear that the act had been written with sufficient care to take in all organizations, large and small and wherever located, actively interested in national legislation, and all agents engaged in lobbying. One would expect from the information so gathered a clear picture of the extent of lobbying before Congress: who the paid lobbyists are, how much they are paid, by whom they are paid, how they spend their money, and what legislation they are interested in. That, certainly, was the intent of the act. But within one year after President Truman signed the act only 898 lobbyists of the thousands known to be active had made the required registrations. Any competent observer scanning the lists in the *Congressional Record* and finding many a well-known lobbyist or pressure group missing knew at once that this was not a truthful picture, even if a little quick arithmetic did show that there were one and two thirds registered lobbyists interested in legislation for every congressman elected to enact it!

The reasons for this situation were not too difficult to find. For one thing the act failed to designate any agency as responsible for enforcing its provisions or for doing anything with the elicited information beyond printing it in fine type in the *Record*. Most students of lobbies and lobbyists had long been of the opinion that the mere filing of information would be useless without an agency to classify, organize, and disseminate the information contained in the reports to the House and Senate. It is quite likely that the committee, charged as it was with "streamlining" a Congress already accused of setting up too many bureaucratic agencies, shied away from perpetrating another. But another more important reason was to be found in the registrations themselves. Many of the registrations as published were filled with deliberately evasive answers and others were marked "Filed under protest," or "I do not think this act applies to me." They had quickly found the loophole, or so they thought. Some critics of the act felt that there would have been less evasion from the start if it had not been called a Regulation of Lobbying Act and if lobbyists had been referred to less harshly as "legislative agents" or some other euphemism.

From the beginning, lawyers for such organizations as the National Association of Manufacturers, the American Legion, or the Congress of Industrial Organizations jumped on the unfortunate phraseology of the act. Section 307 calls for the registration of any "person" (as previously defined) who "solicits, collects, or receives money . . . *to be used principally to aid, or the principal purpose of which person*" is to aid or influence the passage or defeat of legislation.

The wording which I have italicized had been considered in the Report of the Joint Committee on the Organization of Congress. It was there pointed out that certain groups would be exempt from the provisions of the act if they had been "formed for other purposes" and if their "efforts to influence legislation were incidental to the purpose for which they were formed." [1]

Organizations which failed to comply with the act did so in the honest belief, in many instances, that the word "principal" as here used meant "primary" or "major" or "fundamental" or "original." An organization like the American Association of University Women might claim, with good reason, that while it was interested in legislation affecting education the aiding or influencing of such legislation was not the primary purpose for which it had been organized.* By failing to register, several organizations were able to keep the source of their funds and the purpose for which they were spent hidden from Congress and the public.

While many organizations which later came into line did not register, their lobbyists did. One of the most notable standouts was the National Association of Manufacturers. The NAM was determined to prove the law was unconstitutional and denied that its "principal purpose" was aiding or influencing the passage or defeat of legislation in spite of the fact that in its papers of incorporation filed with the secretary of state of New York it sets forth that one of its "general objects and purposes" is "the support of legislation in furtherance of [several duly listed] principles and opposition of legislation in derogation thereof."

Four members of the NAM — James M. Brewbaker, R. T. Compton, Walter Chamblin, and Carey R. Sutlive — were among the early registrants, however. They listed their total salaries as $55,000 annually and their quarterly expenses as $2,806.54. They said they were interested in any legislation affecting the "national labor policy, portal-to-portal wage claims, tax laws, reduction of Federal expenditures, control of atomic energy, Federal subsidization of research, patents and trade marks, and revision of SEC and RFC Acts." [2]

The situation, then, after the 1946 general elections which brought in the Republican-ruled Eightieth Congress, was one of fairly general noncompliance with the law. But with the Eightieth Congress — the one which President Truman was to call the worst

* Although the American Association of University Women (used here merely as an example of a reputable organization of high standing) did not register, its lobbyist, Miss Marjorie L. Temple, did register. She revealed that her salary was $4000 annually and added that "possibly over half of this is for duties in connection with legislative work." As to her expense account, she said she was reimbursed "for occasional expenses, such as 25 cents for carfare (perhaps twice a year), notary fees for any papers that have to be signed (such as the present papers)." *Congressional Record*, vol. 93, no. 148, p. 10723.

in history — it would take a dull observer indeed not to recognize the joy that was written on the face of many a lobbyist, and reflected in the burst of activity by some of the most powerful lobby organizations, registered or unregistered, in the country.

The National Association of Manufacturers, whose advertisements are distastefully remembered by vast throngs of housewives, openly led the stepped-up drive for the immediate revocation of wartime price controls. Joined with the NAM were the powerful lobbies of the cotton and textile industries, the automobile manufacturers and dealers, retail dry goods dealers, and the livestock dealers. In a realistic article Miss Ruth Finney, an able Washington reporter of long experience, wrote:

The amendments which wrecked enforcement of the price control act were written by representatives of these four and other industries. . . . These lobbies coached Congressmen in the meaning of the legislation. One count of lobbyists sitting in the Senators' family gallery during voting on the bill and amendments totaled 39, including the President of the National Association of Manufacturers. A stream of page boys carried notes from the gallery to members on the floor.

Long before the voting began, however, preliminary spadework had been done in every section of the country. Six livestock and meat trade associations had charge of the drive to make the public feel aggrieved about the meat situation. A man who seems to alternate between the public payroll and that of the National Dry Goods Association was counsel for the House Committee that "investigated" OPA.[3]

Later, in the midst of the 1948 campaign, President Truman gave a clear picture of the National Association of Manufacturers' lobby against price controls in his address delivered at Louisville, Kentucky, on September 30, 1948:

Right after the end of the war, big business in this country set out to destroy the laws that were protecting the consumer against exploitation. This drive was spearheaded by the National Association of Manufacturers, the most powerful organization of big business in the country. The NAM boasts a membership of 15,000 industrial firms, but it is dominated by the officers of just a handful of giant corporations. . . .

We know how the NAM organized its conspiracy against the American consumer. One of its own officers was so proud of the work they did that he spilled the story in an interview, which was published after price control was killed. In this interview, the Director of Public Relations told how his organization spent $3,000,000 in 1946 to kill OPA. The NAM spent a million and a half on newspaper advertising. They sent their own speakers to make a thousand talks before women's clubs, civic organizations and college students. A specially designed publication went to 37,000 school teachers, another one to 15,000 clergymen, another one to 35,000 farm leaders, and still another to 40,000 leaders of women's clubs. A special clipsheet with NAM propaganda went to 7500 weekly newspapers and to 2500 columnists and editorial writers. . . .

This is what the NAM had to say about the result of their three-million-dollar propaganda campaign. Their own publicity director said that when NAM started the campaign against OPA, a survey showed that 85 per cent of the people believed OPA was absolutely necessary. In November, 1946, after the NAM campaign, he boasted that only 26 per cent of the people believed that OPA was vital. . . .

The policies of the NAM were carried out by the Republican Party. We have proof of that. Senator Wherry of Nebraska, the Republican majority leader in the Senate, told an NAM group in February, 1948, and I quote him — this is what he said:

"I do not need to remind the membership of this association that it was the Republican leadership in the Senate and the House that was responsible for ending OPA." [4]

Whether or not lobbying was its principal purpose, the National Association of Manufacturers (which a 1948 *Fortune Magazine* poll by Elmo Roper said was known to only 49 per cent of the population, of which 20 per cent were "for" it, 12 per cent were "against" it, and the rest had no opinion about it) [5] was extremely busy on the Washington front. To it must go the major amount of credit or blame for the substitution of the Taft-Hartley Act for the Wagner Labor Relations Act.

According to Representative Arthur G. Klein, a Democratic member of the House Labor Committee, William G. Ingles, a

$24,000-a-year lawyer and registered lobbyist for the Allis-Chalmers Company, the Fruehauf Trailer Company, the J. I. Case Company, and the Inland Steel Company, was the actual author of the Hartley bill. He worked in the House Labor Committee rooms with Representative Ralph W. Gwinn, a Westchester County, New York, Republican. "The bill was actually written with the help of several industry representatives and some lawyers from the National Association of Manufacturers and the United States Chamber of Commerce," Klein declared.[6]

Another lobbyist whom he named as one of the real authors of the act that was to bear the name of the committee chairman, Fred A. Hartley, Jr.,* was Gerald D. Morgan. In what was generally interpreted as an attempt to take the onus of authorship off the NAM, Morgan told a House Labor Committee subcommittee in March, 1949, that *he* was the author of the Hartley version. He said he had been employed for this purpose by the Republican majority in the House Labor Committee in the Eightieth Congress and that his fee of $7500 had been paid by the Republican National Committee (which is not required by law to register as a lobby organization). He said that Theodore R. Iserman, who had first been revealed as one of the authors by Repre-

---

* Hartley was not elected to the Eighty-first Congress. In 1948 he registered as president of and lobbyist for the Tool Owners Union, which had been declared a "fascist" organization by the New York secretary of state, who denied it incorporation papers in New York. He gave his salary as $20,000 a year. The TOU has been active in the fight against repeal of the Taft-Hartley Act. In his registration Hartley said the legislation in which he was interested included "but is not limited to national labor policy, wage and hour legislation, government controls over production and distribution of manufactured products, federal subsidization of research, patent and trade mark legislation." Statement on file with the Clerk of the House and Secretary of the Senate, Washington, D. C.

In June, 1950, according to an Associated Press dispatch, Mr. Hartley resigned from the Tool Owners Union to start "a movement for a right-wing political organization to rival the CIO's Political Action Committee and the AFL's Labor's League for Political Education." Mr. Hartley was quoted as saying that "he was confident there was a ground-swell throughout the United States to organize a right-of-center political group." *New York Times,* June 14, 1950.

sentative Klein, and Gerald D. Reilly, also a lobbyist, had acted as his technical advisers. Representative Klein had said that Iserman, whom he had identified as an attorney for the Chrysler Corporation, had spent two full weeks, during which no committee meetings were held and the Democratic members "were ignored," in helping out the House Committee.* Morgan said that during the drafting of the Hartley version he had conferred with Raymond S. Smethurst, chief counsel for the National Association of Manufacturers.†

The big business lobby got what it wanted from Congress at a cost it is impossible to estimate. It certainly cannot be determined from the statements on file with Congress, but that it was a substantial part of the NAM's and other business lobbies' legislative expense for 1947 goes without question. On the other hand the American Federation of Labor admitted spending $819,648 in its unsuccessful campaign to defeat the bill written by its arch enemy.

---

* Gerald D. Morgan and his law partner, Leonard J. Calhoun, of Washington, D. C., are registered lobbyists. Morgan, who was a former assistant legislative counsel of the House of Representatives, has lobbied at various times for an assortment of firms seeking modification or repeal of the excise tax on toilet goods, the brass and bronze industry, a group of state vocational rehabilitation administrators, and an organization interested in unemployment compensation and social security legislation. Morgan and his partner Calhoun also represented the National Tax Equality League, an active lobby against tax-free cooperatives, at a monthly retainer of $700. Later Morgan was engaged to draft several bills implementing the recommendations of the Hoover Commission.

† It is interesting to note that lobbyist Hartley, in his otherwise revealing "history" of the Taft-Hartley Act, mentions none of these coauthors and is sparing in his crediting Representative Gwinn with a part in the Hartley bill's authorship. See Our New National Labor Policy, by Fred A. Hartley, Jr., New York, 1948. Gerald Reilly, incidentally, is a former New Dealer turned lobbyist and has the General Electric Company and General Motors listed among his clients. The information in this section not taken from the Congressional Record is from the files of Labor, publication of the Railroad Brotherhoods, and from Congressional Quarterly, a factual service for newspapers and commentators. For details on the Congressional Quarterly's magnificent coverage of lobbies and pressures on Congress see the Bibliography.

Other big business lobbies were active at this time but none more so than the various agencies representing the real estate interests. This was the lobby that was to be the most furiously castigated by President Truman. Coordinator of the extensive and expensive lobby was the National Association of Real Estate Boards. When it filed its statement for the first quarter of 1948 it admitted spending $175,000 for lobbying purposes. Working closely with the NAREB were the National Association of Home Builders and the United States Savings and Loan League, which was later indicted for alleged violation of the Lobby Act. Also listed as against administration housing and control measures were the Chamber of Commerce of the United States, the National Association of Manufacturers, the National Lumber Manufacturers Association, the Committee for Constitutional Government, Inc. (of which more later), the National Grange and the American Farm Bureau Federation. These are just some of the better known associations. It was conservatively estimated that the real estate lobby had at least $5,000,000 at its command at the time it was fighting the Taft-Wagner-Ellender housing bill and the extension of rent control.

Working for the housing and rent control measures was a variety of lobbies that ranged from a coalition of the American Federation of Labor and the Congress of Industrial Organizations, through a number of veterans' organizations (including the American Legion, which had opposed the original housing act but later supported it when there seemed a possibility of incorporating in it other provisions it approved), to religious and civic organizations. All of them, as Lowell Mellett put it, made up "a people's lobby, since it represents nobody in particular — just people determined to see a serious effort made to improve the national housing situation." [7]

The foregoing are merely isolated instances of what was going on during the Eightieth Congress. These and others led Miss Finney to remark that "more groups are lobbying, they are spending more money, and lobbies battling for private interests are winning more victories . . . than has ever been seen before in Washington." The Attorney General's office was not blind to the situation and toward the end of 1947 Tom Clark ordered the establishment of a special lobby unit within his department, which was to investigate the extent of evasion of the law and to prosecute malefactors who failed to heed a warning to comply with its provisions. Irving S. Kaufman, a lawyer from New York who was in 1951 to distinguish himself as the Federal judge who tried the atomic spy case, was placed in charge of this temporary unit, which was later to become a permanent division.

To his great credit Kaufman did not engage in headline hunting. Instead he went quietly to work and with noticeable results. He differed with the critics of the act in that he gave a broad definition of the contested "principal purpose" phrase. As he explained it to the Senate Committee on Expenditures in the Executive Departments, which questioned him closely on the efficacy of the act in February, 1948: "It is our position that the phrase 'principal purpose' means any purpose which is not merely incidental to the activities of the person or organization in question. Any other interpretation would make the act meaningless and would clearly defeat the expressed intention of Congress." [8]

The use of the word "principally" went back to 1935 when Representative Howard Smith was sabotaging the antilobby bill in the House. The measure then being debated would have included in its provisions any organization which "in whole or in part" engaged in lobbying, as defined in the bill. Representative Smith sought to amend this by striking out the words "in whole or in part" and inserting instead the word "principally."

"The reason for that amendment," he explained, "is . . . that there are many organizations of national scope who have large memberships of thousands and some of millions of members organized principally for other purposes than affecting legislation, but many of these organizations do from time to time become interested in legislation, and they undertake to do something about it. It was not thought necessary or proper that that class of organization, because a minor part of its funds were devoted to purposes of influencing legislation, should be required to report all of the dues of their thousands of members, and for that reason this amendment is proposed so that it would not apply except where the money is collected for the principal purpose of undertaking to influence legislation or the election of Federal officers. . . ." *

Such a narrow interpretation of the Lobby Act, which, Professor Zeller was to tell the Senate committee, was "a very poor drafting job and not worthy of Congress" [9] — was hardly in keeping with the intent of Congress as far as the 1946 act was concerned. As Senator Homer Ferguson of Michigan remarked, "If we use the strained interpretation you really haven't any law." [10] Such usage would allow hundreds of the estimated 4000 national organizations which engage actively in lobbying whenever there arises a legislative matter affecting their interests (or, the interests of those who "use" them for their own purposes!) to escape registration with its accompanying revelation of their financial setup.

The National Association of Manufacturers, always sensitive to the charge of lobbying, was quick to discover this apparent loophole. Upon advice of its counsel it did not file, taking the stand that the act did not apply to the NAM. At this period Kaufman was following the procedure of delaying prosecution until after consultation with dilatory or defiant organizations, a tactic which had raised the registration of lobbyists to 1016 (representing approximately 750 employer organizations or individuals) by the start of 1948. But he apparently could not convince the NAM immediately. The manufacturers filed a civil suit in the Federal court in Washington in which the NAM claimed the Lobby Act vio-

---

* *Congressional Record*, Seventy-fourth Congress, Second session, vol. 80, p. 4535. Later Smith was to reiterate that the bill he sponsored "does not apply to organizations formed for other purposes whose efforts to influence legislation are purely incidental to the purposes for which formed." *Ibid.*, p. 9751.

lated its "fundamental civil rights." Morris Sayre, then the president of the NAM, explained that it was not bound by the act because it was a service organization with "relatively little interest in lobbying as it understands that term." [11]

In April, however, the NAM filed a statement "under protest" in which it asserted it had spent $146,182.12 for "legislative purposes," a sum which it estimated as 3 per cent of its total 1947 income of $5,145,649.94.

On the other side of the lobby the Congress of Industrial Organizations also followed legal advice and refrained from registering on the grounds that influencing Congress was not its principal purpose. Obviously, an act designed to ensure full reporting of lobby activities which could be interpreted as not covering the CIO, as well as the NAM, had something wrong with it. Within a few months the CIO also filed statements and has continued to do so.

Imperfect though the act might be, it did afford for the first time in the history of Congress a documented if admittedly partial picture of the Washington lobby front. From 1948 on each year's quarter saw the number of registrations increased. During the first quarter of 1948, for example, the addition of 190 lobbyists to the ranks of the registered brought the total to nearly double the number registered in the preceding six-month period. Most of the big organizations, such as the National Association of Real Estate Boards, the Chamber of Commerce of the United States, the Association of American Railroads, the American Petroleum Institute, and the Independent Natural Gas Association, joined the parade.

Early in 1950 Representative Frank Buchanan of Pennsylvania, chairman of a special House committee engaged in investigating lobbying, completed a study of the registrations during the three-and-a-half-year period in which the act had been operative. He reported that 490 pressure groups, registered under the Lobby Act, reported collecting $55,000,000, and the same groups reported spending $27,304,952 in that same period.

These figures, he admitted, were not accurate either as to receipts or expenditures, for two reasons which raise the question of further defects in the law. One reason the figures are incomplete is that not all of the organizations, associations, corporations, firms, and other groups who make up the total of 490 filed for every quarter since the enactment of the act. The largest number to file in one quarter is 219. But more significant is the second reason — the lobbies do not all follow identical practice in filling out their reports. Some include receipts and expenditures of all kinds, whether bearing on lobbying or not. Others, including most of the big lobbies, report only such sums collected as they deem allocable to legislative purposes.

In spite of the incompleteness of the figures the Buchanan report, which brought the total of individually registered lobbyists to 2074 (or three and nine tenths lobbyists for every congressman!), deserved far more attention than it received from the American press. As Buchanan said, the figures "reflect a significant picture of tremendous amounts of time and money being expended by pressure groups and pressure interests throughout the country in seeking to influence actions by Congress."

President Truman Gets Mad

ONE of the clearest thinkers in Washington, as well as one of the ablest reporters, is Thomas L. Stokes, whose daily column is distributed by the United Feature Syndicate. In the spring of 1948, while the Eightieth Congress was still in session, he delivered an address at the University of Minnesota. What he had to say is as pertinent now as it was then:

I have reported for many years on politics and the influences that shape it. That has been much easier in the past than it is today. You are aware of vague pressures against too frank exposition of economic matters and powerful interests that are at work in them. That has disturbed me.

But what has disturbed me most recently was one day when I sat down to write about the Un-American Activities Committee Hollywood investigation, after watching that frightening inquisition perhaps too long, and suddenly found myself wondering whether I should say certain things that I had in my mind and heart to say. It scared me — the fact that Washington has provided such a favorable atmosphere for it (the Un-American, and so forth) tells a good deal about our capital city. For the committee represents a concentration of the pressures that are at work today — pressures exercised also upon other committees of Congress, upon Congress itself — newspapers also feed them.

We went through a peaceful revolution in this country in 1933. We are now in the counterrevolution. We now have back in Washington, back at the battle again, the big economic interests that were restrained somewhat, but never to a degree, as their current balance sheets show, that in any way restricted their own freedom or in any way endangered fair profits. So we see the utilities pecking away on various fronts to check the further expansion of public power. Social security is being attacked from several directions. There is the bill to remove lands in our coastal areas from the control of all the people and return jurisdiction to the states,* where the big oil companies behind this measure hope to have more success in getting their hands on oil deposits in coastal areas. The real estate interests have been busy also, working through one of the most effective and highly financed lobbies now operating in Washington.

The battle rages along the whole front.

It is, truly, a great story, whatever may be the views of any newspaper about the merits of one side or the other. It deserves much better coverage than it is getting in our newspapers today.†

Mr. Stokes was dead right when he said that the story of pressures on the Eightieth Congress was a great story which deserved much better coverage than it received. To tell it adequately would require a book as large as this and the patience of Job on the part of its author. He would find hints of it in the columns of Mr. Stokes, Drew Pearson, and a few others; in the columns of the *Christian Science Monitor, Labor,* the *New York Post,* and here and there in other newspapers; the defunct *New York Star* — the only newspaper in New York City to support President Truman — gave some of it. But the press in general refused to print it, until President Truman, in a series of slashing campaign statements and speeches, made journalistic recognition mandatory.

For those who were interested, the Lobby Act should have made coverage of this "great story" easier than it had been in the past. To give publicity to those interests trying to persuade Congress

* This struggle for the control of tideland oil was, of course, one of the prime economic bases of the Dixiecrat rebellion from the Democratic Party in 1948. It is probable that most of the Dixiecrat financing came from those interested in wresting control of the tidelands from the Federal government.

† Quoted in "The Press," by A. J. Liebling, *Holiday,* vol. 7, no. 2, February, 1950. Thomas L. Stokes has been one of the few Washington columnists who has made any real effort to cover the lobby front in Washington. His columns, which I have followed in that excellent newspaper, which also subscribes to *Congressional Quarterly Reports,* the *Rutland Herald,* have been of great value to me in preparing this book.

on the great variety of legislative problems coming before it was one of the principal purposes of the act. A conscientious reporter, if he is at all familiar with the Washington scene and has enough background in the political and economic history of the country to fit him for the task of covering the national capital, should find many leads to the "story behind the story" in the registrations on file with Congress. Of course, an experienced reporter soon gets to know the sources of the major pressures on Congress. He often fails to report them because such publication would be in conflict with the same sources which bring continual pressure on the American press. The reporter (like Charles Van Devander recently of the *New York Post*, Carleton Kent of the *Chicago Sun-Times*, Clayton Knowles of the *New York Times*, or Richard Strout of the *Christian Science Monitor*) who makes it his business to inform his readers who is "behind" the drive for or against legislation, is the rare exception in Washington. The Associated Press, except in obvious instances, steers away from reporting this part of the news. Of course, when labor or minority pressure groups get active, they are generally given full and usually unfavorable treatment in the press. The late Senator Reed's cynicism — "A lobbyist is anyone who opposes legislation I want. A patriot is anyone who supports me" — is as applicable to the attitude of the average publisher as to that of the average congressman.

The only news agency that faithfully covers the lobby front is Congressional Quarterly News Features, Inc., a small but successful bureau which specializes in a factual and statistical study of Congress in all its phases. It is sold on a subscription basis to newspapers, news magazines, editors, columnists, and commentators. Almost every week it furnishes a special study of "pressures on Congress." It lists all new lobby registrations as they become available, but its more important function is to show what lobbies and lobbyists are lined up for or against every measure as it comes before, and progresses through, the legislative mill. Completely unbiased, the entire *Congressional Quarterly* reports (which are available at year's end in well-equipped libraries in the form of an *Almanac*) alone give an over-all picture of the so-called Third House, as well as the Lower and Upper Houses of Congress.

In 1948 the government sought to enforce the Regulation of Lobbying Act through three court actions. Two were against individuals who allegedly had failed to register as lobbyists, and one was against the United States Savings and Loan League, an integral part of the real estate lobby. At the same time the National Association of Manufacturers brought a civil suit in the Federal Court of the District of Columbia contesting the constitutionality of the act.*

One of the suits brought against an individual is of considerable interest because it resulted in a court decision accepting the constitutionality of one section of the act and, by inference at least, other pertinent sections which were not in dispute in this case. In November, 1948, Roger C. Slaughter, a former Democratic representative from Missouri and a bitter political foe of President Truman, was indicted for violating the act. It was specifically charged that Mr. Slaughter had been employed as an attorney and lobbyist by speculative grain interests in New York, Kansas City, Chicago, and Minneapolis, for which he had drawn large sums of money in fees and expenses, and that in the Eightieth Congress he had lobbied to defeat a Senate bill to increase margin requirements on speculative transactions on the commodity exchanges, to defeat Senate ratification of the international wheat agreement, and to bring about the abolishment of the Commodity Credit Corporation's power to buy or lease grain storage facilities.[1]

Slaughter's defense was that he had merely acted as an attorney for the grain interests and therefore was not required to register under provisions of the act as set forth in Section 308. He contended that he had merely consulted with witnesses for the grain exchanges before they went before congressional committees and had helped in the preparation of these witnesses' testimony. The

* A final decision in this case is still pending as this book goes to press.

judge before whom the final hearings on this case were held agreed with a previous Federal Court ruling that the Lobby Act exemption for those merely testifying at congressional hearings applied also to those helping to prepare such testimony. The court, which heard the case without a jury, ruled that the government's allegations that Mr. Slaughter had undertaken other activities, which would bring him under the purview of the law, were not established by government evidence. Mr. Slaughter was acquitted of the charge of violating the Lobby Act.

The importance of the case does not lie in Mr. Slaughter's acquittal but in Judge Henry A. Schweinhaut's ruling made when he denied Mr. Slaughter's motion for dismissal of the case in a pretrial hearing. (Later Judge Alexander Holtzoff, who heard the case, upheld Judge Schweinhaut's interpretations.) Mr. Slaughter claimed, among other reasons, that the indictment should be dismissed because the act was unconstitutional "as being so vague and uncertain that it fails to meet the due process requirement of the fifth amendment, and fails adequately to inform the defendant of the cause and nature of the charge against him as required by the sixth amendment," and because it also "offends" the first amendment "because it deprives the people of civil liberties thereby defended." [2]

Judge Schweinhaut found that the language of Section 308 was sufficiently clear and definite to be upheld. "The court is of the opinion that this section of the Lobbying Act may stand alone and apart from other provisions and that it is not on its face unconstitutional," he ruled. He elaborated to the effect that the meaning of "engage himself for pay or for any consideration" and of "for the purpose of attempting to influence" is readily understandable. He said "legislation" is broadly defined in the statute (the definition in Section 302 [e] includes "bills, resolutions, amendments, nominations, and other matters pending or proposed in either House of Congress, and includes any other matter which may be the subject of action by either House").

Judge Schweinhaut then held that Section 308, the registration section, "does not abridge constitutionally guaranteed privileges (freedom of speech, press, petition, etc.) since it leaves everyone free to exercise those rights, calling upon him only to say for whom he is speaking, who pays him, how much, and the scope in general of his activity with regard to legislation. This, the Congress should, and in the Court's opinion, does have the right to demand."

In the opinion of the majority of the House committee studying lobbying in 1950, in their final report and recommendations, "this decision strongly supports the constitutionality of comparable language in sections 305 and 307." The report points out that Section 308 contains the phrases "attempting to influence the passage or defeat of any legislation by the Congress," and recalls that Section 305 incorporates by reference the following phrase from Section 307: ". . . to aid . . . in the accomplishment of any of the following purposes. . . . To influence, directly or indirectly, the passage or defeat of any legislation by the Congress. . . ." It comes then to the logical conclusion that if Section 308 is constitutional, as the court has unmistakably held, then Section 305, which calls for the registration of organizations receiving contributions or spending money for lobbying purposes, and Section 307, which contains the act's broad definition of those persons and groups who come under the act, are likewise constitutional. It stresses further that the court's decision was also based on a finding that the definition of "legislation" contained in the act is sufficiently clear and definite to be constitutional.

The committee also recalls that not a single one of the statutes enacted by any of the thirty-eight individual states which have such laws on their books has ever been found unconstitutional by a court, and quotes with satisfaction a 1929 Kentucky decision which says:

The Bill of Rights declares it to be an inherent and inalienable right of all men to apply to those invested with the power of government for all proper purposes by petition, address, or remonstrance. There is no attempt in this law to restrict the legitimate exercise of that right. . . . To protect its members, and for its own information, the legislature undoubtedly had the right to require the registration of special interests and regulate their activities.

Furthermore, the Federal Corrupt Practices Act, on which the Lobby Act was partially patterned, has also been held constitutional. In an interesting footnote the majority report adds:

Sec. 306 of the Corrupt Practices Act requires the filing of a statement by any person who expends more than $50 (other than by contribution to a political committee) to influence elections in two or more states. This makes it necessary to determine whether a given activity is such an activity as would influence elections. Suppose that candidates in two states have become associated in the public mind with a bill which bears their name, and suppose that — during the campaign period — a person expends large sums of money in the two states to circulate pamphlets attacking such a bill, but without referring to the elections. Would this be activity in influencing elections which would require such a person to file a statement of his expenditures pursuant to Sec. 306 of the Corrupt Practices Act? The fact that such a problem could arise did not deter the courts from holding similarly with the Lobby act.*

In February, 1948, at the height of the lobbying activity which President Truman not very much later was to describe as "disgraceful," the Senate Committee on Expenditures in the Executive Departments held a five-day public hearing for the purpose of "evaluating" the Legislative Reorganization Act of 1946. Senator George D. Aiken of Vermont, the chairman and one of the most liberal-minded senators of either party, had the wisdom to invite Dr. Belle Zeller, professor of political science at Brooklyn College, New York, as a witness to the workability of the Lobby Act.

The testimony offered by Miss Zeller added up to a serious

* The committee is here upholding its position concerning "indirect lobbying" by foundations and other lobbying agencies, which is discussed in a later chapter. A discussion of lobbying before state legislatures appears in Appendix B.

criticism of the "defects" of the act and to a series of recommendations which she thought would materially strengthen the act and
make it more effective. Hers were, as nearly as I can determine,
the first incisive criticisms of what Chairman Aiken called "this
rather unsettled part of the Reorganization Act" to have been
made before Congress since the act's passage nearly two years before. The eight points she made are worth consideration, especially since, as we shall see, most of them were to be neglected in
the following year when an attempt was made to rewrite the
Lobby Act.

The first of these was the by-now-celebrated "principal purpose" phrase. Many an organization, as she explained, does perform major services not *directly* related to influencing legislation,
but such legislative activity as it does engage in, even for limited
periods, is often of vital importance to the existence of the organization. As an example she pointed to the American Federation of
Labor. In 1947 this organization spent more than $5,000,000, of
which salaries and expenses for legislative purposes were only
$22,474. Under a "strict interpretation" of the "principal purpose"
clause a case, of course, could be made to excuse the AFL from
registering; but anyone with a grain of common sense must know
that guarding labor's rights from legislative encroachment is one
of the most important tasks facing any labor union, even if, under
ordinary circumstances,* it does not absorb the greater part of its
funds.

"It is difficult, even at times impossible, to separate the so-called
non-legislative from the legislative expenses of any organization,"
Dr. Zeller asserted. She therefore recommended that statements
should set forth the total budget of these organizations, these to
be "broken down into broad categories of expenditures, with a
listing specifically of all items of expenditures labeled *legislative*."
In addition, the names and addresses of all contributors of $500 or

---

* These figures, for example, do not include the sums spent in the
AFL's efforts to defeat the Taft-Hartley Bill.

more in any quarter should be listed, regardless of whether the funds were specifically earmarked for legislative purposes.

The Zeller recommendations called for a listing of the bona fide total membership of organizations, so that the Legislature would have no difficulty in determining just how many citizens the lobbyist actually represented in his appearances before Congress. To this Dr. Zeller added the unusual suggestion that every organization should be compelled to reveal "how its legislative policy is determined and . . . indicate the responsibility of the lobbyist in conveying these views on behalf of the membership of the organizations."

In order properly to enforce the registration of lobbies and lobbyists Dr. Zeller proposed that some specifically designated agency, preferably the Attorney General of the United States, be named for this purpose. She would have all forms filed with the Attorney General as well as with the Clerk of the House and the Secretary of the Senate, and *complete information* on the forms published at regular quarterly intervals in the *Congressional Record*. Realizing that publicity is the main weapon of any lobby act Miss Zeller would have weekly roundups of filed information supplied to all members of Congress while in session and made available to members of the congressional press galleries. In addition she would require the Attorney General to make an annual evaluation of the Lobby Act in his report, which would include an interpretation of the information received as well as suggestions for the act's improvement. (This is required "from time to time" in the case of the Foreign Agents Registration Act.)

Dr. Zeller would not confine lobby registration to persons seeking to influence Congress or its committees but would extend the provisions of the act to all those who "seek to exert influence on any federal bureau, agency, or government official." She would make the employment of lobbyists on a contingent basis illegal. She would extend the present exemption of newspapers and periodicals to the radio industry.

Although the time obviously was opportune for strengthening the Lobby Act Senator Aiken's committee made no move towards this end. And lobbying on the part of private pressure groups continued unabated, providing President Truman with some powerful ammunition for the Presidential campaign of 1948.

At Yonkers, New York, President Truman declared that the Eightieth Congress "was the most thoroughly surrounded . . . with lobbies in the whole history of this great country of ours. There were more lobbyists in Washington, there was more money spent by lobbyists in Washington, than ever before in the history of the Congress of the United States. It's disgraceful. . . ." [3]

Granted that these were campaign speeches and thus subject to hyperbole, they nevertheless were based on truth. The information filed with Congress under the Lobby Act revealed that the obviously incomplete list of lobbies and lobbyists active in Washington spent (or rather admitted spending) $6,741,311 during 1948.

There is no way of determining how much of President Truman's victory was attributable to his attacks on lobbying. He hammered away at them in speech after speech and even after the election returned to them.

It appeared for a time after the election that President Truman's attacks on lobbying might lead to a widespread congressional investigation. Indeed, late in November, President Truman gave his blessing to such a project, saying that such action would have "a very salutary effect." This came about as a result of a resolution adopted by the International Association of Machinists, the largest independent union in the country.

The resolution asked for a joint investigation of the accusations that had frequently been made during this period "that manufacturers spent $100,000,000 to put over the Taft-Hartley bill," charges which, the union said, had never been refuted. The Machinists declared that the public was "entitled to the full facts concerning the lobbying objectives, the identity and interests of individual contributors and lobbying methods" of the following organizations:

> National Association of Manufacturers
> Committee for Constitutional Government
> National Physicians Committee
> National Association of Electric Companies
> National Association of Home Builders
> National Association of Real Estate Boards
> Association of American Railroads

It also called for an investigation of "other lobbies which, while less widely publicized, are working no less assiduously for special interests" to influence Congress. At the same time it self-protectingly stressed that "the spotlight of publicity on these lobbies will not harm any legitimate representation of any group in Washington."

In a letter to President Truman, Eric Peterson, general secretary-treasurer of the Machinists, said that "the voters of the United States, as well as members of Congress" should be made acquainted with "the high-powered lobbying activities which were used so successfully to confuse the members of the Eightieth Congress and deceive them as to the attitude of the majority of voters." He warned that unless such an exposure could be made "these lobbies will redouble their efforts" in the Democratic Eighty-first Congress to block the Fair Deal program.[4]

Thus the way was paved for the first investigation of lobbying by Congress since Senator Hugo Black's exposé of the utilities lobby in 1935. But more than a year was to pass before a select committee of the House began to look into the pressure groups and their agents. In the interim several interesting events occurred.

CHAPTER IX

The Lobby Act Examined

WHEN the Democratic-controlled Eighty-first Congress met in January, 1949, President Truman's blasts against lobbying and lobbyists were still echoing in the national capital. Among the first batch of bills and resolutions dropped in the legislative hopper was a resolution calling for a "comprehensive investigation" of lobbying by the Senate Judiciary Committee. Its author was Senator Harley M. Kilgore, an administration stalwart from West Virginia, who was presumed to have White House support for his measure.

The Kilgore Resolution recognized the imperfections of the Lobby Act of 1946, calling attention to the "confusion" surrounding the act's provisions for registering and reporting, and mentioning the "widespread public belief" that lobbying was still being widely practiced by unregistered persons, many of whom failed to register because they did not believe the act applied to them. It further spoke of the difficulty, even under the Lobby Act, of ascertaining the exact affiliations of many persons who presume to speak for the public, and called attention to the unquestionable need for the complete identification of all individuals and organizations engaged in lobbying.

Senator Kilgore hoped that the Judiciary Committee would establish a subcommittee, of which he would be chairman, to conduct the probe. In this event, he promised, there would be neither a "witch hunt" nor a "smear campaign" (using the two most fashionable clichés of the season) but rather a serious study of the problem that would concern itself with all aspects of lobbying before Congress. He hoped that the result would be a new lobby law that would effectively regulate lobbying in all the branches of the Federal government, thus taking in appearances not only before Congress but before the numerous administrative agencies susceptible to the pressures of private interests. Aware of the growing contention of administration critics that representatives of government were themselves increasingly engaged in lobbying, Senator Gilgore promised that this matter would receive committee attention; but his stress was on the effective regulation of outside pressures. Senator Kilgore pointed out that "legitimate lobbying where the identity, affiliation, and point of view of the lobbyist is fully known" can be helpful to legislators.

The Senate proved to be in no hurry to undertake such an investigation. Over in the House, however, Representative Frank Buchanan of McKeesport, Pennsylvania, a Fair Deal Democrat, was watching the lobbying situation carefully.

Mr. Buchanan, who was then forty-six years old, had many distinctions. In 1941 he became the first Democrat to be elected mayor of the turbulent mill city of McKeesport, across the Monongahela River from Pittsburgh, where he had started his career as a schoolteacher after his graduation from the University of Pittsburgh and graduate work in economics at Columbia University. In a special election in 1945 he was sent to the House to replace Representative Samuel A. Weiss, who had resigned. He was regularly elected in 1946, 1948, and again in 1950. During his first years in Congress he had voted 100 per cent for administration measures and, in his later terms, his percentage of fidelity to the administration never fell below 92 per cent. A tall, handsome man, with a shock of white hair and a mild and friendly manner, he was known as a serious worker for the many causes in which he believed, and he was a willing and able supporter of all labor measures. He was in the forefront of President Truman's fight against the Taft-Hartley Act, both before and after its passage. In the Eightieth Congress he spearheaded the administration's drive to obtain a rent control law that would permit fewer rent rises than the one that Congress passed. Mr. Buchanan did not live to see enacted any of the reforms of the Lobby Act which he had hoped to bring about during the Eighty-second Congress. He was taken ill in March, 1951, and died in the Naval Hospital in Bethesda, Maryland, on April 27, 1951.

As a member of the important Banking and Currency Committee Mr. Buchanan was in a position to observe at first hand the activities of some of the most powerful pressure groups. It was the real estate lobby in particular that eventually spurred him to action. The receipt of a deluge of telegrams and letters, estimated at between 9000 and 10,000, all condemning rent control, aroused his suspicions. Most of them originated in Texas and California, where the real estate lobby was well organized for such a drive. The fact that he got only about 100 such protests from his own district added to his wonderment about the sources of this campaign to convince Congress to bring rent controls to an end.*

While the Senate Judiciary Committee stalled, the House went ahead and on May 18, 1949, passed the Buchanan Resolution calling for a joint investigation of lobbying in all its phases. Three months later, the Senate still having taken no action, the House Rules Committee reported out Buchanan's superseding resolution for the appointment of a select seven-man committee of the House

---

* About this time many newspapers ran stories about a woman in Akron, Ohio, who had written her congressman as a home owner asking relief from rent control. The congressman, Representative Walter D. Huber, investigated, and found the woman was a domestic servant employed by the president of the Apartment Owners Association of Akron. Other similar instances were also revealed. At the same time the AFL was urging 17,000,-000 payers of monthly rent checks to write Congress urging passage of a rent control bill and to defeat the proposed "States' Rights to Kill Rent Control Bill," and the CIO was vigorously lobbying for passage of the "strong" Myers-Douglas bill.

to do the job. The House having decided to carry the ball, the Senate washed its hands of the matter.

Representative Buchanan was named chairman of the committee, which was charged with making "a full and complete investigation of all lobbying activities intended to influence, encourage, promote, or retard legislation" and a "full and complete investigation of all activities of agencies of the Federal Government intended to influence, encourage, promote, or retard legislation." [1] Granted broad powers to subpoena witnesses, books, papers, and documents, the committee was directed to submit its final report to the House, together with "such recommendations as it deems advisable," before the close of the Eighty-first Congress. It was not empowered to report a legislative bill to take the place of the Lobby Act of 1946.

Although Mr. Buchanan was greatly disturbed by Washington lobbying it was obvious to students of the Third House that he had not given the matter, before the opening of his investigation, as close attention and study as it deserved. This was apparent from the nature of a bill he had introduced in July to take the place of the Regulation of Lobbying Act of 1946. The Buchanan Bill, which dropped the word lobby entirely from its context, was based on the assumption that "the Congress finds that acting as legislative representative for substantial compensation with respect to matters pending in Congress and the raising or expenditure of substantial sums of money for legislative representation present questions of grave impending present danger to the Republic." In some respects it did meet certain objections raised against the 1946 act. For example, it eliminated the controversial "principal purpose" clause, but it did so by saying specifically that individuals or organizations need not report their "general assets, income or receipts" if they were "engaged substantially in another business." [2] The Buchanan Bill seemed to leave an even wider loophole than the 1946 act.

The difficulty in separating the legislative from the nonlegislative expenditures of organizations is another weakness in the 1946 act. Most students of pressure groups agree that any organization engaged in lobbying should file a statement of its total budget, including a specific listing of every item spent for legislative purposes. The Buchanan Bill did not call for this vital information. Nor did it call for a listing of all contributors of $500 or more each quarter, a requirement which most students find essential to an understanding of the purposes of a lobbying group. It further failed to require a listing of membership, which is also essential to a complete picture of the nature of an organization seeking to influence legislation. Even more astounding was the fact that the Buchanan Bill failed to provide any means for giving publicity to the lobbies or lobbyists required to register. The 1946 act orders the printing of quarterly registrations and reports in the *Congressional Record*. Under the Buchanan Bill they presumably would have been buried in the files of the House and Senate, available only to those who might go there and ask for them.

The publicity attendant upon registration by individual lobbyists and the filing of financial statements by organizations is, in the final analysis, the most important result of any lobby act. Unfortunately the publicity provisions of the 1946 act itself are not as clearly defined as they might be, although they are far from useless. They do make a vast amount of valuable information available to Congress and eventually to the public. Without them there would be no way of quickly ascertaining who is lobbying and for what. The reports printed quarterly in the *Congressional Record* fill many pages with vital statistics that sometimes are put to good use by the press but which are there in digestible form whether the press chooses to examine and report on them or not. As far as the provisions go they are useful, but they do not go far enough; nor are they foolproof.

The act provides that the financial statements of lobby organizations (Sec. 305[a]) shall be filed for each quarter of the year. These statements, which are designed to show whence comes the flow of money for lobbying, "shall constitute part of the public records" of the office of the Clerk of the House, with whom they are filed, and "shall be open to public inspection [Sec. 306]." But this wise provision is omitted from Section 308(a), which calls for the registration of all persons who, for pay, attempt to influence the passage or defeat of legislation by Congress. It does, however, insist that such registration be made *before* the registrant does "anything in furtherance of such object." The lobbyist, in other words, must state his intentions before he approaches Congress in any way on legislative matters. These registrations must then be printed in the *Congressional Record*, but not immediately. The printing is not mandatory until after the close of each calendar quarter. There is no specific provision in this section of the act which says these registrations shall be considered public records or be open to public inspection, although the reasonable assumption is that they should so be considered.

An excellent test of what can happen when full disclosure of lobbying activities is withheld from the press and public came in the spring and summer of 1950. One of the early actions of the House Select Committee on Lobbying Activities was to prepare new and presumably more efficient forms for registering and filing statements under the Lobby Act. These new forms called for listing not only "the general legislative interests" of registrants but also the listing by name, bill, number, and statute citation of "the specific legislative interests" of the person filing. This was a distinct improvement over the old forms, which did not require such detailed information. For some reason never made quite clear the shift from the old forms to the new created great confusion in the offices of the Clerk of the House and the Secretary of the Senate and while these offices were gearing themselves to the change the files were shut down to public inspection. The "blackout" lasted from May 5 to September 7, a period of four months, which meant that lobby information for more than one quarterly period was kept from the public and presumably from Congress.

The imposition of this "blackout," the legality of which was highly dubious, was first revealed by the *Congressional Quarterly*. Thus deprived of its official source of lobby information it registered, through Clair Johnson, its managing editor, a formal protest with Ralph Roberts, Clerk of the House, Speaker Sam Rayburn, and Minority Leader Joe Martin, stressing the point that legitimate information was being withheld "at a time when vital emergency legislation is being written." [3] The protest pointed out that several lobbyists had already completed their missions to Washington before their registration was made known.* To most observers, this blackout completely negated the intent of the act.

Not until July 14 were reports printed in the *Congressional Record* revealing lobby statements made up to May 5. Upon going over these reports the *Congressional Quarterly* was able to show that several lobbyists, among them representatives of Johns-Manville, one of the corporations that was to refuse lobbying data to the Lobby Committee investigators, had been active on several measures before Congress during the period when registrations had been withheld from public scrutiny. Without the records being available the public might never have known, among other interesting data, that the National Association of Insurance Agents had registered as a lobby against certain aspects of social security and the Commodity Credit Corporation. On August 22 the *Congressional Record* printed 115 more pages of registrations revealing 1017 financial reports and 82 new or revised registrations. [4]

These revelations were not of overwhelming importance, but

---

* There was at least one interesting exception to this rule, according to the *Congressional Quarterly*, which revealed (August 11, 1950, p. 886) that one organization, the National Council of Farmer Cooperatives, published on May 12, 1950, its quarterly release by L. James Harmanson, Jr., analyzing the financial report statement for the first quarter of 1950 of the National Tax Equality Association, its bitter rival in the struggle over repealing all tax exemptions for cooperatives, one of the most vigorous lobby battles in recent years in Washington. "The Clerk's office had made the NTEA report available to NCFC at a time when it was not available to others and at a time when the Clerk's staff had not yet finished processing the incoming forms."

they served to point up the value of the Lobby Act in principle. Without these records the public would not have known that 26 organizations, whose reports were hidden in the "blackout," had admitted to spending more than $700,000 during a part of 1949 and the first quarter of 1950, that the Townsend Plan lobby acknowledged spending $432,110 in 1949, or that the National Association of Manufacturers grudgingly filed papers in which it set forth the sum of $117,230, or approximately 1.5 per cent of its annual expenditures, as the amount "which might be considered as spent for the purposes of influencing Federal legislation within the meaning of the Federal Regulation of Lobbying Act. . . ." [5] If the congressional filings had been open for inspection, the *Congressional Quarterly* revealed, an alert public would have known that many strong lobbies were gathering in Washington to pressure Congress on such matters vitally affecting the general welfare as the Defense Production Act, bills on tax revision, matters affecting transportation, tidelands oil, Communist registration, and the union shop for railway labor. The working press, of course, was — or should have been — aware of the identity of these lobbies and lobbyists, but there, in the files but shut off from both Congress and the people it was supposed to inform, was the exact information needed for the continuous check on the legislative process that must be relentlessly pursued if democracy is to work at its best.*

When the July issue of the *Congressional Record* appeared with 176 pages of registrations and statements Democratic Senator Carl Hayden from Arizona, chairman of the Joint Committee on Printing, objected to the large amount of space devoted to the lobby data. He reported that 176 pages cost $82 each to print, bringing the total to $12,432 for the single issue. In comparison to the amounts the lobbyists spend this does not seem dispropor-

---

* As the Committee on Political Parties of the American Political Science Association succinctly puts it: "Buried data are data withheld." *Towards a More Responsible Two-Party System.* New York, 1950. P. 80.

tionate when the value to the public of this information, otherwise kept hidden, is considered.[6]

In other ways, the proposed Buchanan regulations did not follow out recommendations made by Dr. Zeller and other political scientists. It did not extend its provisions, as many believe a perfect lobby act should, to include lobbying before Federal bureaus and agencies. An analysis of the bill fails to show that it was, in any major aspect, an improvement over the existing act. The bill, fortunately, was not reported out by the Judiciary Committee.

The House debated quite fully the necessity of the lobby investigation, as proposed in the Buchanan Resolution. The debate is worth attention, not because any great originality was expressed on the floor, but because it revealed much about general congressional thinking on the subject. The more ardent support came, naturally, from the Democratic side, which had every reason to believe the investigators would center their fire upon those lobbies which had done the most to oppose the Fair Deal program. Considerable uneasiness was expressed by some Republicans that the investigation would be made a "witch hunt," but the Democratic leadership assured them that this would not happen. As it turned out, the committee lived up extraordinarily well to the promises made in its behalf. In a year which was marked by the hoodlum tactics of McCarthyism the Buchanan Committee acted with remarkable objectivity and restraint.

The argument in favor of the resolution (there was no outspoken opposition once the resolution had come to the floor) was led by Representative Adolph J. Sabath of Illinois, the dean of the House, whose unbroken record as a liberal legislator extends back to his first term in 1906. Long an outspoken enemy of pressure groups, Representative Sabath hoped that the inquiry would "give us an opportunity and basis for proceeding further on corrective legislation designed to eliminate permanently those infamous lobbying practices" which were "annoying and harassing the Members from day to day." He seemed particularly annoyed and harassed by lobbyists for corporations, some of whom received as much as $150,000 a year (or so he estimated) for practicing deceit and fraud upon their employers by making believe they had influence with Congress.

In the course of analyzing what he believed to be the failures of the 1946 act, Mr. Sabath made two pertinent points. He did not feel that the 1946 act had restricted lobbyists; instead, by recognizing them, it had legalized lobbying. With this he had no quarrel for, like most other congressmen, he was aware of the existence of lobbies which were clearly helpful to legislators. More important was his bringing into the open the question, long debated, whether lawyers active on the Washington scene should be required to register as lobbyists. He felt very definitely that they should.

"The majority of the large concerns," he said, "now retain large law firms in Washington and other cities. In these firms is found a partner influential in Washington because he occupied at one time or another an important government position. The compensation these firms receive for lobbying is called a retainer — not lobbying compensation. Hence they do not set forth the amount of retainer or, if set forth, it is charged as fees for legal services [which], they maintain, are not lobbying services. They write briefs, consult with the companies and corporations they represent — send out material for consumption by members of the industry and thus directly and indirectly influence legislation."

It was not, however, the huge coterie of Washington lawyer-lobbyists (some of whom do register, but many of whom do not) that interested two vocal members of the Republican opposition, both of whom were later to be made members of the committee. Nor did the presence of business lobbyists in general seem to disturb Republican Representatives Charles A. Halleck of Indiana and Clarence J. Brown of Ohio, both of whom had been extremely active in opposing the Fair Deal program during the Eightieth Congress. At that time Mr. Halleck was the majority leader. Mr. Brown had been one of the foremost opponents of extension of rent control and the Truman housing program. Both, it might be said, had had extensive firsthand dealings with lobbyists in their time. It was said of them in Washington, that "some of their best friends were lobbyists."

With the aid of James W. Wadsworth, a Republican representative from New York, they had induced the Rules Committee to insert the clause calling for an investigation of the lobbying activities of Federal agencies, a phrase which the Democrats maintained was unnecessary inasmuch as the original resolution had called for an investigation of *all* lobbying, of which this was a part. The reason for this insistence was obviously political to a great extent. It was designed to embarrass the administration, then pushing for the Brannan plan for agriculture and the national insurance health program which the American Medical Association was spending millions to defeat. Majority Leader John W. McCormack of Massachusetts called the House's attention to existing laws making illegal the use of public funds for the purpose of influencing legislative action by Congress — laws on the statute book long before passage of the Lobby Act — but he raised no objection to the phrase's inclusion, and so it remained in. As it turned out, Messieurs Brown and Halleck did try to turn the investigation into an all-out search for "Federal lobbyists" and did their best to put Secretary of Agriculture Charles F. Brannan and Federal Security Administrator Oscar R. Ewing "on the spot" for certain of their activities, but without appreciable success.

In the House debate Mr. Brown was insistent that every precaution be taken by the proposed committee to avoid what he feared might turn into a "witch hunt," for there were, he said, many "good lobbyists" who were "perhaps necessary" to the continuing function of the "rather complex economic system and governmental structure we have created." As he reminded his listeners, "Today any action taken by the Congress may vitally affect some business, or industry, or individual, as well as business or personal investments and income, and all of the varied activities of the business and industrial world." Therefore the committee should be very careful not to do anything that would "embarrass" any "individual or representative group" or that would "smear" or "scare" an "individual businessman" or "any business concern" who might have "the temerity to tell his Representative in the Congress of the United States what he thinks about pending legislation." Far more important than this was the need to look into the activities of the "bureaucratic agencies of our Federal Government," some of which, he warned, were interested in "putting across a certain public health program, or, should I speak frankly and say, socialized medicine."

Mr. Brown wanted a careful investigation of the "use of Government planes and transportation by those public officials who have been running around the country in the last few months busily engaged in building up pressure influence to control the action of this Congress on several pieces of very important legislation." On the other hand Mr. Sabath thought the committee would be better engaged in looking into the activities of the lobbyists who had been so busy in Washington while Congress was struggling with legislation dealing with Taft-Hartley repeal, housing, a minimum wage, increased appropriation for the TVA steam plant, national health insurance, and yellow margarine.

Both Mr. Halleck and Mr. Brown expressed considerable concern over the constitutional rights of lobbyists. Mr. Brown felt that the investigation should be confined to "paid lobbyists" lest it might, as Mr. Halleck feared, "be calculated to deprive the individual citizen of the right that he ought to have to make his voice heard and his influence felt in the affairs of government. After all we do represent the people here and they have not only the right, but the duty, to tell us what they think."

This colloquy brought Mr. McCormack to his feet with the pertinent reminder that "it must be clearly kept in mind that there is a distinction between lobbying and the right of petition. The right of petition is one of the four cornerstones of personal liberty. I do not think any of our businessmen or labor men should be denied the right of petition. My friend from Ohio [Mr. Brown] talked about business; I also include labor, small business, the farmer, and everyone else. They are not violating the law by writing to us or seeing us or contacting us in any way, and certainly none of them need be scared. One thing is certain. According to the records there have been about $40,000,000 paid in for some activities of this kind, and only $9,000,000 per year have gone out for salaries. It might be interesting to know where the other money went."

Primarily of academic interest was the suggestion made by Democratic Representatives A. S. Mike Monroney of Oklahoma (the House sponsor of the Reorganization Act, of which the Lobby Act was a part) and Chet Holifield of California, both of whom, while giving the resolution their support, questioned the necessity of setting up a special committee. Mr. Monroney was of the opinion that Congress should take its obligations under the Reorganization Act* more seriously. He was disappointed that the standing committee having jurisdiction over lobbying activities did not take up the investigation as a part of its regular work. He felt that it was unfortunate that the House did not follow the lines of the Reorganization Act, mainly because, when the proposed committee reported its findings and made its recommendations, it would be without the power of a standing committee to "take that legislation right on through." Mr. Holifield explained that the House Committee on Expenditures was charged with the duty of keeping its eyes on the working of the Lobby Act. He cited subsection (c), which reads, "Evaluating the effects of the laws enacted to reorganize the legislative and executive branches of the government." This committee had never made any real effort to examine the success or failure of the act.

Thus the lines were laid for a lobby investigation. On May 18

---

* One of the major intents of the Reorganization Act was to do away with excess special committees and make the standing committees more efficient.

the House adopted the resolution that would have created a joint committee. On August 12, when it became apparent that the Senate resolution was bottled up in committee, the House, with little further debate, adopted Mr. Buchanan's second resolution, calling for a seven-man select committee of the House. On October 6 Speaker Rayburn appointed the following committee * with Representative Buchanan as its chairman:

Henderson Lovelace Lanham, Democrat of Rome, Georgia; an elderly veteran of Georgia state politics, and former solicitor general of the city court of Rome. He was first elected a representative to the Eightieth Congress. Known as "Judge" Lanham, his fiery Southern temper was more than once to enliven the proceedings of the committee.

Carl Albert, Democrat, Oklahoma; a young lawyer from the town of McAlester, a member of Phi Beta Kappa and a former Rhodes Scholar, who had risen from private to lieutenant colonel in the recent war, and who was a member of the American Legion, Veterans of Foreign Wars, the Masons, the Elks, and the Izaak Walton League.

Clyde Doyle, a Democrat from California, was serving his first term in Congress. A young lawyer, his native wit and legal training were to enable him on several occasions to bring the wandering examination of witnesses back to the matter in hand.

Messieurs Halleck and Brown, Republicans, of Indiana and Ohio, respectively. The former, a congressman since 1935, had been Republican leader in the Eightieth Congress. Like Mr. Albert he was a lawyer and a member of Phi Beta Kappa. The latter, a veteran of five Congresses, was a farmer and publisher of a chain of country newspapers, a Republican National Committeeman, a member of the committee's executive board, and 1946 campaign director for the committee.

* The committee sought $50,000, and was appropriated $40,000. Lucien Hilmer was appointed staff director; Charles B. Holstein research director; and William Earl Griffin clerk.

Joseph Patrick O'Hara, Republican, Minnesota; a lawyer from Glencoe and a former State Commander of the American Legion.

The investigation was to occupy the attention of this committee throughout the rest of the Eighty-first Congress, although, towards the end of the session, when the Korean crisis became acute and the war drive was intensified, it attracted less and less public notice. The public hearings revealed very little that students of government and observers of the political scene had not long known, but they did lay emphasis upon several aspects of lobbying that had not been widely discussed by a reluctant press.

The hearings were conducted with unusual dignity and thus did not grab the headline space, even when the war was still cold, that they might have received had they been stage-managed with this in mind rather than the purpose for which they had been ordered by Congress. They were sandwiched in between the sensational hearings on Senator Joseph McCarthy's unfounded attacks upon the State Department (the House committee made no effort to examine the so-called China Lobby,* which Owen Lattimore charged was at the back of McCarthy's demagoguery) and Senator Estes Kefauver's inquiry into the extent of crime throughout the United States, with its emphasis upon gambling. In one respect this helped the committee, for it was able to go ahead more studiously than most committees have done.

In the long run the Buchanan investigation showed that congressional committees need not, when they are so minded, necessarily alienate public confidence. But in spite of this the objective observer cannot help feeling that if the Buchanan Committee had aimed a little more closely at public disclosure of the existent evils of lobbying, and had hit a little harder, it would have commanded even more respect than it did. As it was it made its enemies and was roundly trounced by the Republican and big business press.

* As this book goes to press, there is some talk of an investigation of the powerful Nationalist China lobby.

Professor Lindsay Rogers of Columbia University, in an enlightening discussion of how Congress "fumbles for facts," recently pointed out that Anglo-Saxon legislatures, by "insisting on their right to compel disclosures by Executive departments and citizens . . . have been less craven and have proved more vigorous protectors of the public weal" than any other legislatures.[7] "It is the legislature," he continued, "which, in Woodrow Wilson's phrase, must demand the examination of 'corners suspected to be dirty' even though to draw the public eye it must 'magnify and intensify the scandal.' " This last the Buchanan Committee failed to do as effectively as it might have done.

Another and perhaps more plausible reason for the negative results can be found also in Professor Rogers's articles. He suggests that Congress is at no time capable of carrying out successfully those investigations which it is continually finding it necessary to make. Major inquiries affecting the general welfare ought to be turned over to an independent outside agency, such as is provided for in New York by the Moreland Act and in Great Britain by the Tribunal of Inquiry Act. Thus political pressure is, to a certain degree, eliminated, and the inquiries can be handled by trained and competent investigators, much as a grand jury operates.

It must be obvious that any investigation of lobbying is, in many respects, an investigation of Congress itself. For Congress is, after all, the party of the second part.

Lobbying is a practice too close to the legislative function for Congress to be able to examine it with the proper perspective. The entire problem of congressional investigations is one which a Congress long jealous of its prerogatives has never properly explored. At a time when so many congressional investigations have ceased to command public confidence, a thoroughgoing study of the principles of the Moreland Act and the British system of inquiry, with an exploration of the possibilities of setting up such a body in Congress, might well occupy the attention of another Hoover Commission. Until such a commission is created it is highly unlikely that all the aspects of lobbying and the constitutional control of pressure groups will be deeply studied by the national legislature.*

The Buchanan Committee, however, began its investigation seriously enough, fully aware of the truth long ago expressed by E. P. Herring. At a time when Congress was busy with another "lobby probe," he warned that such an inquiry can accomplish almost nothing if its objective is the eradication of the Third House of Congress.[8]

---

* In the second session of the Eighty-first Congress both houses had authorized thirty-five committees or subcommittees to make investigations of one kind or another, for which purpose there had been appropriated funds totaling $1,500,000, or about one eighth of the amount admittedly spent for lobbying in 1949. Lindsay Rogers, "When Congress Fumbles for Facts," New York Herald Tribune, March 29, 30, 31, 1950.

CHAPTER X

Lobbying Newly Defined

From the very beginning the committee realized that if it were to carry out the mandate of Congress literally it would be faced with an impossible task. It quickly decided to abandon any thoughts of holding public hearings or of conducting staff investigations on all the thousands of groups then active in influencing legislation. Instead, it decided to split the investigation into two main categories: (1) a broad investigation of certain areas without reference to particular groups or issues; and (2) a more intensive investigation into specific areas and of specific groups. Whether this was the most effective way to bring home to the American public the scope and power of the private lobbies at work upon the national legislature is a question difficult to answer. As the committee in its *Interim Report* [1] pointed out, the scattered efforts of some previous investigations and the extremes of concentration of others marred those investigations and prevented them from being as effective as they might have been. We have seen that none of them succeeded in putting a lobby act through both houses of Congress. But we have also seen that the most concentrated investigations, those, that is, that came closest to intensifying and magnifying the scandal, attracted the most attention and in the long run added the most to our general knowledge of how the process of legislative government works.

Like everyone else who has approached the problem, the committee encountered difficulty in defining exactly the term lobbying. There was nothing in the resolution creating the committee which confined it to the vague definitions of the Lobby Act. (The act, incidentally, was not mentioned in the resolution, nor was the committee restricted to investigating lobbying under the act, although certain minority members acted as if this were the case when it served their purpose.) It found the definitions in state laws were confusing and dictionary definitions too limited in scope to meet modern requirements. Many organizations, however, seemed to go by *Webster's New International Dictionary*, which says that to lobby is "To address or solicit members of a legislative body in the lobby or elsewhere, as before a committee, with intent to influence legislation." As far back as 1908 Arthur Bentley had shown that lobbying was not so cribbed and cabined as that, but with the passage of the Lobby Act the committee found that "numerous groups and persons claimed this definition as their own in an effort to escape full disclosure under the Act." [2] It cited the National Association of Manufacturers as one organization which followed this definition to its logical conclusion when it reported only 1.97 per cent of its $4,300,000 annual budget as allocable to legislative activities, while neglecting to mention its $2,000,000 public relations program or the $395,850 it spent, largely on advertising, in its campaign to abolish price controls.[3]

The committee came to the conclusion, which they could hardly have avoided, that any attempt made for pay or for any consideration to influence the passage or defeat of any legislation, is lobbying. "In the final analysis," it reported, "there are only two practical gauges of lobbying activity — intent and some substantial effort to influence legislation. The means employed are secondary, and any attempt to define lobbying by listing specific methods of influence is inevitably and almost immediately out of date." [4]

Money, of course, is the root of all lobbying. Said the committee, the thing that is "most significant" in attempts to influence legislation, "is the expenditure of money, whether it be used for direct contact of legislators, direct communication with legislators, or in efforts to stimulate grass-roots pressure so that members of organizations and members of the general public will communicate with legislators. . . ." But lobbying — no matter how astronomically its costs may soar, is not something that can be "computed with mathematical precision." The committee made the first official compilation of expenditures reported under the Lobby Act by organizations, groups, and individual lobbyists, and found that from the time of the passage of the act through 1949 the total was approximately $75,000,000. "Lobbying," it concluded, "is an important and usually an honest business, and it is a business that runs on money." But it also concluded that the Lobby Act of 1946, which provides the only official source of information available, only scratches the surface of the vast amounts that are spent throughout the nation each year to influence the Congress of the United States.

The committee did not hold public hearings until late in March, 1950, and by that time it was unfortunately apparent that all was not harmonious within the committee. Two members of the minority, Representatives Brown and Halleck, were obsessed with the thought that the committee members, and particularly the chairman, were intent upon absolving all "left wing" lobbies of wrongdoing, and equally intent upon condemning all "right wing" lobbies. If by "right wing" is meant organizations dedicated to all antidemocratic measures that have come before Congress since 1932, and if by "left wing" is meant labor unions, small business organizations, minority groups, consumer lobbies, and the like, the charge has some validity. But a careful examination of the published testimony taken at the public hearings, and a careful reading of the various reports and documents issued from time to time by the committee, show that Messieurs Halleck and Brown pursued obstructive tactics throughout the investigation and did their best to embarrass the administration at every turn. The partisanship displayed on both sides, but particularly on the Republican side, further emphasizes the fact that Congress is not the body to examine lobbying.

At the conclusion of the public hearings the committee issued a *General Interim Report*. Representatives Halleck, Brown, and O'Hara did not sign it. Instead they issued, through Mr. Halleck's office, a violent statement in which they called it "an attempt to smear American enterprise and to discredit our American system." It was nothing of the kind. It was far from being the "socialistic white paper" the minority called it. The angry dissent, however, was not without its value, for it revealed the state of mind of the minority when it accused the committee of condemning as "vicious" the "privately-financed, dignified, factual, educational campaigns by citizens, professional and business groups, opposed to the socialization of America" — by which Mr. Halleck could only have meant the work of such organizations as the Committee for Constitutional Government, the National Economic Council, Inc., or the American Enterprise Association. Calling the Public Affairs Institute "left wing" because it was primarily financed by the Brotherhood of Railroad Trainmen * was also indicative. And to say that the report "indicates that the majority generally approve as in the public interest all lobbying which favors passage of measures in the program of socialization, and disapprove all activities designed to uphold private initiative and government [*sic*]" suggests that perhaps the minority had read too much of Merwin K. Hart's and Edward A. Rumely's propaganda.

The hearings which led to this *General Interim Report* began with a general seminar on the "role of lobbying in representative self-government," to which several authorities on the subject were invited. Then separate hearings were held on the housing lobby, contingent-fee lobbying, the National Economic Council, the Committee for Constitutional Government, the Americans for

---

* Other "left wing" supporters: United Mine Workers, International Typographical Union, International Brotherhood of Teamsters, United Brotherhood of Carpenters and Joiners, American Federation of Musicians!

Democratic Action, the Public Affairs Institute, the Foundation for Economic Education, the Civil Rights Congress, and on the legislative activities of executive agencies. In addition to these hearings it circularized 173 large corporations in an effort to determine the amount of money spent annually by big business to influence legislation and it examined records of labor and farm groups to the same end.

To the student of political science the opening hearings were of unusual interest, for the committee had before it several distinguished witnesses * who dealt quite realistically with a number of topics relating to lobbying. The 163 pages of their printed testimony [5] reveal at least one interesting and unusual suggestion, offered by Dr. Stephen K. Bailey of Wesleyan University. Much of Dr. Bailey's testimony was devoted to giving a résumé of his book, *Congress Makes a Law*, which is a blow-by-blow description of the metamorphosis of Senate Bill No. 380 — the so-called Full Employment bill of 1945 — into the greatly watered-down Employment Act of 1946, but he went beyond that to set forth a sensible proposal for the revision of present lobby regulations.

"Lobbying," he told the committee, "can be understood only as the reflection of interests shared by shifting coalitions made up by Members of Congress, outside pressures, and executive agencies." He called for an examination of the relationships among private interest groups, members of Congress, and agency personnel, pointing out that lobbying is not a one-way track. In order to facilitate an understanding of these relationships he suggested an

---

* Professor Stephen K. Bailey, Wesleyan University; Dr. Hadley Cantril, director of the office of public opinion research in the Department of Psychology, Princeton University; George B. Galloway, senior specialist in American Government, Legislative Reference Service, Library of Congress; W. Brooke Graves, Legislative Reference Service, Library of Congress; Roger W. Jones, assistant director, Bureau of the Budget; Edgar Lane, instructor in politics, Princeton University; Richard E. Neustadt, member of the Legislative Reference Division, Bureau of the Budget; Frank H. Weitzel, assistant to the Comptroller General; and Dr. Belle Zeller, Brooklyn College.

amendment to the General Appropriations Act which would require from employees of government, including representatives
and senators, information similar to that which the Lobby Act of
1946 attempts to get from lobbies and lobbyists. His proposed
amendment would provide that:

> . . . no part of the funds appropriated under this act may be used to
> pay the wages and salaries of anyone who receives an annual wage or
> salary under this act of $11,000 or more, and who does not by March 1
> of each year submit to the Clerk of the House a statement . . . of
> the amounts and specific origins of all income from sources other than
> the Federal Government. And the Clerk of the House shall have in-
> scribed in the *Congressional Record* not later than April 1 of each
> year, a summary of these statements, and shall make all such statements
> available for public inspection.

This would force executive agency bureau heads, division chiefs,
secretaries, undersecretaries, and all members of Congress, to report the sources and amounts of both their public and private incomes, thus giving the public a chance to check on their possible
partiality towards legislation affecting such sources. It was a sort
of "what's sauce for the goose is sauce for the gander" arrange-
ment. Mr. Halleck was upset. "Are you trying to create the implication," he asked, "by suggesting that amendment, that Members
of Congress are being paid considerable sums of money to influence their action in Congress?"

"No, sir, not at all," replied the professor of government,
". . . All I have in mind here is the fact that it is extremely difficult for anyone, it seems to me, who has outside interests . . . not
to have developed over a period of years what Justice Holmes
once called inarticulate major premises, frames of reference, to
legislation about public policies; and I think in all fairness, if lobbyists are to register because of their interest in some particular
aspect of public policy, then we ought to ask all executive personnel and congressional personnel" to do the same.

Needless to say, this suggestion was not followed up.

The other witnesses at these rather academic sessions helped lay
the groundwork for the more important inquiries into specific lobbies that were to follow. Dr. Belle Zeller gave the committee her
studied evaluation of the lobby acts which have from time to time
been passed by thirty-eight states and the territory of Alaska —
regulations exclusive of prohibitions against bribery, which are
found in all the states.[6] And the gentlemen from the Bureau of the
Budget and the Comptroller General's office acquainted the committee with the scope of the laws affecting lobbying and publicity
methods by executive and administrative agencies.[7]

The lobby hearings came at a time when Washington was still
reverberating with the noise of the "five percenter" investigation
by a Senate subcommittee which had shown that the national
capitol was being plagued by a pestiferous swarm of somewhat
unsavory characters who claimed an ability to snare contractual
and other favors for their equally unsavory clients — for a fee.
During this same period some newspapers * had printed stories
about a pair of "contingent fee lobbyists" which had come to light
through the quarterly listings of lobby expenditures in the *Congressional Record*. These told how one Samuel F. Haines, a registered lobbyist, was working for a group of hotel owners with the
understanding that his $25,000 fee would be boosted to $100,000 if
he succeeded in bringing about the repeal of the 20 per cent
cabaret tax, and how one Thomas J. Downs, another registered
lobbyist, was promised $25,000 in addition to his $10,000 retainer
should he manage the repeal of the 20 per cent fur tax before July
1, 1948.

This kind of lobbying smacked of a return to the old, unbridled days of lobbying when the ethics of the profession were
laxer and the techniques of lobbying less well perfected than they
have become since the end of World War I. Although Dr. Gallo-

---

* E.g., the *Kansas City Star*, May 19, 1948, and other subscribers to the
North American Newspaper Alliance syndicate, carried a Washington
dispatch headed "System of 'Incentive' Pay Enters Lobbying Business."

way of the Legislative Reference Service discovered, from an analysis of the Lobby Act registrations, that not more than 2 or 3 per cent of the total number indicated arrangements for contingent fee payments, the committee decided to peer into this dark corner.[8] Its findings have an interest for students of lobbying particularly because they show the attitude of the courts towards this practice since Justice Swayne's noted denunciation of the hiring of legislative adventurers in 1874.

A number of cases have come before the courts in which contingent fees have been the basis for distinction and, with a few exceptions, an agreement for compensation for services in procuring the passage of legislation has been found unenforceable, as against public policy, if such compensation is contingent upon success. One court declared:

Agreements for compensation contingent upon success suggest the use of sinister and corrupt means for the accomplishment of the end desired. The law meets the suggestion of evil, and strikes down the contract from its inception. There is no real difference in principle between agreements to procure favors from legislative bodies, and agreements to procure favors in the shape of contracts from heads of departments. The introduction of elements to control the action of both, is the direct and inevitable result of all such arrangements.

And another declared:

Bribes, in the shape of high contingent compensation, must necessarily lead to the use of improper means and exercise of undue influence. Their necessary consequence is the demoralization of the agent who covenants for them; he is soon brought to believe that any means which will produce so beneficial a result to himself are "proper means"; and that a share of these profits may have the same effect of quickening the perceptions and warming the zeal of "careless" members in favor of this bill.[9]

An article in the *Yale Law Journal*,[10] however, points out that the courts have not always seen fit to distinguish between cases where the compensation was contingent and those where it was not. While the early practice was to refuse to enforce any contracts for influencing legislation there have been, in recent years, some cases where the courts have enforced the lobbying contract where the fee was not contingent. The *Journal* remarks:

It is questionable if there is any functional basis for the distinction between the two types of lobbying contracts. It is more likely that courts denouncing lobbyists have thought in terms of the corrupt practices of the old lobby, while courts recognizing the less reprehensible lobbying of more recent times as a legitimate occupation have sought a ground for differentiation in the fact of contingent compensation.

Chairman Buchanan felt strongly on the subject of contingent fee lobbying and even before he heard the testimony of Mr. Haines and Julius Green, chairman of the National Fur Industry Tax Committee, he made this pertinent statement:

. . . There is an unsavory fraternity of individuals who represent to businessmen that they can affect Government decisions by pressure, influence, or collusion with Congressmen and Senators. While businessmen would prefer to be honest, they are lulled into an easy belief that Congressmen and Senators can be reached by influence and money, and, as long as it involves no risk on their part, they are willing to pay someone to do a little on their behalf. Does this not lead to a belief that some of our Congressmen and Senators are corrupt?

Even if the lobbyist has influence but exerts it improperly on behalf of a client, or induces his client to believe that he, the lobbyist, may exert his influence improperly, the lobbyist in this way violates the fundamental concept of decent government, and whether it be by reason of politics or personal profit, he strikes at the American way of life.

With this philosophy, and having in mind the laws laid down by the Federal courts that a contract for contingent fees or compensation for the lobbyist's services is unenforceable, as against public policy, regardless of whether corrupt practices are resorted to or contemplated, I would recommend to the Congress that contingent fee contracts for lobbyists be outlawed and that such contracts be held in violation of the Federal law, punishable by fine or imprisonment or both.

Most of the hearings were given adequate coverage by the press and radio, with particular stress, of course, placed upon those where verbal violence occurred, as it did from time to time. During the hearings on the housing lobby and later when Dr. Edward A. Rumely of the Committee for Constitutional Government and Merwin K. Hart of the National Economic Council appeared as reluctant and defiant witnesses, when the close alliance between the extreme right wing and the real estate interests was revealed, a number of shocking statements concerning democracy were put into the record. These received the wide circulation which they deserved. Perhaps most revealing of a state of mind that seems to be prevalent among those who spend millions of dollars lobbying against the progressive and protective measures that have come before Congress during the life of the Fair Deal was a letter found by committee investigators in the files of Herbert U. Nelson, executive vice-president of the National Association of Real Estate Boards. Written in May, 1949, to T. H. Maenner of Omaha, Nebraska, the incoming president of the association, this amazing letter read in part:

I do not believe in democracy. I think it stinks. I don't think anybody except direct taxpayers should be allowed to vote. I don't believe women should be allowed to vote at all. Ever since they started, our public affairs have been in a worse mess than ever.

I don't think any form of government is any good which doesn't recognize merit and ability. I am convinced that our present popularity contests in public life are bound to lead to disaster and to some form of dictatorship as the currency is progressively devaluated by public spending in order to buy votes.[11]

In spite of heated protests by Mr. Nelson's counsel the letter was read into the record and Mr. Nelson later issued an explanatory statement which is almost as revealing as the private letter itself:

We do not have a democracy in this country. We have a republican form of government. My distrust of democracy, the uncontrolled rule of a numerical majority or the dictatorship of the proletariat, was shared by the founders of the Republic, as can be shown from many quotations from their writings.

Frank E. Holman, president of the American Bar Association, recently pointed out: "The United States Army Manual still states: The Government of the United States is not a democracy but a republic, that the word democracy nowhere appears in the Declaration of Independence, in the Constitution of the United States, in Washington's Farewell Address, in Jefferson's Inaugural, nor in Lincoln's Gettysburg Address."

There are democracies in Europe. These governments which depend solely upon majority vote at any given moment and which have no safeguards for individual rights. Both England and France are good examples of such democracies, and one sees the confiscation of properties and the abrogation of personal rights going on now in those countries.[12]

This hatred for democracy was expressed by Merwin K. Hart, who quoted to the committee a speech he made in 1940 before the Union League Club of New York in which he declared:

I wonder sometimes if one of the causes of our trouble today does not arise from the fact that we have been overdrilled into believing we are a democracy. This, too, may be one of the latest "insidious wiles of foreign influence." . . . It is time to brush aside this word with its connotations. It is time for us to return to the conception of a republic.

And the barrage of references to the United States as a "democracy" as though it were an accomplished fact (that the United States is a "democracy") simply camouflages and conceals the efforts of an extremely active group to convert our Republic into a "democracy" — that is, from a representative form of government into a mobocracy, governed eventually by a dictator.[13]

Mr. Hart delved into a long dissertation on the neglect of the word "democracy" by our founding fathers and those who followed in their republican footsteps. He declared it was not "until Woodrow Wilson came along, and why I don't know, but he began talking about the war to make the world safe for democracy. How safe he made it, I leave to you gentlemen to decide."

The word was still in disrepute until Georgi Dimitrov of Bulgaria, "who was a 'big shot' in the Communist crowd," gave the word dubious validity when he used it to describe Soviet Russia in 1935. According to Mr. Hart.

This way of thinking appears continuously in the publications of many of the right wing lobbies, whose stock in trade would seem to be hatred for what most people nowadays think of as democracy. Strangely enough this way of thinking seemed to have permeated at least one member of the committee. When Dr. Dewey Anderson was testifying he sought to explain why the Public Affairs Institute, of which he was the director, had attempted to make a nation-wide study of the registration and voting habits of the American people. The following colloquy took place:

Mr. Doyle. What was your object, Mr. Anderson — what was your ultimate objective? Why make a study of voting?

Mr. Anderson. The hope was, Mr. Doyle, first of all that we would, taking the participation of the various groups in the population in elections, we would reveal, over the nation and for localities, the participation of various groups in elections, who votes and who fails to vote being a matter of great concern to the preservation of a democratic institution.

Mr. Doyle. Why is it?

Mr. Anderson. Because, if you don't exercise this one thing, the franchise, you cannot participate in a democracy, in government.

Mr. Brown. You mean a republic; for this is a republic.

Mr. Anderson. A republic. Let's call it a republic, if you are going to make that fine distinction.

Mr. Brown. I want to be . . . exact.

Mr. Doyle. And I want the record to show that there is a certain nation, Russia, which calls itself a republic. I like democracy, as far as I am concerned.[14]

Such clashes over ideology and terminology were frequent during the hearings, marking the wide contrast between the attitudes of the minority and the majority. A fair reader of the testimony would find it difficult at times to distinguish between the thoughts of Representatives Brown and Halleck and those of Dr. Rumely, Mr. Hart, and others of the John T. Flynn school of political science. In fact, Mr. Flynn and his strange book, *The Road Ahead*, were stamped as the intellectual leader and the bible of the right wing lobbyists and their committee defenders as the investigation of lobbying went its irascible way.

In spite of the intracommittee squabbling, betokening the almost irreconcilable differences of approach to the subject of lobbying by the two sides, the majority — Representatives Buchanan, Albert, Doyle, and Lanham — was able, in mid-October, to reach certain general conclusions.

Events of the past several years point up the conclusion of the committee that pressure groups "thrive on the inability or unwillingness of political parties to exercise the powers of government which they have lawfully won at the polls." The advantages of this situation to the lobbyist, the committee report continues, are obvious, for this lack of cohesion in the parties "enables well-organized private interests to secure some of the advantages of political power without having to submit to the democratic electoral process by which this power is usually attained." [15]

During this period of weak party, if not administrative, leadership the greater weight of the pressure groups has been on the destructive side. The furtherance and even completion of constructive legislation, too often that promised by the party victorious at the polls and therefore presumably the will of the majority, has been hampered and even stopped time and again by the concerted assaults of many lobbies banded together in an unholy alliance. This destructive process is helped rather than hindered by the "necessarily complex structure of our government, with its separation of powers, checks and balances, and bicameral legislature." Nowhere does the committee argue for a change in this structure, even if this complex government does create bottlenecks at which pressure can be "quietly and effectively applied." Because of this situation "the great pressure campaigns of recent years have relied heavily upon the tactics of attrition and delay at every critical spot in the legislative process. The prevention of governmental action, and this is the aim of many lobbies, is relatively easy under the circumstances." It logically follows that some means of exposure and control is necessary if our democratic legislative process is to continue to function even as well as it has in the past.

To any such demands for exposure and control, however, those whose private interests would be the most affected rise up in arms and rush into battle waving the first amendment. In their view, as the committee wisely points out, "lobbying is not a problem of who is to exercise political power, but is, rather, a matter of expressly granted individual rights." To this argument this reply is offered:

. . . the right of petition is cited as both the cause and justification of lobbying, and rightly so. Organized groups of interested citizens have an important informational and representative role to play in our kind of government. Citizens can and should exercise their right of petition individually and through organized groups. Without this constitutionally guaranteed right of petition our kind of free government could not exist. But we often fail to recognize that while lobbying is a necessary right which should not in any way be restricted or abridged, it is a right which is not exercised for itself alone. People and groups seek to influence legislative policy because they hope to gain thereby and not because they want to keep their rights from becoming flabby from want of exercise.

Lobbying as it is carried on in Washington today is, the committee asserts — and all the evidence tends to support the assertion — basically a reflection of the state of our economy. "As the management of this economy has drifted into fewer and fewer hands, so too has pressure on the legislative front been sharply accelerated." The evidence gathered by the Temporary National Economic Committee, and buttressed and brought up to date by the House Subcommittee on the Study of Monopoly Power in the Eighty-first Congress, definitely reveals the acceleration of the concentration of corporate wealth in both the prewar and postwar years.

This fact, the committee asserts, is "one of the most serious problems which large-scale lobbying poses for our easygoing institutional structure." And it continues:

Economic power provides one of the essential raw materials for successful pressure politics; the greater the power, the larger are the possibilities of success. And so to the extent that some groups are better endowed than others, there is a disparity in the pressure which these groups can exert on the policy-making process. . . . "Lobbying for all" may be a sacred right but it is a right which some men can make more meaningful than others. It is said, for example, that the individual consumer and the billion-dollar corporation have equal rights before the law, but are they equal before the lawmakers?

CHAPTER XI

Lobbying by the Billions

In an effort to determine whether the individual consumer and the billion-dollar corporation do enjoy equal rights before the lawmakers, the Buchanan Committee in May 1950 sent questionnaires to 173 large corporations asking for pertinent information relating to their activities in encouraging or retarding national legislation. This was well within the scope of the mandate under which the committee was functioning. Evidence in its files showed that several of the more active lobby organizations existed almost solely because of the generosity of the nation's largest corporations. The committee had also discovered that only 38 of the selected 173 corporations had ever reported their expenditures under the Lobby Act of 1946, and that these 38 had, in the period between January 1, 1947, and June 30, 1950, recorded in their reports a total of only $776,446 spent for lobbying activities.

It does not take a very cynical mind to suspect that this figure barely scratched the surface and that the actual amount spent to influence national legislation and policies was many times that small sum. When the returns were in, coming from all but 22 of the corporations questioned, the committee was able to report the more realistic figure of $32,124,835 as the amount spent for activities which the majority of the committee considered within the meaning of lobbying as defined by the 1946 act. Since there are an estimated 500,000 business and financial corporations in the United States there is every good reason to believe Chairman

Buchanan's assertion that the "business of influencing legislation is a billion-dollar industry." *

It would be interesting to contrast the expenditures of the big corporations with the totals spent by farm and labor organizations. The committee did make an effort to gather some of this data by sending the same questionnaire to four leading farm organizations and to five of the larger labor organizations.† If the total for the corporations seems far too small, the total for the farm and labor groups is equally misrepresentative. The four farm groups reported spending $1,131,952 and the five labor groups reported a total of $1,916,534. While these groups probably do not spend nearly as much as does big business in the course of a year for the direct and indirect persuasion of Congress, it stands to reason that they did spend more than these figures would indicate.

The corporation questionnaire sought information on five fronts:

1. The cost and purpose of all trips made to Washington for legislative purposes and the identity of those making the trips.

2. The cost and a description of the function of company offices maintained in Washington if those offices have legislative functions.

3. Details of all printed or mimeographed material relating to

* *New York Times*, October 22, 1950. The statistical data in this chapter is taken from the 520-page report of the House Select Committee on Lobbying Activities: *Expenditures by Corporations to Influence Legislation* (Eighty-first Congress, second session, House Report No. 3137) and from the *Supplement* to that report in *Expenditures by Farm and Labor Organizations to Influence Legislation* (Eighty-first Congress, second session, House Report No. 3138). Washington, 1950.

† The American Farm Bureau Federation, National Farmers Union, National Council of Farmer Cooperatives, and the National Grange; the American Federation of Labor (which did not answer the questionnaire on the grounds that all pertinent information regarding its lobbying was contained in the filed reports of its registered lobbyists), the Brotherhood of Railroad Trainmen, the Congress of Industrial Organizations, the International Association of Machinists, and the United Mine Workers of America.

public issues prepared or distributed by the corporation (except intraplant instructions on the application of Federal laws and regulations).

4. The date and cost of insertion, description, and place of publication of all newspaper or periodical advertising relating to educational or institutional issues.

5. Detailed data on all other expenditures for the direct or indirect purpose of influencing national legislation.

In connection with the distribution of printed or duplicated material the committee specifically asked the corporations to report all expenditures in connection with the following eight organizations:

American Enterprise Association; America's Future, Inc.; Committee for Constitutional Government, Inc.; Constitutional Educational League; Constitution and Free Enterprise Foundation; Economists National Committee for Monetary Policy; Foundation for Economic Education; and Public Affairs Institute. With the exception of the Public Affairs Institute these organizations are representative of the right wing type of lobby, dependent to a great extent upon corporate generosity for its existence, or they were self-styled "educational foundations" which claimed exemption from taxation. The Public Affairs Institute, supported by several unions, also claimed tax exemption and did not register under the Lobby Act of 1946.

The interrogation was sent to the corporations on May 26 without the approval of the minority members of the committee, indeed over their strenuous protest, and its existence did not become known until about a fortnight later. Although there was nothing in the story to justify the implication, the *New York Times* headlined its story, which led the paper, "House Lobby Unit Weighs Plan to Put Curbs on Industry," [1] and this inference was typical of the reaction of the press in general to this invasion of corporate privacy. Now the press united in vigorous condemnation of the committee. David Lawrence, in his syndicated

Washington column, predicted that "to place any restriction —
even the registration of companies or filing of expenditures — in
connection with the publication of opinions" would be found
unconstitutional by the Supreme Court, and then went on to say:

Businessmen have been reluctant to give out information about these
expenditures, thinking it an unwarranted intrusion in their affairs and
an attempt at intimidation. This is a mistaken view. The businessmen
should help assemble every bit of data so that the American people
may know how trivial, relatively speaking, is the total amount of
money actually being spent to combat the socialistic and quasi-
communistic influences that are trying to undermine the free enterprise system in America. The businesses of America might well consider how far short of a real insurance premium they are spending to
assure survival of free enterprise.[2]

There is a parallel between this observation and the stand taken
by Merwin K. Hart, executive director of the National Economic
Council. He conceded that the committee had a right to investigate lobbying activities, but he thought the committee was going
too far when it asked him for the names of his supporters and of
the purchasers of the material his council distributed by the
bushel. Mr. Hart, who has been tagged a fascist and an anti-Semite
more than once on the floors of Congress, begged the committee
not to let this information "fall into the hands of men and groups
who, by their action and words, have shown that they are willing
to bring about the socialization and in some cases the communiza-
tion of the United States."[3] He also denied being anti-Semitic,
saying, in effect, that some of his best friends are Jews, if they
are Americans first. His plea that the data and names he gave committee investigators were "solely for the benefit of the committee" was not accepted, and from his testimony and the lobby statements of the NEC it was shown that among the large contributors
to the Council were the following:

Armco Steel Corporation; Bethlehem Steel Company; Irenee Du
Pont; Lammot Du Pont; Eastman Kodak Company; Empire State,

Inc.; Joseph R. Grundy; Gulf Oil Corporation; Ex-Senator Albert Hawkes of New Jersey; Lone Star Cement Corporation; Los Angeles Chamber of Commerce; John J. Raskob; W. H. Regnery, Chicago publisher; Standard Oil of Indiana; Sears, Roebuck & Company; Sheaffer Pen Company; the Texas Company; Union Carbide & Carbon; and Robert E. Wood of Chicago.[4]

The *New York Herald Tribune*, on the same day that Mr. Lawrence's column appeared, remarked editorially:

The possible inclusion under the head of lobbying of certain regular business activities begins to touch upon the large issue of free speech. The control involved in registration, and the inevitable taint that attaches to the process of lobbying, can very easily be stretched too far, with results damaging to the whole formation of free opinion in a democracy. . . . The presentation by business, the focusing of attention upon its achievements, have nothing to do with any special interest, but with matters of greatest importance to every American. Institutional advertising, a constructive development of the past decade, is but one of a diversity of means by which business is finding its voice. To have these made the subject of suspicion and perhaps of regulation would be an unfortunate trend. We trust that the special House committee will continue its inquiry with more restraint and with a more defined and limited aim than was indicated by its first sally into this particular field.

William C. Mullendorf, president of the Southern California Edison Company, which was one of the 22 corporations which refused to furnish the requested information to the committee, angrily characterized the questionnaire as "an obvious attempt to use intimidation in limiting exercise of free speech by millions of citizens in opposing or supporting legislation" and expressed in his telegram "deepest resentment and indignation at this brazen attempt at thought control on behalf of the citizens of whom you are the servant and not the master." *

* The *New York Times*, June 12, 1950. Although the committee cited three individuals, who were later indicted, for contempt of Congress for refusing to supply the committee with information from its files or to answer questions, it made no further effort to pry answers from Mr. Mullendorf, or from the 21 other corporations which also refused to answer.

Of the total $32,124,835 spent in three and one half years on what the committee characterized as lobbying activities $26,941,-452 was in the form of contributions to various organizations, some of them registered lobbies, others "fringe" lobbies, and others institutions of purported educational nature. Sixty-five of the corporations spent, according to their own admissions, $2,194,-519 for printing and distributing leaflets, booklets, books, and other material dealing with public issues. Thirty-one reported spending $2,013,369 for advertising dealing with public issues. Sixty-six spent $227,256 sending emissaries to Washington. Seven spent $346,807 on maintenance of Washington offices.[5]

In a newspaper interview Mr. Buchanan said what is pointed up time and again in the *Interim Report* and other publications of the committee, namely that such expenditures were "good and proper and in keeping with our great American rights of free speech and a free press." But, he told the *New York Times* on October 22, 1950:

Congress and the people have a right to know who is behind the gigantic campaigns to influence Congress either directly or indirectly. The replies [to the questionnaire] show very clearly that American business is spending millions of dollars to flood the country with pamphlets, leaflets and books dealing with public issues like TVA, Social Security, labor legislation and the like. Millions of these pamphlets are distributed to school teachers, the clergy, and other local community-thought leaders with the intention of thereby indirectly influencing Congress. Many companies distribute the pamphlets to their foremen and other supervisory personnel as well to influence their thinking and the thinking of those under them.

The corporations that refused an answer were: Allis-Chalmers Manufacturing Company; Armstrong Cork Company; Belden Manufacturing Company; Consolidated Vultee Company; Dow Chemical Company; B. F. Goodrich Company; Harnischfeger Corporation; Inland Steel Company; International Harvester Company; Johns-Manville Corporation; Lone Star Cement Corporation; Marshall-Wells Company; Montgomery Ward; Mountain States Power Company; Kelvinator Corporation; National Steel Corporation; New York Airbrake Company; Pittsburgh Plate Glass; Pullman, Inc.; Southern California Edison; United States Gypsum; Wisconsin Power & Light. *Expenditures by Corporations; New York Times,* October 23, 1950.

John T. Flynn's violent distortion of history, *The Road Ahead*, and numerous publications of such organizations as the Committee for Constitutional Government and the Foundation for Economic Education, have been distributed by the millions in this manner. Invariably they deal with issues pending before Congress and almost as invariably they seek to show that these measures (such as housing, rent control, and excess profits taxes, to name three) are "socialistic" in origin and against the general welfare.* They may not urge direct congressional action, although they often do, and it would be a strained mind which could accept a clean-cut distinction between their ultimate intent and the direct intent of publications from the Political Action Committee of the CIO or the allegedly communistic Civil Rights Congress demanding immediate repeal of the Taft-Hartley Act or defeat of the Mundt-Nixon bill.

In commenting upon the committee report *Expenditures by Corporations*, the *New York Times* raised the question whether the difference between the $32,124,835 admittedly spent on the committee's interpretation of lobbying and the $76,446 reported under the Lobby Act actually showed that "the business of influencing legislation is a billion dollar business," as Mr. Buchanan had said. "It may also suggest," it editorialized, "that there is a difference of opinion as to what lobbying actually is." To sharpen the contrast the editorial went on to say:

Of course the 152 corporations that reported, plus twenty-one (sic) others that neglected to do so, did not do all the lobbying that was done. There are more than 1500 registered lobbyists and lobbying agencies in Washington. Farmers, labor unions, veterans, real estate

---

* "Organizations seeking to protect a privileged status for their members at the expense of the general welfare of all Americans use terms like 'socialism,' 'statism,' and 'welfare state' to forestall rational analysis of legislative proposals which they oppose. We are prepared to risk our national existence against totalitarianism, yet there are those among us who live by the totalitarian principle of the great distortion, endlessly repeated. Political freedom cannot live in an atmosphere of such hysterical oversimplification." *General Interim Report*, p. 65.

owners, doctors, miscellaneous reformers and scores or even hundreds of specialized causes and interests are represented. And the Executive Branch does some lobbying itself, at various levels. If the President invites a delegation from Capitol Hill to come down and see him that action might be described as lobbying.

Lobbying is not a crime, and Chairman Buchanan doesn't say it is. What he does say, and the argument seems reasonable, is that "influencing legislation is an activity that should be carried on in a goldfish bowl." The nature of the pressure and who is paying for it ought always to be public knowledge, and there ought always to be some accurate way of distinguishing between a million dollars and a million votes. If this can be done lobbying can be a part of the democratic process; if it can't some new legislation may be required.[6]

In most enlightened circles the committee's reiterated contention that all substantial receipts and expenditures to influence legislation directly and indirectly should be reported to Congress and the public, was being echoed within a few months of the sending of the questionnaire. There remained little widespread sympathy for the corporations beset by the congressional committee seeking legitimate information. The *Washington Post* felt that the corporations' chief ground for complaint "lies in the odium that is sometimes attached to the word 'lobbyist,' " and continued:

This misconception of the term is most unfortunate, for the task of influencing public opinion is one of the most honorable and important functions that a citizen may perform in a free land. The "molders of public opinion," as they are sometimes called, come into disrepute only when they use underhanded methods. Except for this unfortunate label, it is difficult to see any reason why either corporations, labor unions, professional societies, or other organizations engaged in influencing public opinion should object to reporting their expenditures for this purpose if they are operating in a manner befitting a free society. And of course if they are operating in any other manner, the public ought to know about it.[7]

This change in attitude by a responsible portion of the press, which had greeted the questionnaire with such misgivings a few months earlier, was not shared by Representative Brown of the minority. He called it both an "unfair" and an "un-American action," and his condemnation was shared by Democratic Representative Eugene E. Cox of Georgia and Republican Representative Clare E. Hoffman of Michigan, the latter (whose association with certain lobbies is a matter of record) becoming so incensed that he demanded a special House investigation of the lobby investigation! [8]

This questioning of the corporations was a part of the committee's wider investigation, particularly into the Committee for Constitutional Government, and the National Economic Council, two organizations which, without any exaggeration, can be called a part of the latent fascist element that only the ostrich would deny exists in the United States. Their close alliance — actual or ideological — with big business and with other lobbies for big business, such as the American Enterprise Association and the Foundation for Economic Education, cannot be ignored.*

Deeply disturbing is the fanatical character and utter irresponsibility of these extreme right wing organizations. The National Economic Council is an excellent example. Backed by such corporations as Armco and Bethlehem Steel, Eastman Kodak and Armstrong Cork, Standard Oil and Texas Corporation, the Mohawk Carpet Mills and the Santa Fe Railway, it has indulged in the fascist approach in its publications for many years. "One of its techniques," the committee reported, "is to disparage those who

---

* *Lobbying Direct and Indirect. Hearings* Before the House Select Committee on Lobbying Activities. Part 4, National Economic Council, Inc.; Part 5. Committee for Constitutional Government. The testimony taken at these hearings and at the hearing on the Foundation for Economic Education (Part 7) are summarized to a certain extent in the *General Interim Report* of October 20, 1950, but should be read separately, not only for the facts but for the unconscious humor which they contain. But I would not recommend them to students of the art of cross-examination. Except for Chairman Buchanan all members of the committee had been trained as lawyers, but somewhere along the line they had mastered the art of circumlocution. Every so often, however, either Mr. Doyle or Mr. Albert or Judge Lanham would suddenly come to, and bring the hearings back to the subject of lobbying with some incisive questioning.

oppose its objectives by appeals to religious prejudice, often an ill-concealed anti-Semitism." Many of its backers, who of course must share responsibility for its activities and utterances, probably were unaware of its methods (the committee suggests) and would be opposed to its "appeals to unreason" if they were "fully apprised of them." Indeed, the committee hearteningly points out that it had received evidence that "some corporate contributors" disapproved of the techniques employed by Merwin K. Hart, the NEC's chief executive, and "have recently repudiated NEC." It is probable that the reason why some corporations did not want to answer the questionnaire, thus revealing the names of organizations they backed financially, is the difficulty they would have in justifying these expenditures to their stockholders. It was fear of the defection of blue-ribbon backers that motivated Leonard E. Read, executive secretary of the Foundation for Economic Education, in his unsuccessful attempt to keep their names from appearing in the records of the lobby investigating committee.[9]

Times have changed since Senator Thaddeus Caraway was able to say with some measure of accuracy that 90 per cent of the lobby organizations in Washington were fakes preying upon gullible petitioners, raking in their fees for services they could not perform. Today "soliciting money for lobbying is much more than a device by which a few imaginative opportunists can gull the unwary." It is a big business, conducted for the most part along orthodox lines, following two general patterns that keep the lobby coffers filled. The great majority of legitimate lobbies can be found among the 4000 national organizations, preponderantly serving business, which the Department of Commerce has listed. For the most part these are membership groups which function on the receipts of dues from individuals or local divisions. Except in rare cases, usually when it is felt necessary to conduct an exceptional campaign for or against a specific bill affecting their close interests (such as the hotel owners seeking to repeal the 20 per cent cabaret tax), they operate without special assessments. This method is not confined to business organizations, but is followed by farm and labor groups, veterans' orders, professional societies, and all the other associations which exist to protect private interests. About the only other source of income which these groups have is the sale of their house organs, which in most instances is definitely secondary. Far too few of these organizations are themselves registered as lobbies, mainly because they do not consider lobbying their principal purpose. Some of them keep Washington representatives on their payrolls, and these as a rule do register. But the Congress of Industrial Organizations, which is continually concerned with legislation, has only four registered lobbyists, and the American Medical Association, which admits to spending more money on lobbying than any other group in the nation, has only seven registered lobbyists.

The second general pattern, the effectiveness of which has been shown by two startling examples in recent years, is that of assessment. The National Association of Real Estate Boards maintains a permanent lobby known as the Realtors Washington Committee, which is supported by dues paid from the local boards. But when, as in 1948, it engages in an all-out drive in Congress against Federal housing and rent controls it turns to its grass-roots membership for help. In that year the NAREB demanded of the local boards an amount equaling $5 for each active member. "How your board raises this money is its own affair," the president stated.[10] It collected thousands of dollars this way to be used in one of the most intensive lobbying campaigns in recent legislative history — and incidentally gave President Truman one of the most cogent issues of his campaign that year. Better known to the general public was the 1949 campaign of the American Medical Association which, in the words of the committee, "waged a heavy and generally successful campaign to obtain $25, sometimes not without elements of coercion, from each of its 140,000 members in order to support an all-out drive against national health insurance." [11] Coercion is not generally necessary, however, for the members of most organized pressure groups subscribe so whole-heartedly to the purposes of their organization that they do not need their arms twisted for money to support legislation benefiting their interests or to fight legislation which, in the impressive words of the National Association of Manufacturers, is "in derogation thereof."

Lobbies like the Committee for Constitutional Government or the equally antidemocratic National Economic Council, and lobbies of the indirect variety like the Foundation for Economic Education, are in a different category. In the first place, they represent no particular business or industry, they are not trade organizations, they operate in semisecrecy — or at least did until the Buchanan Committee started its investigation. In some ways they come close to being rackets. They have to "sell" themselves to that part of the public susceptible to their program of action. Their stock in trade is fear — fear of "socialism," "statism," and the "welfare state"; or, on the opposite side, an obsession with the indestructible virtues of a "free economy," "private enterprise," and the "American way of life." Their salesmen spend as much time raising funds as they do creating their propaganda or prose-lytizing congressmen. Some of them do very well at their profession. Mr. Read of the Foundation for Economic Education, which claims exemption from registration on the grounds it is a tax-free educational institution, receives a salary of $25,000 a year. In 1949 Dr. Rumely's Committee for Constitutional Government was listed as the second largest spending lobby, having admitted to spending $620,000 for legislative purposes. And in 1949 Mr. Hart received $17,083.[12]

The leagues, foundations, and institutions, which have multiplied greatly in the past decade and which annually collect millions to "educate" the economically ignorant or "preserve" our socialistically battered constitution, depend very slightly upon membership dues. As the committee explains:

While the labor union or trade association has a specific membership on which it can draw, the foundation or committee seldom has this kind of continuous support. Under these circumstances, it is not surprising to find that the foundation's major fund-raising efforts are directed at those who have the most to give. Lacking a dependable, dues-paying membership, the tapping of individuals and corporations for sizable contributions to the cause becomes the first order of business. The foundation or committee gladly accepts $5 contributions from a sincere believer, but its operations are largely geared to the donor who can give a thousand $5 contributions at once.

But nobody who can afford such largess will make such large gifts without getting something tangible in return. What these large contributors get is "literature." The propaganda mills turn out pamphlets and booklets and releases by the thousands, all bearing on public issues in one way or another. "To most trade associations or labor unions," the committee asserts, "the circulation of house journals, pamphlets, books and reprints is merely a useful incident to the group's work and is seldom a source of support or profit. To the foundation or committee, however, the dissemination of literature is both a reason for the group's existence and a primary means by which it exists." *

Figures unearthed by the committee reveal that from August, 1946, through June, 1950, the National Economic Council had a total income of $2,327,709, of which 59 per cent (or $1,372,047) came from contributions for the distribution of books and pamphlets. A quarter-by-quarter analysis of these figures indicates that such contributions constitute "an increasingly large part" of the NEC's income. For the first two quarters of 1950 — the period in which The Road Ahead was being flooded across the nation — contributions for the distribution of "literature" had mounted to $338,507, or 70 per cent of the NEC's total income.[13]

---

* This is discussed in fuller detail in Chapter XII in relation to the Foundation for Economic Education, and in Chapter XIII, where the distribution of The Road Ahead, by John T. Flynn, is examined. The FEE depends less upon dissemination of propaganda than other "foundations."

The various items of propaganda designed, according to Mr. Hart's statement filed with the committee, "to defeat the Truman program for a socialized 'welfare state,' often called 'creeping socialism,' " [14] are not bought in any vast quantities by the general public. Instead, they are bought by wealthy individuals or corporations which "sponsor hundreds of subscriptions . . . and at the same time enjoy that deep satisfaction which can come only to those who have made a tax-deductible gift to a charitable or religious organization." [15]

Mr. Hart explained the system well to Lammot Du Pont in 1947:

> We have devised a plan that should greatly widen the list of readers of our council publications and strengthen us financially.
>
> We have had legal opinion (I enclose copy) to the effect that a purchase by anybody of subscriptions to council publications to be sent to educational and religious corporations is a gift that is deductible before taxes. Furthermore, as such a gift, it may be for any amount not limited by the $3000 gift tax.
>
> We are already receiving subscriptions along these lines. We have compiled a list of colleges and universities, public libraries and Protestant churches in many sections of the country, and we are going to press this in the hope we can eventually place those publications of ours in the hands of all these organizations throughout the country. That would be of inestimable help.
>
> We have already covered the states of Michigan, Ohio, and Indiana, and most of Illinois, so far as libraries and colleges are concerned, as well as certain other sections.
>
> I write to ask if you would be willing to subscribe for 500 sets of these publications at $10 each on the above lines.[16]

The money which Mr. Du Pont and others gave to the National Economic Council in response to such pleas was used for the general purpose of spreading propaganda for private enterprise, private property, individual initiative, and American independence, and against socialism (of the "creeping" or Truman-Roosevelt variety), world government, the United Nations, a bipartisan foreign policy, and "militant Zionism." Translated into realistic terms this means the NEC lobbied directly and indirectly for a stronger Taft-Hartley law which, in Mr. Hart's words, would "not leave the working people of the country under the absolute domination of a handful of men." * It means the NEC proposed legislation to remove the present Supreme Court from office on the grounds it is socialistic and to bar its present justices from ever again holding judicial office. It means the NEC would limit the government's power to levy taxes by a constitutional amendment which would put a ceiling on income taxes. It means further that the NEC was in favor of withdrawing tidelands from Federal ownership and giving them to the states, that it favored aid to Franco Spain, and that it supported the drive to remove cooperatives from all tax exemption. Those were its affirmative stands.

The list of the legislation which the NEC opposed is longer and it includes nearly all progressive legislative proposals made within the last few years: Federal aid to education; displaced persons legislation; further immigration; public housing and the middle-income housing bill; United States participation in the United Nations, the International Trade Organization, and the International Labor Office; United States ratification of the Genocide Convention; the Fair Employment Practices Act, the antilynching bill, and all other Federal civil rights proposals; rent control and price controls; the Marshall Plan; United States support for an independent Israel; increased social security; farm price support; the Point Four Program; the Reciprocal Trade Agreements Act; the

* In his chapter entitled "Areas of Popular Ignorance" in *The Pollsters*, Lindsay Rogers shows that an analysis of several polls conclusively reveals that there was no great popular demand for the Taft-Hartley Act at the time it was being pressured through Congress by the National Association of Manufacturers, the National Economic Council, the Committee for Constitutional Government, the United States Chamber of Commerce, and several other big business lobbies during the Eightieth Congress. Rogers further shows that there has been even less of a demand for its retention than is popularly supposed. Most political experts agreed after the 1950 election that the labor act was not a supreme electoral issue. *The Pollsters*, pp. 146–151.

Tennessee Valley Authority; the present Atomic Energy Act; and the World Federation resolution.[17]

As Mr. Hart wrote to his angel, Irénée Du Pont, shortly after the demise of the Eightieth Congress: "We have definite evidence in a number of instances that our work with respect to measures before Congress has been decisive in the disposition of these measures. All we need, in order to be of a conclusive influence on a substantial number of measures, is the funds to get additional personnel and to meet other necessary costs."[18] They were forthcoming, as we have already seen. Within the next two years Mr. Du Pont parted with $21,000, bringing his total aid to the council to $31,513.[19]

The high-spending Committee for Constitutional Government has a different method, but one equally effective. It accepts two types of contribution. The first is interesting, for it is obviously designed to escape the provisions of the Lobby Act of 1946 which insists upon a listing of all contributions of $500 or more. Dr. Rumely's organization seeks contributions of $490 or less for its general fund or specifically marked for the distribution of the committee's literature. It also accepts contributions for more than $490, but these are taken *only* for the distribution of books and pamphlets. Presumably any general contributions above the $490 mark are returned if not specifically designated for this purpose. The contributor may distribute these books himself, or, as is usually the case, leave it to the committee to do so. "In either case," the Buchanan Committee reported, "the committee treats the transaction as a book sale which it does not report as a contribution under the Lobbying Act."[20] It also stimulates mass distribution of its propaganda by offering it at low rates to large contributors, as it did with its special reprints of *The Road Ahead*.

Who the large contributors to the CCG are, and the amounts they have given, are not known. This is because Dr. Rumely refused to give the House Select Committee on Lobbying Activities this information. As a consequence of this refusal Dr. Rumely was cited for contempt of Congress. He went to trial in the District of Columbia before Federal Judge Richmond B. Keech and a jury in April 1951. In spite of the fact that Representative Halleck of the Lobby Committee appeared as one of his character witnesses, it took this jury only twenty minutes to find him guilty on three counts of contempt. In imposing upon Dr. Rumely a six-month suspended jail sentence and fining him $1000, the maximum fine, Judge Keech stated that he had given the case "extraordinary consideration" and that "save for this man's age I would commit him." The sixty-nine-year-old Dr. Rumely announced that he would take the case to the Supreme Court on appeal, if necessary.

The committee found that in the course of seven years between 1937 and 1944 the Committee for Constitutional Government had distributed the staggering total of 82,000,000 booklets and other items of "literature" which it characterized as designed to influence legislation. This is fully a million more copies than a magazine like *Newsweek* distributed in the same period. The counsel for the House committee, Benedict F. Fitzgerald, Jr., remarked: "Of particular significance is the fact that Edward A. Rumely and the Committee for Constitutional Government, Inc., in recent years have devised a scheme for raising enormous funds without filing reports pursuant to the provisions of the Federal Regulation of Lobbying Act. This scheme has the color of legality, but in fact is a method of circumventing the law. It utilizes a system whereby contributions to the CCG are designated as payments for the purchase of books, which are transmitted to others at the designation of the purchaser, with both the contributor of the money and the recipient of the books totally unaware of the subterfuge." [21]

The House committee wanted to know to whom these millions of pamphlets and books had gone. Dr. Rumely said he would not give these names to the committtee for fear of exposing them to "the pressure of the labor bosses or the smear of left-wingers." Although such data was demanded by subpoena he ignored the request because it was "an attempted violation of our rights under the First and Fourth Amendments."

"If you persist in demanding these names of purchasers I cannot do otherwise than refuse," he said. "If you cite me for contempt and Congress confirms the citation, I shall again have to stand trial, as I did before, when the jury decided we were within our constitutional rights and brought a verdict of acquittal."

Dr. Rumely took the position that his committee, as publisher, was wrapped in the immunity of the first amendment and that Congress, which can pass no law abridging the freedom of the press, could therefore not ask him any questions which he considered an infringement of that freedom. When the chairman suggested that he was evasive and that his book sales methods were a "phony sales dodge" rather than the "patriotic undertaking" which Dr. Rumely said they were, he declared: "We sell our books at a price so low that it requires a substantial investment of our general funds." In his defense he had the whole-hearted support of Representative Brown, himself a publisher.

MR. BROWN. It is your contention that, inasmuch as you are in the publishing business, that, as a publisher — I want you to get this question very clear: Is it your contention that as a publisher, operating under a constitutional guarantee of the freedom of the press, that you are perfectly ready and willing to submit to this committee any information, any records that you may have, that you feel, or which the committee may feel, after you have had an opportunity to explain, in any way would come under the purview of the Lobby Registration Act, or under the purview of this committee, but that you do not feel you can be compelled to report to anyone as to your activities as a publisher, only as it may be in the direction of influencing legislation?

MR. RUMELY. That is true. That is an exact statement of our position.

MR. BROWN. In other words — and I think the press of the country should pay attention to this — the Congress has a right to investigate and look into, under this resolution, the activities of any publisher when it comes to attempting to influence legislation — perhaps the postal rate bill might be a perfect example — but that no one in the

Congress has the right to inquire into the certain field that has been
held sacred under the constitutional freedom of the press, that is
your right to publish books, magazines, newspapers, or whatever it
is that you may publish legally, so long as they are not subversive or
against the best interests of the United States?

MR. RUMELY. That is exactly the position. . . .*

But this position did not sit well with the Democratic majority
of the committee. In the *General Interim Report* it pointed out
that "There are literally dozens of plain references to specific
measures" in the CCG's publications. Because of these it reached
the understandable conclusion that "under these circumstances,
Mr. Rumely's claim that the first amendment grants him absolute immunity from any inquiry is wanting in substance and must
yield to the rights of the public and the Congress. Not freedom
of the press but simple honesty is at issue here." [22]

Dr. Rumely was extremely adept, as it turned out, in extending
his conception of the freedom of the press to limits hardly im-
agined by the authors of the Bill of Rights. To him it meant also
freedom from paying postage for the mailing of his wares. In
four years time, evidence unearthed by the committee showed the
CCG had mailed between 8 and 10 millions (and perhaps many
more) pieces of "literature" under free congressional frank.

---

* *Hearings*, Part 4, pp. 21-23. Mr. Brown, however, was not always
consistent. When a representative of the CIO was testifying during the
hearings on the housing lobby Mr. Brown cross-examined him closely on a
booklet and demanded to know who purchased them — whether it was "individual local CIO organizations" or "members." When Judge Lanham
chided him by recalling this Mr. Brown angrily replied: "The pamphlets to
which he [Mr. Goodman of the CIO] referred were pamphlets in direct
support of housing legislation and housing proposals then before Congress.
They were not books or booklets of general information. They were used
primarily and only for the purpose of being distributed among those individuals who wished them, and were also presented to members of Congress
in argument as to why housing legislation should be enacted. Therefore, I
think, they generally come under the lobby law." (*Hearings*, Part 4, pp. 26-
27.) A free press for CCG but not for CIO? It was well established that,
although Dr. Rumely said the CCG had never issued "booklets similar to
that," material of the CCG was freely distributed to Congress for the
purpose of influencing legislation.

Because of Dr. Rumely's system, whereby most of the contributions to his organization were earmarked for the purchase and distribution of CCG publications, and because Dr. Rumely on four separate occasions refused to reveal who these purchasers were, the financial backing of the Committee for Constitutional Government remains undisclosed. For this refusal he was cited, and later indicted by a Federal grand jury, for contempt of Congress. Thus the fine distinction which he insisted upon drawing between "publishing" and "lobbying" remains to be decided by the courts.

Representative Doyle, however, did not think very highly of Dr. Rumely's contention that he was a "publisher," and shortly after the doctor's appearance before the committee issued the following statement:

From time to time this organization [the Committee for Constitutional Government] has described itself as an ordinary commercial publisher. This lobbying organization differs from commercial publishers in many respects, some of which are—

1. A commercial publisher takes the normal risks of operating a private business—he does not beg the public for money to help him carry on.

2. A commercial publisher expects to pay income tax on his receipts—he does not seek tax exemption.

3. A commercial publisher is in business for profit; he is not primarily an advocate. He does not constantly grind out pamphlets, leaflets, books, etc., which present only one side of the subject.

4. A commercial publisher does not couple his publishing activities with incessant appeals to the citizenry to bring pressure to bear on Members of Congress in order to influence legislation.

The commercial publishers of the United States are not governed by the Federal Lobbying Act in any way, and need not file reports under it. They are *not* attempting to influence legislation; they are attempting to make money. They should not be confused by attempts of out-and-out lobbying organizations to conceal their activities from Congress and the public.

The Committee for Constitutional Government has also attempted to liken itself to educational institutions; but it ignores the following facts:

1. An educational institution does not spend millions of dollars in pamphleteering campaigns designed to influence congressional action on legislation.

2. An educational institution does not engage in a constant campaign for funds to carry on lobbying activities.

3. An educational institution does not couple its activities with incessant appeals to the citizenry to bring pressure to bear on Members of Congress in order to influence legislation.

4. An educational institution presents both sides of the question in an objective fashion for appraisal. It does not continually present only one viewpoint on each issue it considers.

Considering all the afore-mentioned we can reach but one conclusion: Edward A. Rumely is not an educator. He is not a publisher. He is an ordinary, every-day, run-of-the-mine lobbyist.[23]

These lobbies, which annually spend their thousands of dollars distributing books and pamphlets of their own or others' authorship, are only a part of the big business lobby. But they are an important part, for their aim is to reach the leaders of opinion in the home sectors of congressmen and thus play their influential role in swaying congressional opinion. Invariably they follow the ideological line of the National Association of Manufacturers, which the Lobby Committee did not see fit to examine during its year-long investigation. Conceivably the fact that the National Association of Manufacturers has, in the past, been the target of aggressive congressional attack which has laid bare the tremendous scope of its lobbying activities in other years, and the further fact that it long has had pending a case in Federal Court whereby it hopes to establish the unconstitutionality of the Lobby Act, had some bearing on this decision.

During the course of the investigation, however, the NAM itself filed a belated report covering its 1949 finances, including the amounts it believed were attributable to lobbying expenses. It did not answer the pertinent questions raised at one of the hearings by Dr. Stephen K. Bailey. Using the data assembled in his book *Congress Makes a Law*, Dr. Bailey had shown how the NAM, the United States Chamber of Commerce, the American Farm Bureau Federation, and the Committee for Constitutional Government had jointly engaged in what he called "standard lobbying operations: preparing literature against the [Full-Employment] bill; conducting public opinion campaigns; testifying before Congressional Committees; writing and wiring individual Congressmen; and approaching Congressmen directly." [24] After pointing out the "close connection, or parallelism of ideas" which exists between the NAM and the "opinion centers" in agriculture, and showing that the NAM maintains a Farm and Industry Service, which sends releases to 35,000 farm leaders and "canned" editorials to 7500 rural newspapers, Dr. Bailey urged the Lobby Committee to "make a special study of the National Association of Manufacturers as a possible holding company of seemingly independent pressure groups, and as a conditioner of rural opinion." He added: "It seems to me that this relationship between business and agriculture needs further exploration." The committee did not follow the suggestion and there is nothing deducible from the association's reluctantly filed report to bring further light on this important subject.[25]

The filing of the information reiterated the contention of the NAM, made in 1947 and 1948, that it is not required to file under the act. The organization admitted in a statement filed by Kenneth R. Miller, an executive officer, that the information supplied probably is not "as complete, or in such form or detail, as would seem to be required if it should later be determined by the Courts that the Association is required by law to register and/or file reports subject to Section 305 of the Act." But, incomplete as the information is, it is significant.

The National Association of Manufacturers reported total receipts of $4,480,155 for the year 1949. None of these receipts, it said, was received or earmarked specifically for lobbying. It explained that all its expenditures were on an allocated basis and therefore it broke down its departmental receipts and expenditures and set forth the percentage of each which it believed could be called allocable to lobbying expenditure. It further explained that the Slaughter case decision, previously mentioned, seemed to exempt from coverage by the law not only those who appear before congressional committees but also those who help prepare the testimony for such appearances. Nevertheless, it included this expenditure in its report.

The association's system of allocation of legislative expenses is as follows: A "legislative" percentage, based on the ratio of legislative expenditures to total expenditures, has been calculated and then applied to other divisions "which engaged in no legislative activity," and the resulting figure has been added to the amount reported as "administrative overhead" contributing to the legislative work. The latter figure, for 1949, was $52,037, which, added to the legislative expense indicated, brought the total "lobbying" expenditures to $117,230 or "approximately 1.5 per cent of total expenditures."

Even if this total of $117,230 should be shown not to represent the actual expenditures for lobbying by the National Association of Manufacturers it does place the association within the highest spending lobbies reporting in 1949. These were: [26]

American Medical Association	$1,522,683
Committee for Constitutional Government	620,632
Townsend Plan and Weekly	432,110
National Association of Electric Companies	388,883
United World Federalists, Inc.	291,672
Citizens Committee on Displaced Persons	222,809
Association of American Railroads	194,159
National Small Business Men's Association	192,070
National Milk Producers Federation	178,161
National Association of Real Estate Boards	138,600
National Association of Manufacturers	117,230
Colorado River Association	115,120
National Association of Margarine Manufacturers	101,037

CHAPTER XII

Lobbying by Foundation

THE question of where to draw the line between those organizations which lobby directly, like the Committee for Constitutional Government and the National Association of Real Estate Boards, and those like the Brookings Institution, the Public Affairs Institute, and the Foundation for Economic Education, was one to which the Buchanan Committee devoted considerable attention. As Representative Brown put it: "I wonder where we are going to draw the line even if we do require registration. Suppose we required registration. Where would we stop on these organizations? Could we say the Pope influences legislation? Certainly, the statements he makes influence legislation. Certainly, we cannot go so far as to interfere in the affairs of the church." And later he said of one person: "I don't know of anything that couldn't influence or mightn't influence legislation. You could put in his love letters under that proviso." [1]

The committee did not investigate the Brookings Institution, which has been publishing the results of its research on economic, governmental, political, and legislative issues since its foundation in 1927, and which, upon one important occasion at least, helped draft a highly controversial measure for the Senate. But it did go into the affairs of two other research organizations, one a highly reactionary economic foundation supported by some of the biggest corporations in the United States, and the other a liberal institute whose major financial backing has thus far come from one of the big independent labor unions. Both the Foundation for Economic Education and the Public Affairs Institute attempt to mold public opinion on contemporary political and legislative issues, although neither believes that, as the present law is written, it should register with Congress.

When the Foundation for Economic Education publishes a tract on *Illusions of Point Four* by Henry Hazlitt, who divides his time between *Newsweek*, of which he is a contributing editor, and the foundation, of which he is a trustee, it obviously is trying to influence the legislative mind against any legislation that may be proposed to implement Point Four. When the Public Affairs Institute prepares a critical evaluation of Point Four in its *Bold New Program* series it obviously is trying, as Mr. Halleck put it, to "bring about a better understanding of the Point Four program, and, probably, better acceptance of it in the public mind and, hence, likely, a greater probability of acceptance . . . by the Congress of the United States." [2]

Neither the foundation nor the institute, as far as the testimony before the committee revealed, sought to follow up its pamphlets with direct lobby action. Neither sent agents to the lobbies to browbeat congressmen nor out into the grass-roots districts to intimidate them at election time. But both certainly hoped that congressmen would read and be swayed by their conflicting points of view regarding Point Four. Both pamphlets bore the name of the publisher, the foundation and the institute, but the average citizen and the average congressman has no means readily available of knowing that the Foundation for Economic Education receives its funds almost entirely through the largess of twenty of the biggest corporations in the country and that the Public Affairs Institute receives its funds mainly from the Brotherhood of Railroad Trainmen and, in this instance, from a grant from the Foundation for World Government, another pressure group.

The question of these tax-exempt pressure groups, organized as educational foundations, is a comparatively new one. There is nothing specific in the Lobby Act which exempts such "foundations" from compliance with the act, unless, of course, it is the ambiguous "principal purpose" clause. Rather than chance the revelation of their financial backers under the Lobby Act, or the Corrupt Practices Act, these "foundations" resort to the practice of the Foundation for Economic Education, which states in its certificate of incorporation that its purpose is not to "carry on propaganda or otherwise attempt to influence legislation."[3] In the light of some of their activities it is rather difficult to reconcile this high aim with the actualities. Most of these "foundations" are right wing in their ideology and derive their support almost wholly from corporations or from individuals having large corporate interests, they are antilabor in their approach to economic issues, and some of them are definitely on the fascist fringe. The only "left wing" organization of this kind which the committee seriously investigated was the Public Affairs Institute,* which holds that it is exempt from registration for almost identical reasons: that it is a nonprofit institution set up for "educational, scientific and civic purposes."[4]

---

* The committee also investigated the lobbying activities of the Civil Rights Congress (Hearings, Part 9) but little of significance was revealed at the stormy sessions of August 3 and 4. William L. Patterson, the Negro executive secretary of the Congress, became embroiled with Representative Lanham and each accused the other of lying when Mr. Patterson inadvertently placed the Scottsboro affair in "Judge" Lanham's native Georgia rather than in Alabama. The pair nearly came to blows and had to be separated by the Capitol police. (Hearings, Part 9, pp. 51–52; New York Times, August 5, 1950.) Because Mr. Patterson refused to produce records revealing the financial backers of the Congress and to answer questions as to his affiliation with the Communist Party, he was cited for contempt of Congress. (New York Times, August 31, 1950.) A jury disagreed in his first trial. (New York Times, April 12, 1951.) Another citation of contempt was voted by the House against Joseph P. Kamp, executive vice chairman of the Constitutional Educational League, for refusing to produce records revealing the financial backers of the League. At the time he was serving a jail sentence for refusing to answer questions of the House Campaign Expenditures Committee. He was indicted on his second citation and his trial is still pending as this is written. (New York Times, August 4, 5, 27, 31, September 1, 1950; June 7, 1951.)

Labor groups took notice of these "foundations" a few years ago when the Committee for Constitutional Government and the National Small Business Men's Association, both registered lobbies and, at that time, vocally active in the fight for the preservation of the Taft-Hartley Act, set up as hidden subsidiaries the Constitutional and Free Enterprise Foundation and the Small Business Economic Foundation.

According to a prospectus signed by Frank Gannett, one of the prime movers in the Committee for Constitutional Government, the former sought to raise funds through tax-deductible contributions. It stated that its major purpose was to "indoctrinate 10,000 college students" with "facts" about "their heritage of economic and constitutional freedom" and thus "fortify our form of government against socialistic trends." As one trade-union publication explained: "That's just a fancy way of saying that the foundation will attempt to reach college students with propaganda against President Truman's Fair Deal and any other progressive legislation." [5]

The Small Business Economic Foundation was the brain child of the veteran lobbyist, DeWitt Emery, whose parent organization, the National Small Business Men's Association, spent more than $192,000 for legislative purposes in 1949.[6] The "foundation" sought contributions up to $2500 from corporations and individuals, promising that they would be used to "explain to workers the advantages of our free competitive system of business." Among the corporations which this pleased was the Socony-Vacuum Oil Company, Standard Oil of Indiana, Standard Oil of New Jersey, and United States Steel, according to *Labor*, as quoted from the *Congressional Record*. Whether these "foundations" were lobbying organizations or not is a moot question, but they certainly were interested in indirectly influencing the trend of legislation, if not specific measures before Congress.*

---

* Although Socony-Vacuum was a heavy contributor to other lobby groups it does not give the Small Business Economic Foundation in its list

The Foundation for Economic Education was incorporated in March, 1946, by six men. These were: Donaldson Brown, a member of the board of directors and the financial policy committee of General Motors and E. I. Du Pont de Nemours & Company; Dr. Fred Rogers Fairchild, professor of economics at Yale University; David M. Goodrich, chairman of the board of B. F. Goodrich Company; Henry Hazlitt, former editor of the *American Mercury*, onetime editorial writer of the *New York Times*, and a contributing editor of *Newsweek;* Claude Robinson, president of Opinion Research Corporation, Princeton, New Jersey; and Leo Wolman, professor of economics at Columbia University, who formerly was research director for the Amalgamated Clothing Workers and a member of the National Labor Board and chairman of the Automobile Labor Board.

From the beginning its $25,000-a-year president and executive director has been Leonard E. Read, a vigorous 53-year-old go-getter with many years' experience in the raising of funds and the dispersal of propaganda for the American way of life, Chamber of Commerce style. He spent more than sixteen years on the West Coast as Western manager of the United States Chamber of Commerce and as general manager of the Los Angeles Chamber of Commerce. He came to the foundation after two years with the National Industrial Conference Board. While executive vice-president of that organization in Washington he was closely associated with Donaldson Brown, who was then a director of the National Association of Manufacturers. Mr. Brown was a violent opponent of the full employment bill that, in spite of his efforts,

---

of tax-exempt contributions as reported in *Expenditures by Corporations,* pp. 438–442. Standard Oil of Indiana did not reply to the committee questionnaire. *Ibid.,* p. 449. Standard Oil of New Jersey reports it gave the "foundation" $1600 in two years. *Ibid.,* p. 450. United States Steel denied making any expenditures for lobbying activities, although the committee expressly asked for all contributions to tax-exempt organizations and especially those publishing or distributing matter dealing with public issues. *Ibid.,* pp. 255, 517.

became the Employment Act of 1946. Mr. Read helped Mr. Brown set up an active lobby against the bill, which organized big business opposition and co-ordinated the efforts of the National Association of Manufacturers, the United States Chamber of Commerce, the Committee for Constitutional Government, and the American Farm Bureau by preparing a series of arguments against the bill that were considered of great value to the chairman and conservative members of the House committee.[7]

President Read was also an associate on the advisory committee of Spiritual Mobilizers, a Los Angeles organization which has been active with the real estate lobby, of such gentlemen as DeWitt Emery, Norman Vincent Peale, former chairman of the Committee for Constitutional Government, and Alfred Haake, a former Liberty Leaguer and leader of the Tool Owners Union. Besides opposing Federal housing the Spiritual Mobilizers seek to bring grass-roots pressure on Congress against national health insurance and Federal aid to education.

The Foundation for Economic Education has its headquarters in a rambling colonial mansion, which it has rebuilt complete with a cafeteria for its thirty employees, at Irvington-on-Hudson, a Westchester County suburb about fourteen miles from New York. It operated there for several years without attracting wide attention until Malcolm Logan and Alvin Davis of the *New York Post* discovered it at the height of the 1949 drive to smash rent controls. Even then Mr. Read denied vigorously that the foundation was a lobby and described it as a "university . . . that supplies facts and arguments to persons who oppose control by the state but who stumble and fall flat on their faces when they try to argue their views." [8]

Few "foundations" engaged in this type of work have been as lucky as the Foundation for Economic Education in the choice of financial angels. The foundation has been able to operate on a budget of $300,000 annually since it was started. The names of its sponsors, who have put up from $10,000 to $170,000 apiece since

1946, is most impressive. Many of its contributors also give to such organizations as the American Enterprise Association, the Committee for Constitutional Government, and the National Economic Council, but a breakdown of the figures contained in *Expenditures by Corporations to Influence Legislation* shows that the foundation is a high favorite among the blue-ribbon corporations of the country.

The twenty top contributors to the Foundation for Economic Education and the totals they have contributed to this non-profit, tax-exempt, educational institution, are as follows:

William Volker Fund	$170,000
General Motors Corporation	50,000
Earhart Foundation	45,000
United States Gypsum Company	41,000
Donaldson Brown (loan in 1946)	40,000
Chrysler Corporation	40,000
Consolidated Edison Company, N. Y.	40,000
E. I. Du Pont de Nemours	40,000
Gulf Oil Company	40,000
Marshall Field & Company	40,000
Montgomery Ward & Company	40,000
Sun Oil Company	40,000
United States Steel Corporation	40,000
Republic Steel Corporation	37,500
B. F. Goodrich Company	35,000
National Steel Corporation	22,500
Armour & Company	20,000
International Nickel Company	20,000
Libby-Owens Ford Glass Company	20,000
Alfred P. Sloan Foundation	20,000

Besides Mr. Brown, whose loan was repaid, the following individuals made these substantial gifts:

W. B. Bell, president, American Cyanamid Company	$1,000
Donaldson Brown	2,500
W. S. Carpenter, Jr., chairman of board of the Du Pont Company	4,500

Charles A. Cary, director, Du Pont Company	4,500
Jasper E. Crane, director, Du Pont Company	2,000
Irénée Du Pont	6,000
Lammot Du Pont	19,833
H. B. Earhart, ex-president White Star Refining Company	16,000
B. F. Goodrich	5,000
David M. Goodrich, chairman of board, B. F. Goodrich Company	4,500
L. Albert Hahn	1,000
Ex-Senator Albert W. Hawkes, chairman of the board, Congoleum-Nairn, Inc.	1,000
Atholl McBean, chairman of board, Gladding, McBean & Company	1,250
Joseph D. McGuire, McGuire Press	1,500
Donald R. McLennan, Jr., Marsh & McLennan Company	1,500
Ernest T. Weir, founder and chairman of board, National Steel Corporation	2,500
E. H. Worth	1,100

Other corporations whose contributions range from a top of $17,500 down to a minimum of $5000, are: New York Airbrake Company, Kresge Foundation, Standard Oil of New Jersey, Monsanto Chemical Company, Sears, Roebuck & Company, Detroit Edison, Westinghouse Electric Corporation, Maurice & Laura Falk Foundation, Nash-Kelvinator Corporation, J. L. Hudson Company, Humble Oil & Refining Company, Pittsburgh Plate Glass Company, Owens Illinois Glass Company, Electric Auto-Lite, Champion Spark Plug, S. S. Kresge Company, American Automobile Insurance Company, Ford Motor Company, General Electric Company, Merrill Lynch, Pierce, Fenner & Beane, and Eli Lilly & Company.

In addition to these, fifty-one other corporations and foundations contributed sums ranging upward from $1000. The grand total of receipts by the Foundation for Economic Education, between its founding in 1946 and the spring of 1950, was $1,348,-489.05. Of this amount, $171,772.98 came from the sale of its publications. The rest, a total of $1,175,966.07 was in the form of donations.* It is interesting to note that, of this larger total of donations, $902,859 came entirely from business firms or organizations, and only $141,953 was received from individuals, and of this last sum 51 per cent was donated by only twenty individuals. Teachers, clergymen and students, who are apparently not considered individuals by the foundation, supplied the rest.[9]

In the light of these figures, which reveal that 68 per cent of all the money received during the first four years of the foundation's existence came from only twenty business firms or organizations, it is difficult to take without at least a small grain of salt the foundation's assertion that "It is responsible to no outside person or group — either in government, business, labor or agriculture. Its sole purpose is a search for truth in economics, political science, and related subjects. Its aim is to provoke thought, not to direct political action." [10]

True, the foundation lists no government, labor, or agriculture groups among its contributors. With the exception of a few teachers, clergymen, and students, all those who have given money to the foundation are big business firms, foundations set up to further private enterprise, or individuals who are either owners, officers, or directors of big business corporations. And, as we shall see, nothing except one unfortunate paragraph ever appeared under the imprint of the foundation that was in any way distasteful to these interests, that did not espouse their economic beliefs, and that did not, at least indirectly, seek to influence not only the people but their representatives in Congress. That the foundation felt a responsibility to business — a perfectly legal and proper responsibility — is obvious. Its rather sullen efforts to hide this responsibility, to keep the names of its sponsors hidden from sight, is more difficult to understand.

In its *Interim Report* the Buchanan Committee took cognizance of this reluctance:

* Plus $750 listed as "honoraria."

We would be less concerned with the propriety of corporate donations to these groups if either the corporations or the foundations were willing that these donations should be a matter of readily available public record — to the stockholder as well as to the public at large. But this does not appear to be the case. Full disclosure, we are told, would mean "half-truths" and "oversimplifications" which would be dangerous for all concerned. We reject this view. . . . The right to privacy must yield to full disclosure of the salient facts in a matter so obviously clothed with the public interest.[11]

The committee, in making this appraisal, was referring to Mr. Read's general defense of secrecy which he made at the hearings on July 18, 1950, a statement which seems to express with exactitude the general views of these opinion-forming foundations which depend upon the quiet generosity of big corporations and wealthy individuals for their existence. None of them are self-supporting through their publications.

Mr. Read was frank enough when he commenced his testimony with the declaration:

I believe the pursuit of such a policy would lead eventually to the destruction of many such institutions. The public reporting . . . would present a single fact — the amount of a contributor's donation — to casual readers, persons having only a cursory interest in the matter at issue, persons who would not and perhaps could not possess all the facts. These folks of the so-called public thus receive only oversimplifications or half-truths from which only erroneous conclusions are almost certain to be drawn. If there is a public interest in the rightness or wrongness of corporate or personal donations to charitable, religious or education institutions, and I am not at all ready to concede that there is, then that interest should be guarded by some such agency as the Bureau of Internal Revenue, an agency that is in a position to obtain all the facts, not by Mr. John Public who lacks relevant information for the forming of sound judgments. . . .

. . . Half-truths submitted to the public, bearing the names of contributors, cast suspicion on the contributors. Many corporate contributors, for instance, are extremely sensitive to the position they occupy with the public — their market. They will not long endure any such risk. Donations to eleemosynary institutions are marginal expenditures with many and are cut off with the slightest provocation. Public reporting of a half-truth is indeed a significant provocation. I repeat, it would gravely endanger the existence of institutions such as ours, for there is no means to correct the unnumbered misunderstandings public reporting of mere donations would create.

I cannot in this statement delve into one of the most important points of all, the right of a person or corporation to do with the fruits of his or its labor as he or it pleases as long as the actions are devoid of fraud, coercion, conspiracy, or predation. Securing privacy in the affairs of men is a point not lightly to be tossed aside. Establishing a situation in which men begin to think in terms of how they are doing with a governmentally created and therefore artificial public instead of how they are doing with their own personal consciences is seriously to be guarded against.[12]

Here we have compactly an expression of a philosophy that has long been indicative of the business mind, a philosophy that Arthur M. Schlesinger, Jr., exposes with clarity in his book, *The Vital Center*. It consists of a distrust of democracy, of the "folks of the so-called public," sneeringly referred to here as Mr. John Public; timidity, and fear that revelations of sources of income will displease the customer and the stockholder; a sense of guilt that to be "found out" will bring desertion and disaster; and a quasi-reliance upon the "rights" of the individual as opposed to what others might recognize as the common good.

Since no "duress" is employed in seeking funds from contributors who are "responsible for their own actions," therefore (in the Read philosophy) "the public does not need to be concerned about them." As far as the recipients of the foundation's ideological products — their pamphlets against rent control, the Marshall Plan, Point Four, and the rest of the list — are concerned, the great bulk of them are on the foundation's mailing list "by personal request" and "it is presumed they [the subscribers] wish no protection against their own judgment." But what if this ideological product should fall into the hands of others, "like the employees of a corporation"? Well, they can as easily "put their faith in their respective managements who conduct and stand responsible for the distribution" as they can put their faith in "some public agency whose interest in them is assuredly even more removed." Public officials like congressmen — who can always hold an investigation and ask questions! — should be "quite able to take care of their ideological selves." As to the "millions who are not donors or recipients" — but just members of the great American public — "I cannot conceive what it is they need protection against." Certainly it is not against "our trustees, men of character and good repute, occupying positions of confidence and high esteem in the educational and business world" who testify by "their interest and trusteeship to the integrity of our activities."

Before exploring further the question of whether or not Congress and the public should be empowered to demand the source of funds of a "foundation" which claims to be "operated exclusively for educational purposes" it is necessary to examine what these educational purposes actually consist of. Unlike certain other organizations, the Foundation for Economic Education has little direct contact with Congress and a case might be made out for exempting it from the provisions of the Lobby Act of 1946 were it not for the saving clause, Section 307 (b), which includes any organization which receives money to be used *indirectly* to influence the passage or defeat of *any* legislation by the Congress of the United States. The moot questions affecting the Foundation for Economic Education and, it might well be, such organizations as Brookings Institution, the Russell Sage Foundation, the National Planning Association, the Public Affairs Institute, and many others, would seem to be whether their funds are used principally for the indirect influencing of legislation and does Congress have the constitutional right to demand this information?

As revealed by the committee the major function of the Foundation for Economic Education is "the preparation of pamphlets, booklets and articles presenting one side of public issues." An examination of the product shows that this is a fair description. Nearly all of them deal with matters of general public interest, and many with issues that were actively being considered by Congress at the time of publication. The following titles are revealing of the "educational" interests of the foundation: *So You Believe in Rent Control?, Price Supports, No Vacancies, Roofs or Ceilings, Industry-Wide Bargaining, The TVA Idea, Wages and Prices, Will Dollars Save the World? Liberty and Taxes, High Prices, Illusions of Point Four.* From these it can be seen that the foundation was interested in such legislative matters as housing, rent control, taxation, wage and price controls, foreign economic policy, and government ownership of power. Each took a definite stand, often discussing actual legislation, but even those that dealt mostly in generalities expressed a definitely conservative point of view.*

* The foundation distributed almost 4,000,000 booklets and pamphlets during the first four years of its existence. Its articles were used in nearly 400 newspapers and magazines, and one of its releases was reprinted in so many magazines, journals, and newspapers that it was estimated it reached an audience of 100,000,000 people. This particular article did not deal with legislation.

According to Read's testimony, the foundation maintains a mailing list of about 30,000. Although Read was friendly to Dr. Edward A. Rumely of the Committee for Constitutional Government, he did not agree with the latter on the efficacy of having the foundation's material reprinted by friendly congressmen in the *Congressional Record,* thus making it available for mass distribution under free congressional frank. His aim, apparently, was to hit at the top executives and business leaders of the country, and not at the masses through the kind of demagogic appeals favored by Dr. Rumely. He thought most people threw *Record* reprints away unread, anyway. Rumely wanted him to have his booklet on *Industry-Wide Bargaining* inserted in the *Record* and offered the use of his mailing list to have it sent to 13,000 or 14,000 editors and publishers of newspapers, 38,000 farm leaders, and 100,000 clergymen, preceded by a postcard asking them to distribute it further. He also wanted it sent to all members of the American Bar Association. "It would not be too burdensome to reach a quarter of a million with the booklet, and we have mailed tens of thousands of franked releases, and our experience with them is that when put out under the news they can be highly effective," Rumely wrote to Read. Read's response to this suggestion is not given in the record of the *Hearings.*

Hearings, Part 8, pp. 120–124, 127; *Interim Report,* pp. 33–34.

"It is difficult," said the committee, "to avoid the conclusion that the Foundation for Economic Education exerts, or at least expects to exert, a considerable influence on national legislative policy." [13]

"Is it the intent of the Foundation that its publications should have no influence whatever?" the committee wondered. "If so it is difficult to understand why these publications all relate to what Mr. Read . . . calls 'subjects high in current interest and discussion.' It is equally difficult to imagine that the nation's largest corporations would subsidize the entire venture if they did not anticipate that it would pay solid, long-range legislative dividends." [14]

Representative Albert, a majority member, took a blunt view of the foundation's literature. "Every bit of this literature," he said, "is along propaganda lines," [15] which seemed to shock Mr. Read, who perhaps recalled the injunction in the foundation's certificate of incorporation that "the corporation shall not carry on propaganda or otherwise attempt to influence legislation."

Certainly its booklet, *Roofs or Ceilings*, was definitely propaganda and sought to influence legislation. Nor could it be said to conform with Read's assertion about the educational status of the foundation. "In my opinion," he told the committee, "no primary or secondary school, no college or university or other institution of learning in this country is more genuinely, and with any more uncompromising honesty, dedicated to the search for truth in economics, political science and related subjects than is the Foundation." [16] This booklet was printed in bulk by the foundation and half a million copies were sold at cost to the National Association of Real Estate Boards, which had them widely distributed throughout the country by its far-flung network of local member boards. The foundation probably hoped that the realtors would remember its injunction in its pamphlet *On Distributing Literature:* "In offering literature to others, whether employees or friends, any semblance of the offering as a 'must' activity is not good. Such an attitude creates an unnecessary resistance. Rather, keep the effort in the realm of a voluntary opportunity. 'It's yours if you like it.' . . . Literature should not tell the reader what he ought to do or how he ought to think. This approach is generally resented. Convictions are self-formed. . . ." [17]

"Although groups like the National Association of Real Estate Boards have a natural advantage in secondary distribution of materials, other groups without comparable Nation-wide organizations have achieved similar results by careful focusing of efforts," the committee remarked. "As organizations like the Committee for Constitutional Government, the National Economic Council, and the Foundation for Economic Education draw their major financial support from relatively narrow and well-defined sources, so, too, are their materials directed at those persons and groups, which are expected to have an important influence upon opinion within their communities. True, the pressure group seeks maximum distribution for its product, but it seeks this distribution in terms of status and position first and in terms of ordinary people last. . . . Where the Committee for Constitutional Government strives to saturate the thinking of the community, the Foundation for Economic Education is content with a sprinkling." [18]

This, of course, is not a new discovery, nor does it apply only to pressure groups. The weekly news magazine *Newsweek* for many years did not aim at mass circulation. Staff meetings were continually adjured, and the magazine's promotional material echoed it, to aim at "the top 700,000." Its writers were continually told to keep the business executive in mind, the well-to-do leaders of the community. In this connection it is interesting to note that the magazine, which each week features the reactionary column on economic matters by Henry Hazlitt, trustee of the Foundation for Economic Education and also of the American Enterprise Association, derives its financial support in good measure from the advertising, often institutional in nature, of those very same corporations which contribute so generously to Mr. Hazlitt's private enterprises.*

Representative Lanham cut to the heart of the matter when he said: "It means something to me to know who is financing this organization. . . . I know that Mr. Read's organization is supported by big corporations and no labor unions, and I know what to expect in the literature. I may agree with part of it and I may disagree. However, I think that the public ought to be able to tell, when these organizations mail out this stuff, who is financing it." To Mr. Read's objection that the foundation is required to file with the Bureau of Internal Revenue the names of all big donors, Mr. Lanham replied, "That list is not public, it is secret. I want something that these newspaper reporters, the honorable gentlemen of the press who are always snooping around as they should do, can get, and let the people know about. I do not want something in the secret files of the FBI or the Department of Internal Revenue. . . . I do not want to keep you from dissemi-

---

* As book critic for *Newsweek* for nearly six years I was, especially after World War II, frequently subjected to executive pressure to pay less attention to books of a liberal nature and more to those by such writers as Henry J. Taylor and John T. Flynn. When Von Mises's *Human Action* was published in 1949 I was directed to ignore it inasmuch as Henry Hazlitt would review it in his column "Business Tides." It was not until I read the testimony before the Buchanan Committee that I learned that Hazlitt was responsible for its publication. Correspondence and the minutes of the board of trustees of the Foundation for Economic Education show that the FEE, at Hazlitt's insistence, arranged with the Yale University Press for the subsidized publication of *Human Action* (*Hearings*, Part 8, p. 39) and for its subsequent promotion by the foundation (*ibid.*, p. 42). There was no indication either on the jacket of the book nor in its contents that the book was subsidized by the foundation, nor was this explained in Mr. Hazlitt's review. The foundation bought 1140 copies of *Human Action*, which retailed at $10, at the cost of $7150 (the money was put up by an unidentified member of the board of trustees), and sent a copy to "each of the country's university and college libraries." Jasper E. Crane, a Du Pont director and financial backer of the foundation, who said "I suppose I ought to read it," wrote Read: "Every economics department should be put on notice that its members need to read and study this book, or they are not up to date"! (*Ibid.*, p. 131.)

nating your views, but I want to know who is financing what you people are sending out." [19]

In 1946, just after the incorporation of the Foundation for Economic Education, Herbert U. Nelson, executive vice-president of the National Association of Real Estate Boards and one of the highest paid lobbyists in Washington, was leading the fight against rent and building controls and pressing for the abolition of the Federal rent control act by the following March. This is the gentleman who was to write his association president a few years later: "I do not believe in democracy. I think it stinks." [20] In May, 1946, Nelson suggested to Read the preparation of a pamphlet with "some such title as 'The Case Against Federal Rent Control.'" Less than a month later the "educator" and the lobbyist were on a "Dear Herb–Dear Leonard" basis and Nelson had already distributed thousands of foundation pamphlets which Read had sent him without cost. They were now busily co-operating on the new project which the foundation had engaged Milton Friedman and George J. Stigler to write. It was to be called *Roofs and Ceilings* and it was to be an outright attack on rent controls.

When Nelson received a copy of the manuscript he wrote Read to say, "The pamphlet . . . is a dandy. It is just what I wanted." Evidently Nelson had not read it as closely or as critically as Read, for the latter hurried off a letter calling attention to a paragraph "that worries me, as well as the rest of us here." The worrisome paragraph was:

The fact that, under free market conditions, better quarters go to those who have larger income or more wealth is, if anything, simply a reason for taking long-term measures to reduce the inequality of income and wealth. For those, like us, who would like more equality than there is at present, not alone for housing but for all products, it is surely better to attack directly existing inequalities in income and wealth at their source than to ration each of the hundreds of commodities and services that compose our standard of living. It is surely the height of folly to permit individuals to receive unequal money incomes and then to take elaborate and costly measures to prevent them from using their incomes.

Mr. Read, faced with the unhappy fact that the authors stubbornly refused to allow the deletion of this subversive paragraph, wrote a footnote "to take care of any criticisms," although he did not think anyone "except a sharp free enterprise economist" would catch the "offending paragraph." "But then," he added in a letter to Nelson, "our works are supposed to be above any criticism by a free enterpriser." [21] The footnote, which he assured Mr. Nelson would be in all his 500,000 copies, read as follows:

Editor's note: The authors fail to state whether the "long-term measures" which they would adopt go beyond elimination of special privilege, such as monopoly now protected by government. In any case, however, the significance of their argument at this point deserves special notice. It means that, even from the standpoint of those who may put equality above justice and liberty, rent controls are the height of folly.

It undoubtedly was literature like *Roofs and Ceilings* that inspired Dr. Royal Wilbur France, the president of Rollins College at Winter Park, Florida, to write his Yale colleague, Dr. Fairchild, from the start a trustee of the foundation:

I have no special quarrel with the purposes of the organization and certainly concede its right to carry on propaganda on behalf of the beliefs of its members: but there is a wide difference between propaganda and education. It is the use of the word education in the title of the organization that I am questioning.

After suggesting to Dr. Fairchild that the foundation be made a "truly educational institution of the American people" by broadening it to have others of different viewpoints also give their ideas on each subject in the pamphlets put out by the foundation, so that both sides would be covered — a suggestion Dr. Fairchild flatly rejected — Dr. France said:

If the trustees of the Foundation for Economic Education have deep convictions of the rightness of their views, and I believe they have, they should have confidence in the strength of these views to stand up in a fair field and win out over what they deem error. They will only have a really convinced and informed following if that following is satisfied that it has made up its mind after hearing a fair presentation of all sides of the case. Apparently the foundation has funds and there is a great opportunity here for democracy in action.

What did the foundation think of this suggestion for the use of the corporative wealth at its command? V. O. Watts, in an inter-office memorandum to Mr. Read, put it succinctly:

It is precisely because Dr. France's pusillanimous attitude toward the fallacies of collectivism has so corrupted the schools and colleges that our work is necessary.[22]

An attitude towards education, lobbying, and the role a "foundation" plays in these fields which is far different from that professed by Mr. Read was set forth by Dr. Dewey Anderson, trustee and executive director of the Public Affairs Institute. Testifying before the Buchanan Committee on July 14, 1950, he said:

The utmost disclosure should be a must in any legislation in this vital field [of lobbying] where a people in a democracy must make up their own minds, form their own judgments, and act thereon. They have a right to know the source of support of those agencies which put out the facts on which they must act. Requirement of such disclosure would not be anything new. The free press of this nation — magazines and newspapers — are required . . . to print a sworn statement of their management and ownership, revealing to the people if any special interest controls exist. Undeniably research studies have some ultimate influence on policy making in this nation. It is always well to provide a mechanism which will reveal if the springs of our educational materials should become polluted.[23]

The Public Affairs Institute was founded in 1947 through a trust agreement signed by Dr. Anderson and the late A. F. Whitney, president of the Brotherhood of Railroad Trainmen, and the latter supplied the funds which were the core operating budget for the first three years. This has amounted to $157,597, parceled out between October, 1947, and March, 1950. Most of the institute's other funds have come from labor unions, some of them general contributions for operating expenses, but mostly funds earmarked for specific research projects.

Dewey Anderson is a man probably heartily disliked by the distinguished gentlemen of Mr. Read's list, for he was the executive director of the Temporary National Economic Committee set up by Congress under President Franklin D. Roosevelt to investigate the concentration of monopolistic power in the United States. He held a similar position with the United States Senate Small Business Committee until that fell into Republican hands with the Eightieth Congress, and he served with the Board of Economic Warfare and the Office of Foreign Relief and Rehabilitation Operations. President Roosevelt named him to the White House Conference on the Care of Children in a Democracy, and he was relief director during the depression in California.

Dr. Anderson believes firmly that the institute which he heads is — despite its affiliations — independent in outlook and rigorously scientific in its use of the techniques of research and in the publication of its findings. He told the Buchanan Committee:

The Public Affairs Institute operates strictly as a nonprofit research agency. It initiates its own program. It does not sponsor specific legislation. It does not seek the passage or defeat of legislation by the Congress of the United States. As with . . . other similar nonprofit active educational and research organizations, the Public Affairs Institute develops specific recommendations flowing from the research and study of a problem, recommendations which may require substantive legislation and changes in public administration to be effective and to make the conclusions of the research done of practical value. We do not shrink from this use of the research technique: on the contrary, it is our means of influencing the course of events and helping to shape public policy. That is what the application of social science is all about, and it is what distinguishes a research approach from a propagandist approach to social-economic-political issues.[24]

Not only was Dr. Anderson's conception of the purposes of his organization different from Mr. Read's but the amounts donated to the institute and the sources of the donations were in contrast with those of the Foundation for Economic Education. Although the ideological uses made of them were different in each instance, the expressed purposes of the two organizations as pure research institutions were almost identical. If steel and oil and other large corporations were the predominant source of income for the foundation, labor unions were the predominant source for the institute, as the following table [25] shows:

Donors, from October, 1947, to March, 1950	Amounts
Brotherhood of Railroad Trainmen *	$157,597.00
Christian Social Justice Fund *	500.00
Max Udell & Sons, Inc.*	100.00
Stein, Hall & Company *	500.00
Gramercy Park Clothes	50.00
National Farmers Union †	1,000.00
International Typographical Union ‡	4,000.00
United Brotherhood of Carpenters and Joiners ‡	4,000.00
United Mine Workers ‡	4,000.00
United Steelworkers ‡	4,000.00
Textile Workers Union ‡	2,000.00
International Brotherhood of Teamsters ‡	4,000.00
Amalgamated Clothing Workers ‡	2,000.00
United Automobile Workers ‡	2,000.00
American Federation of Musicians ‡	4,000.00
William C. Whitney Foundation *	4,000.00
Congress of Industrial Organizations *	800.00
Congress of Industrial Organizations ‡	1,652.68
CIO Political Action Committee §	2,000.00
Foundation for World Government ‖	39,900.00
Receipts by sale of pamphlets	1,848.89
Brotherhood of Railroad Trainmen †	2,500.00
Total receipts	$242,448.57

* for operational expenses
† for Missouri Valley research project
‡ for labor-management research project
§ for registration and voting research project
‖ for Point Four research project.

Thus the Brotherhood of Railroad Trainmen gave $157,597 for operational expenses for the institute and $2500 that was earmarked for special research projects and the remainder of $82,351.57 came from eighteen other contributors and from the sale of pamphlets. These other contributors included one farmers' organization, nine labor unions, one labor political action committee, one private foundation, and one organization that can be considered a lobby for the cause of world federation. With the exception of the Brotherhood of Railroad Trainmen no contributor came anywhere near matching the large contributions from General Motors, Chrysler, United States Steel, Du Pont, and the other corporations that supported the Read organization in New York.

This money has gone for research projects and the production of pamphlets upon a variety of subjects, many of them of current legislative interest. These include European recovery, the role of collective bargaining in a democracy, conservation of natural resources, the Hoover reports, distribution of the costs of health insurance, unemployment, the distribution of Series E savings bonds, an "action program" for the redwood forests, the economic reports to the President, inflation, medical care for the individual, and eight pamphlets on the so-called *Bold New Program* or Point Four.[26] Approximately 45,000 copies of these publications have been sold or distributed gratis to the press and radio, labor and other organizations, members of Congress, members of the Cabinet, heads of administrative agencies, economists, teachers, clergymen, and the institute's own sponsors.

At present there are sixty-five of these sponsors, but at the beginning there were twenty-three: [27]

A. F. Whitney; Morris L. Cooke, first REA administrator; Morris L. Ernst, lawyer and author; John M. Carmody, former United States Public Works administrator; T. J. Kreps, Stanford University; James H. McGill, chairman of board, McGill Manufacturing Company; James G. Patton, president, National Farmers Union; Abe Fortas, former Undersecretary of Interior; Alvin Johnson, New School for

Social Research; J. Franklin Carter, former columnist; Fowler Harper, Yale Law School; Morris Rosenthal, president Stein, Hall & Company, Inc.; Senator Hubert Humphrey; Thurman Arnold, former Assistant Attorney General; ex-Governor Chester Bowles; J. F. Burke, president, Standard Broadcasting Company; Representative Hugh B. Mitchell; Bryn V. Hojde, New School for Social Research; Charles A. Murray, assistant to Senator James E. Murray; H. W. Schacter, president, Kaufman Straus Company; Paul S. Taylor, University of California; Cass Canfield, chairman of board, Harper & Brothers; Jerome I. Udell, president, Max Udell & Sons, Inc.

From these names it can easily be seen that the institute is as "liberal" in its approach to contemporary problems as the foundation is "reactionary" and it is quite probable that, while the trustees of the latter would scoff at the institute's claim to impartiality and objectivity, the sponsors of the former would heartily subscribe to Dr. Anderson's declaration that the Brotherhood of Railroad Trainmen:

. . . has been motivated solely by a deeply felt concern for the public interest and its conduct [in financing the institute] stands forth as a glowing example of what an enlightened, responsible organization of working people can accomplish for human welfare. In no instance has the Brotherhood sought to dictate the problems to be studied by the Institute . . . or to determine its activities or its product. In fact, a preponderance of the work done by the Institute is in fields in which the Brotherhood members take their part strictly as private citizens along with the rest of the public the Institute seeks to serve.[28]

The interesting point brought out by the Buchanan Committee in contrasting these two organizations so dissimilar in ultimate aims but so similar (on the surface, at least) in the use of techniques, is that both tax-exempt bodies do not believe they come under the registration provisions of the Lobby Act. Dr. Anderson, however, had some doubts, as a colloquy between himself and members of the committee showed.[29] They had been discussing an institute publication, *Role of Collective Bargaining in a Democracy*.

MR. LANHAM. To go back to distribution, you list here as Government, President's cabinet, members of Congress, 765. Did you mail any of those to Congressmen and Senators without request?

MR. ANDERSON. Oh, yes.

MR. LANHAM. Isn't that lobbying in a sense — you are seeking to influence views, the opinions, of Congressmen and Senators?

MR. ANDERSON. I don't know whether it is lobbying or not. I think that is one of the reasons for the existence of this committee. . . .

MR. LANHAM. You understand, I am not criticizing, but I want your opinion as to whether that could be called lobbying: could that be called indirect lobbying, or is it lobbying at all?

MR. ANDERSON. There is no question but what, both in the case of our own distribution of pamphlets and the distribution of this particular document, and as in the cases of the Committee on Economic Development and the National Planning Association, that all of us are motivated by the same purpose.

We spend hundreds of hours on a project of this character; solidly do it. We come to conclusions and state them positively — as this one does.

This one is filled with legislative intent.

And then we seek to have that material used in whatever way you choose to use it. We don't dictate that, or try to. We seek to have that used by you as you see fit.

We likewise seek to have it used by a college professor as he sees fit.

Now how that can be brought under the scrutiny — because it could be subject to great violation of reasonable intent — how that could be brought under the scrutiny of the Congress and of the American people, I don't quite see; but I think it should be.

MR. O'HARA. In this connection, Mr. Anderson, of course, no matter how objective you are, or dispassionate you are in your viewpoint, when your institute gets out an article, you are writing it for a purpose, aren't you?

MR. ANDERSON. That is right.

MR. O'HARA. That objective was to influence thinking — I am not saying this critically.

MR. ANDERSON. That is right.

MR. O'HARA. When you sent those pamphlets to Members of Congress, naturally, you are hopeful this work you had done and which is contained in that pamphlet will have an impact and an influence upon the Members of Congress.

Now, do you feel that that is lobbying in a sense?

MR. ANDERSON. Well, if that is lobbying, I would urge upon the committee a clearer definition of lobbying than is contained in the law. I think that ambiguity of the law needs clearing.

After further discussion, during which it was brought out that the Public Affairs Institute had never filed any information with the House or Senate, and that the subsidy of the institute by the Brotherhood of Railroad Trainmen had not been publicly known until disclosed at the hearings, Dr. Anderson said:

I think I ought to be forced, as the exictive officer by law held responsible as the executive officer of this institution, to file a financial statement. I think Brookings [institution] should be required to do the same. I think that applies to any organization that is engaged in this field in any way. And that is where I come back to a definition of what you call lobbying. I would get a more dignified word. It even hurt me to be put in that category, but the Brookings people would have fits if they were called lobbyists. . . .

I believe it is a necessity of a society like ours to devise a means; starting with a definition, it can be done. Surely any responsible organization seeking to influence your judgment, or my judgment, as a citizen, should stand up and account for it.

MR. DOYLE. Do you mean, Dr. Anderson, that those groups trying to do that should be compelled by law to divulge the source of their income?

MR. ANDERSON. That is exactly what I mean.

MR. DOYLE. Including the names of persons or groups that give them the money or buy their books?

MR. ANDERSON. That is right.

MR. DOYLE. Would that be a violation of the Bill of Rights, in your opinion?

MR. ANDERSON. I don't see it that way.

CHAPTER XIII

The Road Ahead

IN the winter of 1949–1950 it was almost impossible to wait for your turn at a doctor's or dentist's office without coming under the influence of one or another of the pressure groups that fell beneath the scrutiny of the Buchanan Committee. In neat piles on waiting room tables, where they could not escape the attention of the bored and apprehensive alike, reposed countless copies of a book that became, if not the most widely read book of the year, one that was at least the most widely distributed. Behind this book, which in several different formats was free for the taking, lay one of the most disturbing manifestations of the lobbying technique, as practiced by a coalition whose main purpose was the disruption of American democracy and the furtherance of a neofascist political party within the United States.

The book that was seen by so many millions of people that it is impossible to estimate the true extent of its influence upon the American mind was *The Road Ahead*. Its author was John T. Flynn, renegade New Dealer, former America Firster, and articulate Roosevelt hater, whose violent diatribes, *Country Squire in the White House* and *The Roosevelt Myth*, stand out as two of the great biographical and historical distortions of our time.

When *The Road Ahead* was first published in October, 1949, I wrote in a review that it was "one of the two most important books about the contemporary American scene" that we would have that year — not because of its intrinsic worth, which was negative, but because it was an extreme manifestation of "an endemic hysteria presently affecting a considerable segment of our society." * Quickly thereafter it achieved fabulous sales and even more fabulous free distribution, thus spreading this hysteria among those who have been called "the educated ignorant" who are so large a part of the worried middle class. It was reviewed by women's clubs, discussed in high schools, and, as the *Louisville Courier-Journal* said, was "read with bewilderment by thousands of good people who had innocently supposed until now that we were doing pretty well."

Mr. Flynn's book was written to scare people. Composed with

---

* In its February, 1950, issue the *Reader's Digest* printed a condensation of *The Road Ahead*. Among other "tributes" to the book it used the following: " 'One of the two most important books about the contemporary American scene that we will have this year' — Karl Schriftgiesser in the *New York Times Book Review*," thus distorting the meaning of my review. This falsification aroused the ire of the *Times*, whose Sunday editor, Mr. Lester Markel, sent his vigorous objections to the *Reader's Digest*. The May issue of the magazine contained a correction: "This did not fairly represent Mr. Schriftgiesser's opinion, for in his review he had gone on to say that the importance of the book lay in the fact that it was a 'manifestation of endemic hysteria.' The Editors of *Reader's Digest* regret this inadvertent error." The editors then said: "But it is only fair to the author of the book to point out that a most impressive number of Americans do not accept Mr. Schriftgiesser's opinion. *The Road Ahead* has made a tremendous impression; each month it is more widely read, more widely discussed; it has appeared week after week on the best-seller lists of both the New York *Times* and *Herald Tribune;* and the *Reader's Digest* has received orders for an unprecedented number of reprints — *over two million as we go to press.*" (My italics.) The *Digest's* distortion of my review received some attention in the press. The *Louisville Courier-Journal* said, among other things, that the misquotation was "deliberate dishonesty." The *Digest* did not say who the two million who requested reprints were, but the Lobby Committee showed that many of the requests were for job lots and that they were bought not by individuals but by lobbying organizations. I received several letters from people who had read the review and were indignant at the *Digest's* "deliberate dishonesty." A few wanted to know what the other book was. Reluctantly, for it is an even more poisonous piece of propaganda, it was *Politics Has No Morals* by Norman Beasley.

Sources for this chapter are: *The Road Ahead* by John T. Flynn, New York, 1949; files of the *Reporter*, the *Nation*, the *New York Times* (my review was in the issue of October 2, 1949), the *Louisville Courier-Journal*, the *St. Louis Post-Dispatch;* columns by Marquis Childs and Thomas L. Stokes in the *Rutland Herald;* Friends of Democracy's *Battle; Congressional Record; Hearings*, Parts 2, 7, 8; *Interim Report.*

the skill of an experienced distortionist, it painted a frightening picture of a decaying America that most people should be too intelligent to accept. Its main thesis, so at variance with historical facts, is that while we have been absorbed with our fears of communism we have neglected an even more serious menace, the "hooded socialists" who are leading us "not in the footsteps of Russia, but in the footsteps of England" down the dreadful Fabian Way, gradually but inevitably into the Welfare State. President Roosevelt fell victim to the wiles of these hooded men, who never openly use the word "socialism" but who are devoted to its ends, nevertheless, and President Truman has followed with willing recklessness in his destructive path! Within ten years, said the flagrant Flynn, "our whole way of life" will have been destroyed.

There is, however, a way out, this Jeremiah explained, although not by any ordinary means. As Mr. Flynn, who has no faith in the democratic process and who apparently distrusts our constitutional system, puts it: "We cannot depend on any political party to save us. We must build a power *outside the parties* so strong that the parties will be compelled to yield to its demands." (My emphasis.)

The leadership of this power, which he never quite defines, "must pass into the hands of men who understand" how to fight against "the one big war against our civilization" that has been in process in Washington since 1933. Who these "men who understand" may be he does not say, but in this era of "guilt by association" it is not difficult, after examining the evidence before the Lobby Committee, to see whom he means.

The author of this tract for revolution from the top has been spouting his hatred for democracy for many years. By 1949 he had become the darling of the most reactionary forces in the United States. His book was planned as an *Uncle Tom's Cabin* in a civil war against liberalism and progressivism for which Mr. Flynn has long been preparing the way. His associates have collected and spent thousands of dollars to spread his doctrines throughout the country with the help of some of the most dangerous pressure groups of our time.

In the early days of the New Deal Mr. Flynn was as articulate an economic liberal as could be found among all the bright young men. His articles in the *New Republic* had wide influence in Washington and in editorial offices. As he said of himself, he was well left of center, and he often chided President Roosevelt for being, in his opinion, too far to the right. He helped the Senate investigate the stock exchanges and contributed to the writing of the Securities and Exchange Bill. Always an Anglophobe, the first indications of his pronounced isolationism came when he associated himself with Senator Gerald K. Nye in the investigation of the munitions-makers. By 1940, while still pretending to despise fascism, he had swung far to the right. In the summer of 1939 the scholarly *Yale Review*, then being edited by Wilbur Cross following his defeat for re-election as Governor of Connecticut, printed a violently partisan article entitled "Mr. Hopkins and Mr. Roosevelt." This led President Franklin D. Roosevelt to write a "personal protest" to Dr. Cross, an old friend, as follows:

I love controversy — whether it be in literature, in economics, in sociology or in education. To us controversy is grand. You and I have reveled in it for many decades.

But it is your concept and mine, I think, that controversy is not merely a question of pro and con in any field of human endeavor.

Controversy, as I take it, concerns itself primarily with problems that call for answers. It is not controversy for one side to say in such a case, "I propose the following solution of the problem" — and to have the other side say merely, "I am opposed to that solution." I have watched John T. Flynn during these many years and the net answer in my mind is that he has always, with practically no exception, been a destructive rather than a constructive force.

Therefore, Q.E.D., John T. Flynn should be barred hereafter from the columns of any presentable daily paper, monthly magazine or national quarterly, such as the *Yale Review*.

Yours for construction. . . .[1]

Eventually Mr. Flynn became chairman of the New York chapter of the America First Committee and national chairman of the Keep America Out of War Congress. Coughlinite and Bundist publications praised him. The seditionist, William Dudley Pelley, quoted him frequently.

Mr. Flynn disappeared from public view after Pearl Harbor, but in 1944 he broke his silence with the publication of a strange little book called *As We Go Marching*. In this he argued that fascism had been inevitable in Italy and issued a warning that the policies of President Roosevelt were leading towards totalitarianism in this country. This book impressed Merwin K. Hart of the National Economic Council and that little group of unreconstructed Liberty Leaguers who, as we have seen, were Mr. Hart's corporate sponsors. It was not long before Mr. Flynn, who no longer seemed able to get his books published by the respectable New York publishers, was writing pamphlets for this "hate-mongering outfit," as Representative Sabath has called the National Economic Council, as part of his crusade to prove that President Roosevelt plotted our entrance into World War II.

Within the next few years Flynn's association with these individuals and groups became closer. He was on the executive committee of American Action, Inc., a postwar revival of the America First Committee, which was set up as a "political action committee" until it was exposed to ridicule by a congressional committee. Among its backers were Colonel Robert McCormick, publisher of the *Chicago Tribune*, General Robert E. Wood, Lammot Du Pont, Ernest T. Weir, and several notorious anti-Catholic and anti-Semitic propagandists. In 1946 and 1947 Flynn contributed frequently to the *Chicago Tribune* and to the Hearst press.*

* It is interesting to note that Mr. Flynn's most recent books, *The Roosevelt Myth* and *The Road Ahead*, were published by the Devin-Adair Company, a small New York firm which also published George Morgenstern's *Pearl Harbor*, which follows the Flynn-McCormick line of Rooseveltian war guilt, and Frank Hughes's answer to the Hutchins report on press freedom, both of which were written, on assignment from the *Tribune*, by members of its staff.

Back in 1937, when President Roosevelt was trying to bring the Supreme Court to its senses, another lobby with which we are familiar — the Committee for Constitutional Government — was founded by Frank Gannett, a newspaper chain publisher, and heavily endowed by him and other wealthy reactionaries and large corporations. This was later to become closely, but not officially, associated with Mr. Hart's National Economic Council. It lobbied extensively for the defeat of the Roosevelt "court-packing" bill and took unto itself much of the credit for its defeat. After this victory it stayed on to continue its badgering of the New Deal. Reluctantly and after considerable prodding by the Justice Department it registered under the Lobby Act and in 1949 it was listed as the second largest spending lobby in the nation.

From the beginning the executive head of the Committee for Constitutional Government was Dr. Edward A. Rumely. After World War I Dr. Rumely was convicted of violating the Trading with the Enemy Act when it was alleged that in 1917 he had purchased the *New York Mail* on behalf of the German Government and had concealed the true ownership of the newspaper. President Coolidge eventually pardoned him for this felony.* In 1944 he refused to tell a congressional committee the names of contributors of $100 or more to the Committee for Constitutional Government for use in the Presidential campaign and was cited for contempt of Congress. A jury in Federal Court acquitted him of the charge after a first jury had failed to reach a verdict. Dr. Rumely was a promoter of vitamin foods before entering the presumably more lucrative business of lobbying. His assistant has

* When questioned about this episode in his past by a member of the Buchanan Committee, Dr. Rumely said: "There is no proof whatever that that paper was financed by the German Government. After the conviction, the Attorney General, Harlan L. Stone, recommended to Coolidge, on the ground that we had been innocently convicted, that a pardon be granted, and when the jury saw the evidence that was suppressed, 11 of the 12 jurors petitioned that their verdict be set aside, and President Coolidge did everything he could to right that wrong; and you have no business to bring that up here." *Hearings*, Part 4, pp. 23–24.

long been Dr. Willford I. King, a former professor of economics.

After the surprising election of President Truman in 1948 Dr. Rumely realized there was a lucrative field for his activities among the members of the middle class who were frightened by the refusal of the American people to desert the principles of the New Deal. He had long watched the successful operations of the Political Action Committee of the CIO and now set out, through the Committee for Constitutional Government, to establish a similar organization throughout the country, with bases of its so-called "grass-roots organization" set up in what seemed to be the more susceptible congressional districts. The CCG believed that if it could corral small groups of frightened voters, mainly among professional people and businessmen, and collect sufficient funds from them, it could win elections for the "strong men" it would pick to run for Congress. To carry out this purpose it established a subsidiary organization called Fighters for Freedom.

Through this new outfit, Dr. Rumely published a pamphlet which called for an organization of 2,000,000 people — which is under 2 per cent of the national population — in an adhesive group. This, the prospectus observed, would be a nucleus just large enough "to tip the scales at the bar of public opinion" and "turn the tide" away from "creeping socialism." It asked for contributions — which it hoped would exceed $8,000,000 — of any amount, but as we have noted, it suggested the sum of $490, which of course by Dr. Rumely's reasoning would allow it to evade, by $10 per contributor, the provisions of the Lobby Act.

At this time Mr. Flynn came back into the picture. The CCG was trying, not very successfully, to sell through Fighters for Freedom a book ostensibly offering proof that the entire New Deal was "unconstitutional." This book lacked the necessary "scare appeal," for it was pretty difficult to get most people stirred up about such an academic danger to the American way of life. Something much more frightening was needed. Mr. Flynn was not the first to find this frightening something, but once it was found he made the most of it.

The first to offer it was a Hoosier from Westchester County, New York, Representative Ralph Waldo Gwinn, whose close alliance with the real estate lobby is a matter of public record. A stanch Republican of the most reactionary brand, Mr. Gwinn was a regular contributor to the clipsheet published by Fighters for Freedom. For this he received expenses for "research" but no salary. Mr. Gwinn had been an active member of the House Committee on Labor and Education in the Eightieth Congress when Chairman Hartley had invited the National Association of Manufacturers' lobbyists and lawyers to help write the Taft-Hartley Act. He was well impregnated with antiliberal virus. Reviewing for the clipsheet the 1948 elections he discovered that 189, or more than two thirds, of the newly elected representatives had been sent to Washington with the connivance of what he called "the labor socialists."

Mr. Flynn took it up from there. The Gwinn thesis fitted the Flynn pattern of thought. Long a hater of everything British Mr. Flynn now joyously and with customary irresponsibility seized upon the rise of the Labor Party in England and combined it with his horrendous predictions of things to come in the United States. The result was *The Road Ahead*. It was published in October, 1949. Neither the jacket of the book nor the newspaper advertisements mentioned any connection between Mr. Flynn and the Committee for Constitutional Government, Fighters for Freedom, or the National Economic Council.* It appeared as another

---

* When subpoenaed before the House Select Committee on Lobbying Activities Dr. Rumely said: "I am willing to produce the records of loans within the designated period, except a few that related to the promotion of *The Road Ahead*, and advertising Fighters for Freedom, which had nothing to do with lobbying." At no time while a witness would he testify concerning the financial arrangements for this book. He testified (*Hearings*, Part 4, p. 21) that the bookstores had sold about 70,000 copies. If Mr. Flynn received a straight 15 per cent royalty on the retail sales of the regular trade edition his book netted him about $26,600. What percentage he re-

trade book, retailing at $2.50 a copy. Enough people bought it at
this price (if they had waited they could have got it for nothing!)
to propel it onto the best-seller lists. At least 60,000 copies of the
regular trade edition were sold.

There was, of course, nothing illegitimate in this, although the
ethics of the publishers in refraining from informing potential
readers anything about Mr. Flynn's significant background may
be questionable. Soon after *The Road Ahead* appeared on the
market Fighters for Freedom began its campaign to place this new
Uncle Tom's Cabin before the 2 per cent of the people it hoped to
form into that "power outside the parties" that Mr. Flynn proposed. "Millions of copies of *The Road Ahead* must be sold
quickly to save our constitutional system of free enterprise" and
to "save our country from destruction," it screamed in sales letters sent to its vast mailing list.

Within two months of publication *The Road Ahead* was, in
Dr. Rumely's phrase, "taken up" by the Committee for Constitutional Government, which sold 600,000 copies within the next
five months. In spite of Dr. Rumely's reluctance some interesting
details about the committee's methods of distribution were ex-
tracted by the Buchanan Committee. The first thing the Rumely
group did was to cut the price. A single copy of the CCG edition
was available for $1. Amounts of from 2 to 15 copies could be
got for 70 cents, while the price for 25 to 100 copies was dropped
to 60 cents, and on down the line until lots of 1000 or more were
to be had for 50 cents each. The committee sought to sell the book
in any amounts but, of course, it preferred mass sales. It was sometimes so anxious to spread the message of Flynn that it occasionally cut the price even below the 50-cent mark. The Lobby Committee unearthed a letter to a member of Congress from Dr.
Rumely saying:

ceived from reprints, condensations, and so forth, is not known, but it is
reasonable to assume that so able a private enterprise economist as Mr.
Flynn did not allow this phenomenal distribution of his brain child without
due compensation.

Attached herewith are copies of letters we have written to Hugh R. Cullen urging him to finance the distribution of 100,000 copies of *The Road Ahead* to clergymen and educators, and naming the special price of 30 cents per copy, our bare cost. A letter from you to him emphasizing the importance of this distribution might be extremely helpful.[2]

From the Committee for Constitutional Government's own booklet, *Needed Now — Capacity for Leadership, Courage to Lead*, which was published in 1944 when the CCG was a mere infant of seven years, the Lobby Committee drew the believable boast that Dr. Rumely's outfit had distributed 82,000,000 pieces of literature, 760,000 books, 10,000 radio talks "on national issues," 350,000 telegrams to citizens "to arouse them to action on great issues," "many thousands" of releases to daily and weekly papers, and "full-pay" advertisements in 536 different newspapers with a combined circulation of nearly 20,000,000. And yet it also boasted, at the same time, "Throughout its seven years, the committee has not spent one dollar for lobbying!" It is doubtful if at any time during this extraordinary performance the CCG concentrated more ardently on any of its publications than it did in 1950 on *The Road Ahead*. On June 28 Dr. Rumely testified that up to that date his committee had sent out 3,500,000 post card advertisements of Flynn's book. The first million, he said, had resulted in sales of 175,000 copies. He hoped, before the campaign ended, to place a copy of *The Road Ahead* in every fifth home in the nation, or more than 8,000,000 copies. Perhaps that goal has already been reached, for other lobby groups have distributed copies, and the various condensations in the *Reader's Digest*, the Hearst press, and elsewhere, add up to a staggering total figure.

The Lobby Committee had no doubts in its majority mind * that this huge distribution of this book, as well as the other pub-

---

* There were plenty in Mr. Brown's, and he expressed them so vigorously and so often that Mr. Lanham was constrained to ask him upon one occasion, "Is the gentleman representing the persons subpoenaed here? It would appear so." *Hearings*, Part 4, p. 5. The above figures are from *Interim Report*, pp. 30–31, 35; *Hearings*, Part 4, pp. 23, 27–28; *Hearings*, Part 5, p. 442.

lishing activities of the organization, was lobbying. The CCG also widely distributed copies of other publications, of which *Why the Taft-Hartley Act*, *Compulsory Medical Care and the Welfare State*, and *Labor Monopolies or Freedom* were representative examples. These facts and figures, said the committee:

> . . . are more than enough to establish that the Committee for Constitutional Government exerts "substantial effort" in connection with national issues. What of "intent to influence legislation"? We submit that any fair-minded person who has the time and patience to read a substantial part of the publications distributed by the Committee for Constitutional Government can reach no reasonable conclusions but that such intent is present in overwhelming abundance.[3]

It would be interesting and valuable if there were some apparatus available to measure the extent of influence upon the public mind of these CCG publications, to determine what effect they have had upon the national Congress and upon the public in general, and upon the outcome of national elections. The committee's aim was to circulate *The Road Ahead* "among clergymen, businessmen, large and small, heads of service groups, farm leaders, editors and publishers, public officials, judges, governors, and particularly, regardless of party, Members of Congress — Senators and Representatives." It should go to "everyone in a position to disseminate ideas, to foremen, supervisors, salesmen, insurance agents and, when these have been reached, to housewives and industrial employees. So that, if possible, every family in the Nation may have a copy." More than half of these people, it can safely be said, would never recognize it for what it is — the propaganda of an antidemocratic lobby. A recent survey — a poll conducted by the American Institute of Public Opinion in 1949 — showed that fully 45 per cent of the cross section of citizens questioned did not know what the term "lobbying" meant. On the strength of this is it safe to conclude, as Dr. Dewey Anderson quizzically did, that the "Flynn study cannot do harm in an enlightened, intelligent citizenry"? [4]

The Committee for Constitutional Government had untold aid in spreading the Flynn theory of the creeping socialization of America across the country. The American Medical Association, with its huge war chest for fighting the national health program sponsored by the administration, quickly found *The Road Ahead* a tract for the times. In December it mailed copies of the trade edition to every member of Congress. A short time later Dr. Rumely told a reporter for the *St. Louis Post-Dispatch* that a leader of the Oregon State Medical Society had taken 5000 copies for distribution. Soon physicians active in the AMA were distributing free copies throughout the country. Another wholesale distributor was Ernest T. Weir of the National Steel Corporation.

In February came the condensation of this book, which the *Louisville Courier-Journal* called "grossly biased and misleading," in the *Reader's Digest*, with its enormous circulation of 9,000,000. Senator Owen Brewster of Maine, chairman of the Republican Senate Campaign Committee, was so impressed when he read it that on March 3 he asked unanimous consent to reprint the condensation in the *Congressional Record*. He told his colleagues — under the rules and not from any sense of virtue — that the cost for printing the 14½ columns in the *Record* would be $348.50. Senator Scott Lucas, then the majority leader, remarked, "I have read the book and I do not agree with the Senator that it's worth it. I do not think the *Reader's Digest* article is worth $348 of the taxpayers' money, but if the economy-minded Senator from Maine wants to spend that amount of money I am not going to object."

It was printed. When Mr. Brewster announced that he was going to buy 50,000 copies of the reprint for distribution the official publication of the American Federation of Labor chided him for supporting "socialized printing" instead of depending upon "private enterprise" — pointing out that the cost for the reprints at the Government Printing Office would be about $500, whereas in a privately owned plant the charge would be $1500!

Talking to a reporter Dr. Rumely said: "It has snowballed on something like the old chain-letter principle. A physician, a lawyer, a businessman, or maybe a minister, would order a copy and after reading it would order five, ten, twenty-five or maybe a hundred copies. They in turn would order more copies and send to friends." Other organizations of the extreme right helped spread the book. One of them was the so-called grass-roots movement of American Guard, Inc., which was launched in Anderson, Indiana, "to arrest the current trends towards socialism in America." Members of the Daughters of the American Revolution were officially told that it was required reading. A Nashville, Tennessee, minister condensed it, with lurid additions, and printed his brimstone version in the *Presbyterian Tower*. Several newspapers ran reprints of it. In Texas a Republican who used it as a campaign textbook became the first member of his party to win a congressional seat from a Texas constituency in nineteen years.

It has been impossible to determine exactly the number of copies of *The Road Ahead* that have been circulated in various editions and condensations throughout the country. Twelve million to date would probably be somewhere near the right figure. It undoubtedly made a substantial bundle among the millions of "pieces of literature" mailed by this lobby under congressional frank. Dr. Rumely himself estimated that if the CCG had paid the postage, which the taxpayers of America paid instead, it would have cost his organization between $240,000 and $300,000.*

---

* The Committee for Constitutional Government was not the only lobbying organization to make use of the free franking privileges of congressmen. Leo Goodman, legislative agent of the national housing committee of the CIO, told the committee that he knew of a case where 4,000,000 copies of House speeches, all of them opposing public housing, continued rent controls, or Federal aid to education, had been mailed out to the country under the frank of one or more members, a total of seven carloads. Another witness, Francis Biddle, former Attorney General and national chairman of Americans for Democratic Action, testified that the ADA at one time had 10,000 copies of speeches supporting the Full Employment Bill distributed under the frank of Democratic Senator James E. Murray of Montana, the author of the legislation. When Representative Halleck pounced on this admission Mr. Biddle pointed out that 10,000 speeches in four years was

During 1949 Dr. Rumely's friend and associate, Representative Gwinn, had sent out 2,450,000 free mailings, including reprints of *The Road Ahead*, under his frank. He was not the only legislator to lend his franking privilege to the Committee for Constitutional Government. During the first four months of 1950, a breakdown by counsel for the committee showed, Senator Harry F. Byrd, leader of the so-called "economy" bloc in the Senate, sent out 70,000 mailings under his frank. Senator James O. Eastland, a Democrat from Mississippi, sent out 40,000 mailings; Representative Wint Smith, a Republican from Kansas, sent out 100,000; and Republican Representative Clare E. Hoffman of Michigan sent out two lots, one of 100,000 and the other of 165,000.

In the light of these revelations many people will agree with Representative Wright Patman of Texas that the Committee for Constitutional Government is an important part of "the most sinister lobby ever known." If not the most sinister, it has been the most active on the far right, and its fantastic flooding of the nation with copies of *The Road Ahead* is an accomplishment that even the well organized Communist Party at the height of its activities could look upon with envy. Mr. Patman may not have been too far from the truth when he contemptuously called it "that fascist group." [5]

"infinitesimal" compared to the 8 or 10 million pieces of literature franked by congressional friends of the Committee for Constitutional Government in the same period. *New York Times*, April 26, 1950, and July 12, 1950.

CHAPTER XIV

The Perfect Lobby

In 1932, while the Hoover administration was still fumbling with disaster, the editors of *Fortune* published a study of housing in the United States, in which they told their jittery readers that "at least half of America's 30,000,000 families are not even decently housed." In June, 1933, the Roosevelt administration set up the Home Owners Loan Corporation, which in the three years of its existence granted over 1,000,000 loans and assumed nearly one sixth of the urban home-mortgage indebtedness in the nation. Even then, in his second inaugural message President Roosevelt was still able to speak with dreadful truth about the one third of the nation that was still ill-housed as well as ill-clad and ill-fed. But in that period some effort at stimulating private construction and reforming the dire housing situation had been made. Under the direction of the Public Works Administration, slums in Atlanta, in Cleveland's notorious Whisky Island, and in Brooklyn's infested Williamsburg area had been cleared and decent homes had been found for a few thousand of the 30,000,000. And under the Federal Housing Authority more than a billion dollars had been lent to finance the repair, renovation, and enlargement of existing living quarters.

The extensive building of low-cost housing became one of the principal aims of the New Deal. The United States Housing Authority, established in 1937, was the Roosevelt administration's declaration of war on the national disgrace of the slums in the great cities from coast to coast. The Resettlement Administration was the New Deal's sortie against the rural slums in all the soil-eroded sections of the land. Under the administration of the former agency nearly 200,000 family units had been provided, making life better for that portion of the lower middle class. But the sum of Federal housing activity was small compared to the nation's needs, although it was far greater than anything attempted by private enterprise, which stood almost stock-still except for a few corporations like the Metropolitan Life Insurance Company. The New Deal came nowhere near reaching its goals in housing.

With the approach of war building came to a virtual standstill except in those areas where it was necessary for the national defense effort. When the national emergency was declared rents were frozen to protect millions of people from the cupidity of landlords. The end of the war found the nation even more desperately lacking in housing facilities and landlords avidly awaiting the day when controls would be lifted and they could boost rents to whatever heights they desired. This was the situation that faced the Eightieth Congress when it convened in 1947, with President Truman prepared to go forward with the delayed New Deal program which he now called the Fair Deal.

Although Democratically controlled, the Seventy-ninth Congress had failed to respond to President Truman's demand for general housing legislation. But the war was now over, citizens everywhere were crying for places in which to live, veterans were without homes to go to in city or country. A real emergency existed. A year earlier the Special Committee on Postwar Economic Policy and Planning, with Senator Robert A. Taft of Ohio as chairman of its subcommittee on housing, had started an extensive survey. After months of public hearings conducted by Senator Taft, Senator Robert F. Wagner of New York, and Senator Allen J. Ellender of Louisiana, a mass of evidence was assembled which showed conclusively the desperate need for better housing. The bill which resulted from this great report passed the Senate but died in the Banking and Currency Committee of the House in the second session of the Seventy-ninth Congress, primarily because of the delaying tactics employed by Republican committeemen friendly to the real estate lobby, which even then was recognized as one of the most active in Washington.

Although a similar bill was in the hopper during the first session of the Eightieth Congress, and was even reported out by the Senate Banking and Currency Committee after valiant efforts by Senator Charles W. Tobey, Republican, of New Hampshire, all moves to get the bill on the Senate calendar were stymied by Republican Senators Joseph R. McCarthy of Wisconsin (the same who later was to become notorious as the tool of the so-called "China Lobby") and Harry P. Cain of Washington. Instead Congress, in the closing days of the session, set up a joint committee, with an appropriation of $100,000, for another investigation of housing. In the debate over this in the House Representative Sabath, the veteran Illinois lobby fighter, declared:

Such a resolution would not have been necessary if the Republicans had not been swayed and influenced by one of the rottenest and most powerful lobbies that ever infested Washington. The real estate and building lobbies have claimed that if controls were removed they could build plenty of homes to meet the acute need, particularly for veterans.

The result of the removal of housing controls, he said, had resulted in housing which few veterans or other citizens of average means could afford and he prophesied that any legislation arising out of the investigation would provide no housing but only more profits for developers and promoters.

The joint committee took from early September, 1947, to mid-March of the following year to make its report. Its eighteen recommendations included five that actively encouraged public housing and slum clearance. Senator McCarthy issued a separate report asking that all the public housing features be eliminated from the bill. Shortly before these reports were made President Truman again asked Congress for an "integrated program to assist in obtaining more housing at lower cost, both in the immediate future and for the long run." Prodded by Senator Tobey and Senator Ralph E. Flanders of Vermont, two rugged Yankee liberals, the Senate committee reported out soon thereafter the Taft-Ellender-Wagner bill, with its public housing and slum clearance features intact in spite of heavy pressure on the committee for their elimination.

In the committee the fight against the long-range housing bill was led by Senator McCarthy; on the floor Senator Cain was the outstanding legislative advocate of the anti-housing lobby. Together they tried to amend the measure to death. Cain's tactic was to try to bring defeat through division: low-rent housing, he said, was not a housing problem at all, but a "social welfare problem." Therefore, get rid of it now and come to it at some later time. He offered an amendment to that effect which was rejected, after bitter debate, by a vote of 49 to 35. Two Republican Senators, Kenneth Wherry of Nebraska and Homer Ferguson of Michigan, also took a lead in fighting the housing proposal. When the former asked, "What assurance have I that any housing will come to Nebraska?" Senator Tobey replied:

The time has come in this country to pass fundamental social legislation. Our small, individual states are not all-important, after all. The whole is greater than any part. This is a national problem. The social implications of public housing and the eradication of slum conditions should appeal to everyone in connection with the elimination of juvenile delinquency and marital infidelity. Good housing is fundamentally needed in America. We must improve conditions over a period of years. So let us not quibble over small details.

For this and other heretical expressions of an honest and enlightened opinion the real estate lobby was to pour thousands of dollars into the campaign of 1950, when Senator Tobey was running for re-election, in an almost successful effort to defeat him. The lobby did not forget that he had cried out against it in the Senate when Senator McCarthy had revealed an alleged "deal" in which he quoted Representative Jesse P. Wolcott, chairman of the Committee on Banking and Currency, as saying: "We [the House] will give you gentlemen of the Senate a blank check in drafting housing legislation if you will keep out of this bill provisions as to public housing and slum clearance, and if you do not go too far in the research section. . . ." To this charge Senator Tobey had answered: "Let us find out who is controlling the interest of humanity in this country. Where has government of the people, for the people, and by the people gone if one man, the head of a powerful committee of one branch of the Congress, may say, 'We will not let the people's representatives vote on public housing, slum clearance, and urban rehabilitation'?"

In the House the lobby had been successful. After conducting hearings lasting more than five weeks the House Banking and Currency Committee rejected the Taft-Ellender-Wagner Bill as amended and sent on from the Senate. In its place was the so-called Wolcott Omnibus Bill, which eliminated provisions for public housing, slum clearance, and urban redevelopment. But the pressure by the pro-housing lobby was growing in strength, and three Republican committee members succumbed, along with the Democratic minority. These features were restored by a margin of just one committee vote.

But the fight was by no means over. In the last week of the session, which was about to adjourn for the Republican Convention, the Rules Committee blocked sending the amended Wolcott Bill to the floor, and a new Wolcott measure, with several new items favorable to the real estate interests inserted, was introduced. The Rules Committee suspended rules on the introduction of bills, leaving to the discretion of Speaker Joseph W. Martin, Jr., of Massachusetts the right of an individual member to call up a bill. Wolcott, having refused to recognize any amendments or points of order, called up his bill at the last moment, and although the housing bloc was furious, there was nothing to do but vote on the crippled measure. As Sam Rayburn said: "I impugn the motives of nobody, but if I were to vote for this bill, under these conditions, I would feel that I was perpetrating a fraud upon the American people, for the simple reason that I know that this means there will be no housing legislation at this Congress."

The House passed its bill on June 18. Congress adjourned, but was called back into special session by President Truman. On August 6 the Senate amended what was now known as the Wolcott-McCarthy Bill. The House accepted the changes the following day. There were no sections in the bill President Truman signed calling for Federal aid for low-rent housing, slum clearance, or urban rehabilitation. The housing and real estate lobby had won.

On another field it was less successful, mainly because in fighting for the complete elimination of rent control it was going against the demands of a large section of the population in an election year and because it was seeking to destroy a tangible measure already on the statute books. Realizing this, the real estate lobby sought to turn rent control back to the individual states. The purpose was obvious. State legislatures are even more easy to control than Congress, and local lobbies were hopeful that they could defeat rent control, especially in those states where rural-minded legislators were more powerful than those from urban areas.

As usual the lobby concentrated its attention on the House. There it succeeded in passing a measure completely decontrolling building materials and not just those to be used for the building of schools, churches, and welfare centers. It also removed housing "new on the rental market" from controls, and rooms in private homes and trailers. The Senate subcommittee wrote such a strong decontrol bill that the full Banking and Currency committee felt constrained to rewrite it. Senator Cain, taking his arguments almost straight from such books as the Foundation for Economic Education's *Roofs or Ceilings*, led the Senate floor debate with the strange declaration that there really was no housing shortage, but only a shortage of rental units, which of course was caused only by rent controls. The act that was finally accepted by Congress allowed some rental increases but continued most of the controls for another year.

The charge that the housing and real estate lobby had the Eightieth Congress in the hollow of its hand was made so frequently (and with such telling effect by President Truman in his campaign speeches) that the House Select Committee on Lobbying Activities would have been remiss if it had failed to look at its operation in detail.*

"Members of Congress," the committee reported in its *Interim Report*, "are used to being sought out in their offices, in their homes, in the corridors of the office buildings and of the Capitol, in the cloakrooms and restaurants, on the floor of the Chamber itself. They expect and welcome letters, telegrams, and telephone calls from constituents and from those outside their districts as well. In an age where the actions of Congress directly affect the lives of so many, legislators depend on these communications in a very real and immediate way. They are both the pipelines and the lifelines of our kind of representative government." [1]

Representative Brown waggishly remarked that he could smell the difference between spontaneous and genuine communications and those that were inspired by special interests. It was because Representative Buchanan found a bad smell clinging to hundreds

---

* Part 2 of *Hearings* before the House Select Committee on Lobbying Activities, Eighty-first Congress, second session. Housing Lobby. Washington, 1950. The information in the foregoing section of this chapter is from various sources. The best brief legislative history of the Housing Act and the extension of rent control can be found in *Congressional Quarterly Almanac*, vol. IV, pp. 137–143, 339–344.

of telegrams and letters sent him during the debate over rent control and housing that he originally brought the need for a lobby
investigation before the House. He found that this barrage, in the
committee's words, tended to "degrade the right of petition into a
solemn-cynical game of blindman's buff, a test of wits between
the lobbyist and the legislator." As an example the committee
offered a letter sent by the National Association of Real Estate
Boards to realtors throughout the nation. It was a form letter,
very personal and friendly in tone, designed to be used as a guide
for letters to be sent to the recipient's own congressman. One
sentence read: "Recently I met with some of our good friends,
including —— ——, and we discussed what best should be done to
correct the injustices being practiced in the name of controlling
rents." It then had sections for the insertion of other names of
local businessmen who presumably had influence with the congressman, making it look as if every one in town was against rent
control. Then followed a place for the insertion "in your own
words" of some of the "Fifteen Points" (supplied by the
NAREB!) "which you think will appeal to him most." Heading
this suggested letter was the warning: "NOTE. Be sure to change
form and ideas into your own words, rearrange, omit some parts,
and add personal experiences." [2] Mr. Buchanan at last knew where
all those letters had come from.

Only when a lobby has sufficient funds, a national organization
through which to work, and a large staff of workers with plenty
of time to plan the campaign, can this type of approach be used
with effect. But it is widely used by private pressure groups on
both sides, just as hurried telegrams to interested people are used
when time is limited, as this telegram from Nathan E. Cowan,
lobbyist for the CIO, to the heads of CIO unions and state industrial councils, shows: "Telegraph or, if possible, telephone your
congressman urging that he be on hand if the bill comes out for
a vote. Demand that no weakening amendments be added during
debate." [3]

The National Association of Real Estate Boards has thousands of members all over the country upon whom it can depend for funds and moral support. During the legislative battles over housing, rent controls, price controls, and all other matters even remotely affecting real estate or housing interests, they can be depended upon to flood Washington with letters and telegrams. Its trained staff of lobbyists is ever ready to prepare communications for local members to submit to their senators and representatives. Through its local member boards it has developed remarkably extensive and well documented lists of congressional "contacts," made up of individuals who are presumed to wield influence for one reason or another with their representatives in either house. James J. Spatz, executive secretary of the Dayton real estate board, sent Calvin K. Snyder, lobbyist attached to the Realtors Washington Committee, its active lobbying agency, a list of persons "who might carry weight with Senator Taft" — a man "prominent in town, has entree to Taft," a former state senator, a Shriner, a "well-known realtor, experienced in legislative matters," and the president of the Dayton Board of Education! [4]

Since housing bills and rent control bills are in the hands of the Banking and Currency committees of both houses, the NAREB keeps a "special list," fully detailed as to contacts "back home" and presumably as to the financial and social status of those opposed to its interests, of all members of this committee. It does the same for the Rules Committee which, in the House action on the Housing Act and the rent control measure, played its important delaying role. It also has a valuable list labeled "Key Senate Phone Contacts." [5]

At crucial moments during a legislative campaign these local contacts are rushed into action; the pressure is put on by the political, business, or personal acquaintances of the legislator whom the contact has previously lined up. There are between 600 and 700 such "contacts" making up the membership of the realtors Washington Committee. Their work has been described by Herbert U. Nelson, executive secretary of the NAREB:

The specific objective and activity of the enlarged committee is to wire or write their Senators or Representatives regarding any critical matters which may arise from time to time that seriously affect the real estate industry and where quick action is required. Only those who have shown a willingness or desire to render support in this manner, or who are closely acquainted or have personal contact with Members of Congress, have been appointed on the enlarged committee.[6]

It works on both sides of the fence in the same way. When pressure was needed a Florida citizen, pressed into action by the National Housing Conference, Inc., a pressure group opposed to the NAREB, induced the mayor (who was also a contractor), a railroad union leader and city commissioner, two bank presidents, an attorney and large property owner, several executives of local Chamber of Commerce groups, an "outstanding physician and surgeon" (who was also a "large property owner"), a lumberman, and a general contractor, to bring individual pressure on their representative to vote for slum clearance and "additional public housing" for his district.[7]

With 1115 real estate boards scattered throughout the country, claiming a membership of 44,000 individuals, and six highly trained, well-paid registered lobbyists working in Washington, the pressure which the NAREB was able to exert was tremendous. Most of these member-lobbyists worked without compensation and even paid their own expenses. One was so willing to help fight rent controls that he wrote Mr. Nelson: "I believe our case opposing the extension of rent control would be helped tremendously if we could parade in a few small property owners from around the country, a little bedraggled and run-down-at-the-heels-looking, who could get their story over to Congress that the small man who owns a little property is taking one hell of a beating."

This suggestion of the vice-president of the Detroit Trust Company was brushed aside by Mr. Nelson, who told him that "there isn't a member of Congress that isn't well up on all the techniques of presentation." [8]

Although the National Association of Real Estate Boards carried the brunt of the lobbying during 1948, and has continued to do so during all subsequent attempts to maintain rent controls and forward the administration's housing program, it was able to enlist the help of at least eighteen other strong groups. The Committee for Constitutional Government and the National Economic Council gave valiant help, circulating thousands of pieces of literature. Other powerful lobby groups included the National Association of Home Builders, the National Lumber Manufacturers Association, the National Grange, the American Farm Bureau Federation, the United States Savings and Loan League, the National Apartment Owners Association, numerous local apartment owners' associations and "taxpayers' defense leagues," and powerful segments of the Chamber of Commerce of the United States and the American Bar Association.

These, Mr. Nelson showed, were often called in for consultation, while they lobbied on their own initiative and collected their own funds. He denied there was any compact, over-all lobbying organization or pooling of strategical directions.

The greatest strength of the pro-housing and pro-rent control lobbying came from the CIO, the International Association of Machinists, the Brotherhood of Railroad Trainmen, the National Farmers Union, veterans' associations, the Federal Council of Churches of Christ in America, numerous other Protestant and Catholic church groups, the League of Women Voters, groups interested in municipal problems, consumers' groups, and the like. The fight, however, was led by the CIO. The lobbies supporting the administration's program were not nearly so well coordinated as the NAREB-led lobby.

When Leo Goodman, registered lobbyist for the National

Housing Committee of the CIO, testified, Representative Halleck asked him:

Would it be fair to say that your techniques were designed to create a feeling among members of Congress that if their votes on housing matters met with your disapproval, they might expect reprisals at the polls?

To this Mr. Goodman replied:

That is not a technique of mine. Our Washington committee prepares the records and sends them to unions at the local level. The voting for members of Congress is done at local levels. The decision is made at those points as to whether the CIO voters like or dislike the records of past performance.

That the political pressure technique was used by both sides is obvious.

Other techniques used by the real estate lobby, as set forth by the Lobby Committee evidence, included the following:

1. Seeking out *financial backers* of members of Congress who were viewed as "enemies" of the real estate lobby's program and making efforts to have these backers apply pressure on the members of Congress to make them "friends."

2. Conducting campaigns in which "everybody who can read and write" is organized to blanket Congress with telegraphed or written pleas or demands concerning votes on highly technical and complex questions involved in the legislation.

3. Linking lobbies that were against "socialized" housing with lobbies against "socialized" medicine, and terming housing measures "communistic" in origin. The Rumely and Hart lobbies were especially helpful on this score.

4. Providing arguments against public housing to such organizations as parent-teacher associations, to offset textbooks which, according to the lobby, were written by "pinkos" who opposed "the private enterprise system."

5. Reaching "private enterprisers" in the American Legion and

other veterans' organizations to induce them to put forward resolutions condemning Federal aid to housing.

One of the most active private lobbies against public housing for years has been the United States Savings and Loan League, which was indicted for violation of the Lobby Act. This association is composed of more than 3700 savings and loan associations, co-operative banks, and their co-operating organizations. The Buchanan Committee found it has resources of $13,000,000,-000, largely for making long-term loans for the buying and building of homes. Its active lobbyist in Washington is Morton Bodfish, who got Representative Everett Dirksen to have printed by the government 85,000 copies of anti-housing speeches he made in the House in 1947. The league paid the charges. Bodfish also suggested to Mr. Dirksen that he get the Republicans to "do something on slum clearance." His clever thought was a bill which would restrict Federal expenditure for housing to funds from "the liquidation of government-owned real estate mortgages, etcetera." He even had such a bill drafted and passed on to Mr. Dirksen for study and polishing by "the legislative counsel." [9]

As late as June, 1950, Mr. Bodfish was boasting, in a "confidential bulletin," of the close association between the league and "its long-time friends," Representatives Spence (Democrat, Kentucky), Wolcott (Republican, Michigan), and Senator John Bricker (Republican, Ohio), who could be counted upon "whenever legislation affecting our institutions or their instrumentalities in Washington is in the hopper." [10]

The political operations of the real estate lobby are not confined to bringing pressure upon its "friends." It has intervened in specific electoral contests in support of its supporters and in purging its enemies and deserters. It has also found it "equally important to take a hand in shaping the issues on which these contests are waged." [11] In the early summer of 1948, flushed with its victories during the Eightieth Congress, the National Association of Real Estate Boards took its fight against public housing to the Republican National Convention. Calvin K. Snyder of the Realtors Washington Committee wrote his boss, Herbert U. Nelson:

But the public housing lobby did not let up with the adjournment of Congress. They carried their fight to the Republican Convention. And there, with the help of Dave Childs, and others, we were able to get a housing platform. . . . Still the public housers were fighting away. In the closing hours of the Republican Convention an innocent-looking little resolution almost got by. It said in part that, irrespective of the platform adopted by this convention as the policy of the National Republican Committee, the convention go on record in favor of public housing, slum clearance, and all the rest. It was an 8-point program and would have repudiated the action taken by the platform committee and unanimously approved by the convention. There were less than 500 delegates and alternates on the floor when these resolutions were offered and practically railroaded through. But the alertness of a Congressional friend stopped this resolution from seeing the light of day. In less than 15 minutes the convention was over, without endorsement of public housing.[12]

Once groups like the NAREB find it necessary to enter the local lists they have various ways of fighting. Mr. Snyder, in 1947, wrote a letter to the Columbus, Ohio, real estate board praising it for "the job you are doing on Senator Taft," coauthor of the Taft-Ellender-Wagner Bill. "The quiet and easy way you are handling your political contacts there is quite disturbing to the Senator," he continued. "The more subtle you can be, the more effective you are. You do not need to exert a public-relations campaign in the press or radio. That only helps the Senator. The behind-the-scenes operations with his political cronies are what counts. In my opinion this is no time for public opinion pressure. It is time for political infighting without fanfare." *

* *Hearings*, Part 2, p. 885. The Lobby Committee reported that it "is convinced that most lobby groups of any consequence are to some extent involved in influencing elections." After quoting a telegram from Nathan Cowan, CIO lobbyist, to executives and legislative representatives of his

But when the time comes for public opinion pressure such well-financed and tightly knit lobbies as the NAREB and its satellites in the lumber, building, home-financing, and allied industries are well equipped for the job. Their public relations setups are well organized. Their literary mills are constantly grinding out editorials, news releases, statements, letters to the editor, speeches, and every conceivable kind of written material that might possibly find its way into the newspapers. These seldom are sent out directly, but are "spotted" in the press by local bigwigs who have them copied verbatim and sent out under their own names. When newspapers refuse to use the canned editorials, some local real estate agent talks the editor into using it as a letter, or, if he is really persuasive, induces an editorial writer to recast it in his own form. Local lobbyists are continually told that "Congressmen read their home-town papers carefully. They follow trends as reported in the press." They are reminded that if "your Congressman sees stories in the papers emphasizing the failures of public housing, he will be more inclined to vote against the pending measure." [13]

They flood the newspapers with free material. The column "Sylvester Says" of the National Retail Lumber Dealers Association, which is distributed by the Western Newspaper Union, is

---

unions, which said: "In every letter, every wire, every phone call, remind your Congressman we'll remember the record in November," the committee said: "Today's legislative stakes are too high for such groups to abstain from working for the election of candidates most likely to favor their demands. This positive participation in influencing elections is an important consideration often ignored by political scientists. More important, however, is the negative participation of pressure groups in elections. The very essence of a pressure group is that it is a body of people who want something. If the present object of their pressure does not give them what they want, they may turn to another candidate at the next election." The Committee then quoted a letter from Joseph T. King, lobbyist for the National Retail Lumber Dealers Association, to an Akron, Ohio, lumber dealer: "I guess you will have to purge Mrs. [Frances P.] Bolton [Representative from the Twenty-second Ohio District and a congressman since 1940] as she is the only Republican that deserted the Ohio delegation." *Interim Report*, p. 45.

said to reach an audience of 4,000,000 readers, mostly through the rural and small-town papers, not one of which is ever informed of the source of the propaganda. If this were paid for as advertising matter, as it decently should be, it would cost the dealers $272,500 a year, their own lobbyist estimated.[14] In recent years these pressure groups have turned to paid advertising, as everyone knows who has read the advertisements of the National Association of Home Builders, with their warnings that public housing is pure socialism. They prepare radio material, all carefully disguised as "entertainment" or "educational material," and they even write textbooks for schools and colleges.

As the Lobby Committee says repeatedly in its *Interim Report*, none of this is illegal. It is sustained by the constitutional guarantees of freedom of the press, of speech, and of the right of assembly. It is lobbying most perfected. The National Association of Real Estate Boards "is by no means the only lobbying organization to recognize that every method of reaching peoples' minds is of some utility in the effort to create a reservoir of public support for group aims. But NAREB has been unusually successful in translating this conception into action. Aided immeasurably by the financial and human resources of its Nation-wide organization, NAREB has fitted every conceivable media of communication into its over-all planning. Its plans are not necessarily more ambitious than those of other groups; it has simply had better opportunity to realize them." [15]

CHAPTER XV

Recommendations – Pro and Con

THE House Select Committee on Lobbying Activities held several public hearings, the results of which were printed in ten volumes, and it issued twelve printed reports before it was through. It investigated the housing and real estate lobby quite thoroughly, as an example of an active lobby concentrating upon actual legislation before Congress. It looked into the affairs of such organizations as the National Economic Council, the Committee for Constitutional Government, the Public Affairs Institute, and the Foundation for Economic Education to show how important a part in legislative matters these "indirect lobbies" actually play. It made a gesture at investigating "left wing" as well as "right wing" lobbies and followed the prevailing pattern by citing William L. Patterson, the Negro leader of the Civil Rights Congress, for contempt of Congress not only because he refused to supply requested information but because he would not say whether he was or was not a Communist. It also dusted the surface of lobbying by Federal executive agencies, as directed by the resolution creating the committee.

Of all the documents emanating from the committee the *General Interim Report* and the *Report and Recommendations on Federal Lobbying Act*, which was submitted on the last day of the final, extended session of the Eighty-first Congress, are of the most lasting value. They contain the findings of the majority members of the committee. The minority refused to sign either, and issued a brief, caustic dissent entitled *Minority Views*, which is also of interest to students of the legislative process as an expression of a point of view prevalent, it seems probable, among many conservative members of Congress.

One thing stands out from the investigation and, although it is by no means an original discovery, it bears repetition. The present system of pressure politics has assumed extraordinary proportions in recent years and it is now assumed to be not an evil but an important and necessary ingredient of democracy. This system is bound to expand in the future. In its expansion it may well challenge the existence of representative government as we have known it. Nevertheless, the constitutional right of petition must be preserved, no restriction should be imposed upon legitimate lobbying. This, the committee concludes, is one of the most pressing problems facing the lawmakers in Washington today.[1]

Several approaches to the problem were considered by the committee, which as we have seen had the advantage of listening to some of the keenest minds among political scientists as well as some of the most successful practicing lobbyists representing a wide variety of private interests. A number of these are worth discussing.[2]

It has been suggested, "seldom with any clear outline for practical implementation," that government should support those important interests which do not have adequate resources so that they can contend on an equal basis with groups that are well supplied with funds. Donald C. Blaisdell makes this suggestion in his TNEC monograph, *Economic Power and Political Pressures*, and it has often been recommended by persons interested in the representation of minority and consumer interests. The committee does not explore this suggestion widely, but dismisses it on what seem to be valid and understandable grounds. Although it admitted that this approach might help solve the problem of the "present imbalance between various groups," it felt that quite likely it would result in more rather than less pressure on policy making. Furthermore, it predicted that it would be almost impossible to select reasonable criteria on which such support could properly be based.

Because most lobbies represent large and important economic interests and play such an increasing role in ultimate lawmaking it has frequently been suggested that organized groups be given a formal and recognized place in the policy-making process. This has been tried, without much success, in various European countries,[3] where experience with economic councils (a practice associated with the Hitler regime of Germany) has shown that they do not fit into our concept of democratic government. In this country several of our administrative agencies recognize the existence and value of various advisory councils, and, of course, the private pressure groups are forever appearing openly before congressional committees preparing major legislation. Business, labor, and farm groups, representing all shades of opinion in our three largest economic subdivisions, find no difficulty in presenting their cases to Congress. Consumer groups, on the other hand, are as often as not unrepresented at hearings because they have no organized body to make their wants known. Labor groups, however, frequently take the consumers' side. The committee believes this is as far as the system should be extended, once again stressing the difficulty of determining the criteria on which any formal group representation could equitably be based. The establishment of any such procedure would, in the committee's judgment, be "yielding to pressure groups rather than coping with them."[4] Our popular representation system with its geographical determination seems to preclude the necessity for any further steps in this direction.

The need for "streamlining" the legislative and administrative process is stressed in the reports. But in neither is any blueprint offered beyond the committee's final recommendations for revising the Lobby Act of 1946. They merely point out that pressures "thrive on Government" when government becomes "too complex for ordinary citizens to understand." In recent years we have made some strides in the right direction. The Lobby Act provision of the Legislative Reorganization Act of 1946 is, of course, a case in point; and the recommendations of the Hoover Commission, when and if fully enacted, may be helpful. It is a little strange that the Hoover Commission itself did not send one of its "task forces" into the lobbies to make its suggestions as to improving the relationship between pressure groups and Congress. Its only recognition of lobbying seems to have come after the reports were submitted. Then Herbert Hoover assailed the powerful lobby of the Army Engineers Corps — which is an open alliance between the corps, private builders, and certain members of Congress — at a time when this lobby was vigorously fighting certain of the Hoover Commission's proposals.*

More important for the proper control of lobbying, the committee finds, is a change that has been stressed throughout this book: the need for stronger political parties and party discipline. "This," it says, "is basic."

Political scientists in recent years have emphasized this need, which is one that should be obvious to anyone concerned with making our democratic political system work to the best advantage of all concerned. We have shown time and again that it is when party leadership and party responsibility are weakest that the lobbies are strongest and get away with the most. "Much of the present onus placed on partisanship in politics overlooks the fact that if the parties don't accept responsibility the pressure groups will move in by default."

Strong party platforms and programs and a determination to carry them out through disciplined party action, with the parties

* See "The Lobby that Can't Be Licked: Congress and the Army Engineers," by Robert de Roos and Arthur A. Maass, *Harper's Magazine*, August, 1949, for an excellent account of this lobby. The Citizens Committee for the Hoover Report, a privately financed pressure group, has lobbied valiantly for the recommendations of the Hoover Commission before Congress, using many of the accepted tactics of direct and indirect lobbyists.

making up their minds about the problems of the day and then living up to their commitments, would weaken the threat of government by pressure. Whether such party discipline is attainable in this country is a question that cannot be answered offhand, but the need for it has been obvious in recent years. (The Republican-Dixiecrat coalition is an instance of party weakness which has allowed freer play for pressure groups whose activities might have been checked if a strong Democratic Party, driving cohesively towards definite goals under determined leadership, had been in existence.) The alliance between pressure groups and parties is often well known. Certainly the real estate lobby has an easier time during Republican domination of Congress; but the inability of the Democratic Party always to hold its lines against strong, organized pressure groups has affected legislative results more than once. The Buchanan Committee, echoing the findings of the Committee on Political Parties of the American Political Science Association,[5] questions whether a stronger sense of party cohesion can be achieved — "for most Americans seem to like their parties as they are" — but it adds that ultimately responsible parties are "an essential requisite for responsible government." [6]

Realistically the committee rejected any lobby reform that called for more than a revision of the Lobby Act already on the book. Its final conclusion in its *Interim Report*, later to be buttressed with concrete suggestions, is worth pondering:

We need more information on lobbying and lobbyists. This, at the moment, is the most feasible approach. Every group has the right to present its case, but at the same time Congress and the public have a right to know who they are, what they are doing, and where the money is coming from — in a word, full disclosure of the relevant facts. Such disclosure is thoroughly in accord with our system and principles and has already received legislative recognition in the Regulation of Lobbying Act. What is needed is that this act be equipped to fulfill more effectively the purpose for which it is designed. . . . The act as it stands is a workable and valid piece of legislation. . . . The act does not seek to regulate but to inform.

It works on the simple premise that Congress and the public have the right to full information on those who actively attempt to influence the decisions of government.

No one of these approaches alone is equal to the magnitude of the problem we face; but together they are the first steps which must be taken if special interest groups are not to ride roughshod over a public interest which may often be inarticulate.[7]

The old-fashioned "pressure boy" type of lobbyist, the rugged individualist seeking to coerce or corrupt Congress in behalf of his private clients, is not the menace or the great problem he once was. "Our investigation has convinced us," the committee said, "that the business of influencing legislation is dominated by group effort, and that individual activities by persons known as 'lobbyists' are subordinate." Faced with the fact that there are nearly ten registered lobbyists for every elected congressman, and that many of them are highly paid and vigorously active individuals, the committee did admit that the activities of individual lobbyists must not be disregarded; but it insisted that "the printed word is much more extensively used by organizations as a means of pursuing legislative aims than personal contacts with legislators by individual lobbyists." Much of the testimony to which it had listened, as we have seen, does lend weight to the assertion that "lobbying activities of this kind increasingly overshadow the traditional techniques of contact and persuasion."

Lobbying of this kind wraps itself in the close protection of the first amendment, under which armor the American tradition of group activity has increasingly flourished. Thus there has grown up in this country an almost countless variety of pressure groups, and each of them is convinced — or seeks to convince others — that when it exercises its right of petition it does so in the general interest. Because of this there has developed a tendency to divide lobbying into two parts, just as the cynical Senator Reed did with his distinction between lobbyists and patriots. Each group considers itself a "good lobby" and those who oppose its aims "bad lobbies." For the same reason members of the public in general invariably classify pressure groups as "good lobbies" or "bad lobbies" according to their stand on the legislative programs the lobbies are working for. Lewis Haney, writing in the Hearst press from the eminence of his position as professor of economics at New York University, recently sought to tell his readers how to distinguish between good and bad lobbies:

The basic test of the goodness of lobbying is truth. . . . Lobbying that is not for truth is bad . . . lobbying on behalf of the rights of all men as individuals under fair competition to choose, to earn, to own, is ethical. Lobbying against such rights is bad. . . .

Lobbying for the maintenance of a representative republican form of government under a constitution is good, and vice versa.

Lobbying in favor of a voluntary competitive system of market values as the basis for a price system, is good.

Lobbying for freedom of worship is good.

Anyone should be free to teach, preach, or lobby for objective truth, including established American ideals.

But lobbying for special advantages for laborers, farmers, businessmen, races, or religious sects, as classes, is antisocial, radical, and bad. And above all, lobbying on behalf of Communism and "Communist-front" organizations which would revolutionize our freely adopted institutions, treat unequals equally, and distribute income without due relation to productivity — this is bad.[8]

To such distinctions the committee gives short shrift. The attempt to classify pressure groups as "good lobbies" and "bad lobbies," is, in the committee's "considered judgment," unnecessary, inadvisable, and indeed impossible. "Distinctions as to 'good lobbies' and 'bad lobbies' can be made on a subjective basis only, but in framing a statute the criteria must be objective," it wisely concludes.[9]

The rejection of any legal distinction between good and bad lobbies simplifies rather than complicates the problem of legislating on the subject of lobbying. Any act which had this in mind would be a regulatory act, and (in spite of the fact that the

1946 law is termed "regulation") the committee firmly insists that no act should in any way prohibit pressure group activities. "Congress and the people can evaluate group pressures properly, provided they know the identity and financial participation of those who support such operations." Beyond that, it would not go. And that, it continues, is what the present act does, to a highly successful degree. Furthermore, in doing so it is entirely within the constitution, as the so-called Slaughter case (already examined in these pages) amply shows.

The recommendations of the committee, therefore, do not call for any drastic changes in the act in spite of the fact that such critics as Professor Belle Zeller on the one hand and the National Association of Manufacturers on the other have called the act "poorly drafted." After examining the act almost word for word and finding that it "presents no difficulty when an honest effort is made to arrive at a sensible over-all construction" the committee makes the following suggestions for its improvement:

1. It would eliminate the word "lobby" from the title on the ground that the word has a "stigma" attached to it. It would call it "An act to require the reporting of certain information on efforts to influence legislation," with a "short title" amended to "Legislative Interests Reports Act."

2. It would add television and radio broadcasting stations to the press as explicitly exempt from provisions of the act.

3. It would eliminate the punitive clause (Sec. 310 [b]) which forbids persons convicted of violating the act from appearing before committees of Congress for a period of three years after such conviction. It would keep violation of the act a misdemeanor with its present penalties (Sec. 310 [a]).

4. On the grounds that such a change would substantially reduce the amount of detailed reporting required, it would raise from $10 to $50 the amount of the minimum individual expenditures which must be reported quarterly by lobbies, with names

and addresses of donors (Sec. 305 [a][4]); but would continue to require all lobbies to preserve receipts for expenditures of $10 or more (Sec. 303 [b]).

5. It would make contingent-fee lobbying illegal by an amendment to the Criminal Code.

6. It would amend the act so that the act would "not be applicable to a person in a year in which such person neither receives nor expends as much as $1000" for lobbying purposes.

With these changes, the majority of the committee felt that the Lobby Act would continue to serve its major purpose of supplying Congress and the people with the necessary information concerning the pressures continually being brought to bear on Congress in the performance of its legislative duties.

The committee made several recommendations about the administration of the act that bear examination. Perhaps the soundest is the suggestion that the Senate and the House designate standing subcommittees to provide for continuous analysis and evaluation of the Lobby Act filings. In the House it would set up a subcommittee of the Committee on House Administration whose members would act as a supervisory body to the Legislative Reference Service and the Clerk of the House. The former would be charged with making quarterly indices and analyses of the lobbying activities from the data filed with the latter, thus making available a continuous flow of information regarding the receipts and expenditures of various categories of lobbying groups. The committee also recommends a system whereby copies of filings be made more quickly available to the Department of Justice, charged with enforcing the act, than is the case at present.

Recognizing that it was confined to investigation of lobbying before Congress only, the committee also recommends another congressional investigation of attempts to influence action by executive agencies. "In these critical times," it warns, "special attention in such an investigation should be given to various aspects of our defense program such as efforts to obtain Government contracts, priorities, etc."

Certainly there was nothing startling or radical about any of these recommendations. They are based on a presumption that the act, as written in 1946, is basically sound. They even accept, by indirection at least, the conclusion that even the "principal purpose" phrase (which, as we have seen, has long been in controversy as to its meaning and has frequently been used to evade the act) is neither vague nor ambiguous. The gist of the committee's argument is that there is more to lobbying than meets the eye — that lobbying includes every act, whether direct or indirect, that is deliberately aimed at influencing Congress. Direct lobbying is easily recognizable, but indirect lobbying often is not. It is the latter which the majority of the committee believe is the more costly and the more influential and in the end the more dangerous to the democratic process.

None of this set well with the minority members of the committee. In a separate, brief dissent, issued under the signature of Representative Halleck, they questioned both the motives and the tactics of the majority in reaching their recommendations — which the minority contemptuously dismissed as having been hardly worth the time and effort and expense of the investigation. They centered their fire on the majority report on three fronts. Not only did the majority approach their task with a "misconception" of the intent of the Lobby Act of 1946 and of the meaning of lobbying itself, but they were so lacking in "objectivity" and possessed of such "political bias" that they completely evaded the instructions of Congress as set forth in the resolution creating the Buchanan Committee. Furthermore, they failed to "examine closely the present language of the statute" and therefore were able only to recommend a "series of comparatively insignificant amendments changing the name of the law and increasing exemptions under it in an entirely unrealistic manner." The majority also succumbed to the blandishments of the "overzealous" staff which, the minority members imply, was a rather radical group of young men.*

It is a little difficult to accept the charge that the majority misconceived the purpose of the investigation inasmuch as the original demand for an investigation was made by Representative Buchanan himself. And it is certain that, in the light of the record, the majority were no more "politically biased" than the minority. Both sides were politically biased, both sides being made up of politicians conducting an investigation in an election year. The wonder is that more "politics" was not played. A careful reading of the testimony taken at the open hearings cannot fail to convince the open-minded reader that Messieurs Brown, Halleck, and O'Hara sought at every possible turn to stymie the investigation, to "protect" those whom it said the majority members were "harassing," and to turn the investigation into an assault upon the administration. On the other hand, the majority played "politics" by defending Secretary of Agriculture Brannan, Security Administrator Oscar Ewing, the State Department, and the Housing and Home Finance Agency from the "attacks" of the minority, and by exposing the lobbying activities of the real estate and building interests and putting their major emphasis on those right wing foundations, committees, and institutions which have spent vast sums opposing the basic programs of the New Deal and the Fair Deal. The millennium would have arrived had it been done otherwise.

Unfortunately the minority saw fit to deal only in generalities and failed to answer the majority report point by point. Although their report says that "substantial legislative recommendations should have been forthcoming" in the face of "overwhelming opinion that changes are necessary," they fail to make any suggestions on their own account. "We are convinced that the pres-

---

* Lucien Hilmer, staff director; Thomas F. Flynn, Jr., assistant staff director; Joseph F. Dolan, counsel (he replaced Benedict F. Fitzgerald, Jr., and Louis Little, who served earlier); Edgar Lane, consultant; Charles B. Holstein, consultant; and William Earl Griffin, clerk.

ent Regulation of Lobbying Act is vague, ambiguous, uncertain, and seriously in need of amendment," the Halleck report declares.

Although it does not offer specific recommendations, the Halleck report does reveal its own aims when it says:

We would like to emphasize . . . the difficulties of attempting to legislate in this field. We doubt whether the so-called indirect lobbying, which, on the surface at least, is no more or less than constitutionally protected freedom of speech, can, or should be, regulated by the Congress. We do feel that those individuals whose principal purpose is to attempt to persuade individual members of Congress to follow a certain course of action might well be required to identify themselves and their source of support. Whether any lobbying statute should go further than this is seriously open to question.

Thus the minority members would, if they had their way, make little or no effort to find out the sources of the pressures continually beating on Congress. They would ignore all indirect lobbying. They would make casual inspection of some individuals engaged in making direct contacts with congressmen. Beyond that they would not go.

Lobbying, we said at the beginning of this book, is as old as legislation. It would seem, too, that the effort to understand it, to seek to resolve the problem within our constitutional framework of government, will last as long as legislation continues to be made by a Congress elected by the people.

CHAPTER XVI

Lobbying and the Atom

How can the ordinary, intelligent citizen hope to pass judgment on the control of atomic energy, the most overwhelmingly important question facing the peoples of the world today? Who but one steeped in the mysteries of nuclear physics can decide with any degree of intelligence whether any of the brave proposals for this eventually inescapable necessity would, if adopted, accomplish their avowedly beneficial purposes? The gap between amateur and expert thinking in this complex and esoteric field is still enormous — and necessarily so, in spite of all the education we have been subjected to in the last few years.

The ordinary citizen and the expert had better get together soon and close this gap if atomic energy, which was brought to penultimate perfection only through the expenditure of billions of the ordinary citizens' dollars, is not to be stolen from them. The lobbies are already at work.

As far as the ordinary citizen is concerned, there is at the present moment less need for specialized information about atomic energy than there is need for a wider understanding and deeper knowledge of the everyday political process. Atomic energy has long been wrapped in a frightening secrecy and mystery. But one fundamental fact about it can and should be grasped by everyone. And that is very simple: *Energy, whatever its source, is energy; and energy is power.*

History long since has proved that where there is power there are private interests ready and avid to use any means they can get away with to obtain it for their own personal profit.

During the last few years it has been stated over and over again, by scientists and statesmen alike, that the future existence of the United States and even the whole world is more dependent upon the outcome of atomic energy *control* than upon any other single factor, political, economic, social, or scientific. The potentialities of atomic power are so tremendous that it is no exaggeration to say that when and if we come to our senses a whole new world may evolve from its humane use. We are told that these potentialities are limitless — so vast that they can eventually be expected to replace the world's rapidly dwindling reserves of power-producing fuel. Of course, all this is contingent upon whether we blow ourselves off the face of the earth in the meantime, which the scientists say is possible, and which up to now has seemed highly probable.

We can, if we want to do so, preserve the limitless power for the people. But if we do, it will have to be done not in the laboratory but in the legislatures. Fundamentally the great problem of atomic energy is no longer scientific but economic. And being economic the technique of its solution automatically becomes political. For this obvious reason the future of atomic energy lies in the hands of those most able to persuade the lawmakers as to its disposition. This is as it should be in a democracy.

The electorate, using the admittedly imperfect processes of democratic politics, created the Atomic Energy Act at a time when far less was known about atomic energy in every way than is known today. The story of how this law came into being is a study of lobbies and lobbyists that may some day be recognized as a classic of its kind. It is a rare and stimulating example of how a "peoples' lobby" defeated the "vested interests" with their own weapons. But it is even more a thrilling and heartening example of how a democratic government can function in behalf of the general welfare. Its lesson should not be forgotten when the statesmen and journalists of the world get over their jitters, and atomic energy, we may hope, is at last put to those constructive uses for which, the scientists so wistfully tell us, it is intended.

The compelling need for some form of drastic control of atomic energy was apparent almost immediately after the horrifying implications of President Truman's first announcement of the existence and use of the bomb began to sink into the national consciousness. The search for it became a matter of paramount legislative interest with the close of the war. Hiroshima was destroyed on August 6, 1945. President Truman signed the Atomic Energy Act just one week less than a year later, on July 30, 1946. Thus at least one "decadent democracy" acted without undue delay. The passage of this law, certainly one of the most important actions in the history of Congress, has been rightly called "as radical and unprecedented as the scientific discovery that occasioned it" and an action "without precedent in the legislative history of this or any other country."

It is no exaggeration to say, as the first historians of this act have said, that never before:

have men in any state, standing on the threshold of a new technological era, attempted to provide in advance for rational control of the forces to be unleashed. And never before in the peacetime history of the United States has Congress established an administrative agency with such portentous responsibilities as those conferred upon the Atomic Energy Commission. The Act creates a government monopoly of the sources of atomic energy and buttresses this position with a variety of broad governmental powers and prohibitions on private activity. The field of atomic energy is made an island of socialism in the midst of a free enterprise economy.[1]

This chapter of our history is all the more exciting and heartening when we consider the position the United States found itself in at the time when the Senate was charged with writing the first atomic energy control measure. Since the Civil War the growth of corporate concentrations had proceeded without many effective restraints. Powerful economic interests had sought to dominate American life, and they had generally succeeded until first slackened by the New Freedom under President Wilson and later by the stronger central controls of the New Deal. Then the awarding of war contracts prodded the latent economic concentration and strengthened the financial positions of the largest business and industrial interests. Occupying as they did their most formidable fortress since 1932, these interests cherished a dream of a return to that state of Normalcy which they had experienced with relish in the 1920's. As the end of the war came closer they prepared to reassert their power. Their first objective was the abolishment, at whatever cost or inconvenience to the public, of all Federal controls. As we have seen, the great business and financial lobbies descended upon Washington in force to lead the battles against such socialistic nonsense as price controls, rent controls, public housing, and corporate taxation.

Those whose duty it was to write an atomic control bill had to face the fact that atomic energy, of which neither they nor anyone else outside the secret laboratories knew very much, "could not be contained within the framework of existing institutions." A fundamentally conservative Congress, beset by conservative pressures, was faced with a more drastic problem than any that had been wished upon that body since the adoption of the constitution. The problem was threefold.

First, and seemingly most important, was the question whether Federal control, which was universally recognized as necessary, should be exercised by military or civil authorities. Second was the question of the extent to which restrictions should be placed over scientific activities. And then came the third question which, in the end, may turn out to be the most important of all: How far should private commercial activities in the field of atomic energy be controlled?

None of these questions was fully resolved at the time, nor could they be under the circumstances surrounding them then.

Only the first question was widely debated in Congress and by the press; in a world suddenly and dramatically "at peace" and yearning to get out of its collective uniform as soon as possible, that seemed transcendent over all others. At the close of a war fought against three great military dictatorships, the debate over the issue of military versus civilian control was understandably passionate. Involved also were such issues as freedom versus authority and nationalism versus One World. But the main concern of the people was to find some means for keeping power over so strangely lethal a weapon away from the military and of vesting it, in accordance with our democratic tradition, in the hands of civilians.

For several months before the people knew there was such a thing as an atom bomb the more enlightened scientists who had been working to make it a destructive reality had been growing more and more concerned with problems not usually associated with the laboratory. They had been studying and preparing memoranda not only on the potential results of using the weapon but also on the probable international political effects its use might have. Such speculations were inevitable. But the peacetime applications of atomic energy which might be anticipated were also very much in the forefront of scientific thought; although, in the mind of a public so badly frightened by the destructive elements of this new phenomenon when the news of Hiroshima was finally made public, such possibilities were put to one side. Would there be a world in which to enjoy them? That became the universal question.

This question, of course, was very much in the minds of the political leaders who made the decision to use the bomb against Japan. In the fateful spring of 1945, even before the first experimental bomb had been dropped in the New Mexican wasteland, Secretary of War Henry L. Stimson had, with the approval of President Roosevelt, appointed a committee of civilians which was charged with the extremely difficult task of recommending legislation for the domestic control of atomic energy. This committee, which was composed of Assistant Secretary of State Will Clayton, Dr. Vannevar Bush, James F. Byrnes, Dr. James B. Conant, Dr. Karl Compton, and George L. Harrison, studied the problem for two months.

In the meantime the War Department also had legislation under consideration. Few of the scientists working on the atomic project were then aware of this. There was little they could have done at this time to make the military subordinate to the civilian authority which would be established by the forthcoming recommendations. Apparently the Stimson Committee was not then overwhelmingly convinced, or it was unable to make its considered views on this aspect of the problem acceptable to the bill-drafters in the War Department. All this, of course, was taking place under the same rules of secrecy that made the development and eventual use of the bomb the best-kept secret in military history until President Truman shocked the world with his historic announcement on August 6, 1945.

Shortly afterward the Smyth Report was released, with its astonishing array of what hitherto had been considered the most highly classified material. Then a strict censorship was clamped down on atomic information by the army. In spite of the latter, or perhaps because of it, the scientists realized that unless an educational campaign were instituted to disseminate information from reliable sources the world would live in an atmosphere of terror which, at that moment, was unnecessary. In Chicago, Los Alamos, Oak Ridge, and Manhattan, the atomic scientists quickly organized, hoping that through their concerted efforts the weird and dangerous conclusions that were being formed throughout the country might be dispelled.

While such erroneous beliefs as that only three people in the world knew the secret of the bomb, that we should not give our "secrets" away, and that the navy possessed a "defense" for the bomb, gained rapid headway, the results of the War Department's thinking and the Stimson Committee's recommendations were incorporated in a legislative bill. Introduced early in October, 1945, by Senator Edwin C. Johnson of Colorado and Representative Andrew J. May of Kentucky, its provisions stunned the scientists, who were, after all, the only people in the world who really knew what was being provided for.

The May-Johnson Bill, which was referred to the House Military Affairs Committee, of which the egregious Mr. May was chairman, proposed the establishment of a part-time commission for the domestic control and development of atomic energy, to make and enforce security and safety regulations, and to make arrangements of unlimited scope with private individuals and institutions for exploitations in this untouched field. The bill emphasized the military applications and even went so far as to place the domestic uses of atomic energy under military control. Throughout the bill, the emphasis was shifted away from "the future essential peacetime developments" and nowhere in it was there adequate recognition of the "intertwining of domestic and international problems in the field of atomic energy." [2]

The explicit provision that members of the Atomic Energy Commission might be officers of the army or the navy and the obvious fact that Congressman May was trying to jam the bill through his committee without adequate hearings created an immediate furor and set the stage for the bitterest legislative battle since the slaughter in the Senate of the League of Nations. As James R. Newman and Byron S. Miller wrote in their excellent study:

The historian who attempts to recreate this drama is appalled by the confused and chaotic nature of the action. The scene that confronts him resembles the description of the Battle of Borodino in Tolstoy's *War and Peace*. The hosts gather, impelled by some deeper impulse than any they comprehend, seeking a goal they do not altogether understand. The struggle that ensues takes on a life of its own, independent of any individual's will or direction. The conflict swirls and eddies and becomes not one but scores of battles, each appearing crucial to its participants. The field is a confused jumble of motion, the whole is obscured in smoke, and even the commanding generals have little understanding of developments, much less any effective control over them. The motives of the contestants are frequently obscure; the action is extended over weeks or months, rather than hours; there are sometimes not two but several armies engaged; alliances are shifted in the heat of battle; and in the end the issue is not decided on the field at all but in some clandestine meeting among the rival leaders.[3]

The scientists, bewildered and without a leader, came out of their laboratories. Fortunately there was in Congress at that time a sounding board from which they could express their viewpoints. President Truman, early in September, had urged upon Congress the enactment of legislation which would place the resources of the Federal government at the disposition of scientific research. Senator Harley M. Kilgore of West Virginia introduced a bill which would have realized this objective through the establishment of a national science foundation, whose task would be the promotion of scientific research in the national interest. The hearings before Senator Kilgore's subcommittee gave the scientists a forum for their rapidly forming opinions relative to the need for domestic legislation affecting science that would be acceptable to a nation which was, so they thought, dedicated to an extended period of peace.

The Kilgore Bill passed the Senate, but the big business–private enterprise lobby, the National Association of Manufacturers, and other lobby groups, vigorously opposed any national science foundation. They got to the House committee to which the bill was referred and succeeded in smothering it. Their attacks, though covert, were effective, and it was not until the closing days of the first session of the Eightieth Congress that a national science bill was adopted. This, the so-called Smith Bill, was so riddled by restrictive clauses and was such an "administrative monstrosity" that President Truman wisely vetoed it.[4] It was during the debate over the Kilgore Bill that it first became apparent that our political leaders must turn to the scientists if they were to produce a measure at all worthy of the tremendous discovery which they were charged with controlling.

Led by scientists from the University of Chicago, a small group of able men formulated their principal grievances against the May-Johnson Bill, outlined what they believed was a more satisfactory measure, and laid the groundwork for what later became the McMahon-Douglas Bill, out of which the Atomic Energy Act was hewn.

Some time in October scientists then unknown but whose names were later to become familiar to everyone — Doctors Leon Szilard, E. U. Condon, Harold C. Urey — arrived in Washington. Their aim was to defeat the May-Johnson Bill and bring about the establishment of a congressional committee on atomic energy which would give the subject the intelligent attention it deserved. Thus the first atomic lobby came into being. Within the next few months it was to accomplish most of its purposes. It was to do this through the application of all the techniques of lobbying which, over the years, had been exerted for less worthy reasons by pressure groups seeking private gains at the expense of the general welfare.

On November 1, 1945, scientists from all the atomic centers — Oak Ridge, Los Alamos, New York, Chicago — met in Washington and formed the Federation of Atomic Scientists. In a borrowed office and with one secretary they went to work to correct the appalling lack of information on the part of members of the administration, representatives, and senators. They were determined to remain on the scene until they could bring about a satisfactory understanding of the mysterious new problem, which would enable those responsible for its solution to write an act that recognized the international and domestic, the military and peacetime potentialities of atomic energy.*

* On October 3, 1945, President Truman told Congress: "Scientific opinion appears to be practically unanimous that the essential theoretical

The first thing to be done was to defeat the May-Johnson Bill. Its opponents were quick to charge that this measure would lead to an authoritarian, repressive, and militaristic system. In reply the supporters of the bill had little to offer except that those who opposed it were irresponsible and subversive radicals whose only aim was to jeopardize the welfare of the nation. In this supercharged atmosphere the Federation of Atomic Scientists (now known as the Federation of American Scientists) held its first press conference. The pioneers of this lobby — four politically inexperienced young scientists led by Dr. Lyle Borst — met with hard-boiled Washington newsmen in the Senate office building on November 4 and with refreshing candor told them, "We got

knowledge upon which the discovery is based is already widely known." He also said: "The hope of civilization lies in the international arrangements looking, if possible, to renunciation of the use and development of the atomic bomb, and directing and encouraging the use of atomic energy and all future scientific information toward peaceful and humanitarian aims." On November 15, 1945, the joint statement of President Truman, Prime Minister Clement Attlee, and Prime Minister Mackenzie King started the problem of atomic energy on its way to the United Nations. The Truman and the joint statements helped sway the public away from the false concepts under which it had been laboring and spurred the process of education so necessary then — and now. *New York Times*, October 4, 1945.

The Truman-Attlee-King statement may have been affected by one of the first actions of the atomic lobby. Before the tripartite conference was held the newly formed federation prevailed upon Mrs. Helen Gahagan Douglas, congresswoman from California, to introduce a resolution urging President Truman to call a meeting of Russia, the United States, and Great Britain to initiate discussions leading toward world control of atomic energy through the United Nations. The federation, seeking its introduction in the Senate by a bipartisan group, had more trouble there; while negotiations to this end were proceeding the conference was announced. The resolution had wide circulation on Capitol Hill, where ignorance about atomic energy was widely and freely admitted, and undoubtedly had been pondered at the White House. "Notes on History of Federation," by W. A. Higinbotham. Manuscript. John A. Simpson, "The Scientists as Public Educators: A Two-Year Summary," *Bulletin of Atomic Scientists*, vol. 3, no. 6, September, 1947. Memoranda in manuscript from files of Michael Amrine, who was public relations director for the Federation of Atomic Scientists, of which W. A. Higinbotham, then of Los Alamos, New Mexico, was the first president.

mankind into this crisis and now we want to help get you out."
They blasted the beliefs that the bomb was a secret and that adequate defense against it could be created, and they spoke impressively about the necessity for world control. The meeting did
not make many headlines, but Richard Strout of the *Christian
Science Monitor* suspected, and wrote, that this was the beginning of "the revolt of the scientists."

Soon the scientists, who had no funds as well as no experience
in the political maelstrom, found good advisers in such men as
Raymond Swing, the radio commentator, Michael Amrine, a
free-lance magazine writer, Alfred Friendly of the *Washington
Post,* and Mr. Strout, who taught them the way around the capital and introduced them to the politicians and statesmen. They
worked from cold rooms in an old brownstone house, they paid
secretaries out of their own pockets, and lived on their savings
while on leaves of absence from their laboratories. Dr. Higinbotham, Dr. Szilard, Dr. John Simpson of Chicago, Dr. Urey,
and Joseph H. Rush were the lobby's nucleus. Father Edward
Conway, secretary of the Catholic Association for International
Peace, was adviser and raiser of funds.

It did not take this "league of frightened men," as one reporter
named them, long to become wise to lobbying techniques. Scientists from the scattered atomic groups, physicists from New
York, radar experts from Cambridge, Massachusetts, worked
with the same unison of purpose as the Washington Realtors
Committee of the National Association of Real Estate Boards. In
Washington Dr. Condon conducted what was known as his
"night school for senators." Unofficial symposia of various kinds
were held to which congressmen of every shade of political
opinion were invited. Cocktail parties, dinners, luncheons were
given at every opportunity. Dr. Urey went around telling meetings of legislators that "we scientists speak as citizens who have
had more time than the rest of you to think about your problems."

Amused though they sometimes were, and astounded as they often were, Congress listened to the scientists. As Messieurs Newman and Miller have said: "It may be that they were grossly naïve in politics, but there is no denying that they showed a capacity for improvisation and prompt action beyond anything the economic groups involved in the legislation were able to muster." The lobbies of private enterprise, operating with their huge funds through experienced lobbyists, were no match for these tyros who were the first to enter the field and who stayed on to see their battle won. Under the auspices of the National Committee on Atomic Information, local groups throughout the country were formed and these in turn formed citizens' committees which flooded Congress with appeals to defeat the May-Johnson Bill and — after its introduction — to support S. 1717, which was the McMahon-Douglas Bill. In the ranks of this army of untrained lobbyists were liberals, conservatives, and reactionaries "who rallied to the defense of the traditional Constitutional principle of civilian supremacy." The military features of the May-Johnson Bill were roundly denounced by newspapers. Some sixty professional societies, women's clubs, church federations, labor unions, veterans' groups — all the organized and unorganized pressure groups except those of big business, which were silenced by the avalanche — labored with results.

The May-Johnson Bill, which never had the support of the Truman administration, was successfully bottled up in the House. In the Senate controversy raged over whether to refer an atomic control bill to the Foreign Affairs Committee or the Military Affairs Committee, with the result that a Senate Special Committee was set up. This latter, after protracted public hearings, produced a tentative measure, the famous S. 1717, which contained as general principles provisions for a full-time civilian commission, the stimulation of research, government ownership and operation of strategic phases of atomic energy, the prevention of monopoly, the direct Presidential control of the use of atomic weapons, and a minimum of secrecy consistent with national security. The bill was then taken into closed sessions of the McMahon Committee, as the special committee was known. The closed hearings took place just at the time the Canadian spy case broke hysterically in the newspapers, thus making easier the adoption of the controversial Vandenberg amendment, which provided a military board with broad review powers over all decisions of the Atomic Energy Commission and the right to carry complaints to the President — which again placed atomic energy under military control.

This amendment, adopted by a committee vote of 10 to 1, was generally considered worse than the May-Johnson Bill. Again the atomic lobby went to work. Mass meetings were held, the mail reached a new volume, and the sounds of protest in Washington from the grass roots grew so loud that the Special Committee was forced to reconsider its action. A compromise was reached. The new provisions confined the operations of the military liaison committee to the area of "military applications" and gave the full-time commission the responsibility of keeping the armed services informed of its activities, while the army and navy were also enjoined to report on their activities to the AEC.

To this peoples' lobby must go the major credit for the passage through Congress of the Atomic Energy Act. Dr. Simpson has said that "our ability to reach both major parties was . . . partly due to the fact that the men in Washington could not determine whether atomic energy belonged to the Republican or Democratic party." If nothing else this statement shows how quickly and how well the nuclear scientists had come to absorb the basic facts of political science. "We found in Washington," he continues, "that many political organizations wished to join with us or to include us in their program. It required considerable watchfulness to prevent our group from becoming attached to any political organization. Pressure was applied at various times, but we resisted it successfully."

The victory of the scientists was a great one, and even more astounding when we realize that here was a pressure group that had come into being for no reason except the general welfare, that was without private ambitions, that had no profit motive, and that was able to put to rout the well-organized private interest lobbies. Whether these latter failed to recognize the profitable implications of atomic energy or whether they were merely temporarily stunned and impotent in the face of an aroused citizenry is difficult to determine. It probably was a little of both.

Although the military aspects then held the public imagination (as they continue to do in the troubled world of today) it is those provisions of the Atomic Energy Act which directly deal with the role of private enterprise that must interest us here. For it is precisely in this field that we must eventually expect the great struggle of the pressure groups to take place. A brief survey of the act (which thus far has withstood all major assaults) shows that there are several sections on which private enterprise is bound to turn its guns as soon as it thinks the time has come when such raids will have a chance of success.*

The scientists of today are even more convinced than many of them were in 1945–1946 that the information provisions of the act are repressive as far as scientific development is concerned. There has, indeed, been in the last five years (a brief period, historically, it is true) but little indication of the practical development of atomic energy for those "peacetime uses" so freely and so frequently mentioned. And this is in spite of the fact that the AEC was deliberately designed as the "stimulator,

---

* The major attacks to date have been upon the personnel of the Atomic Energy Commission. This was apparent in the bitter assaults in Congress upon the integrity and usefulness of David Lilienthal during his chairmanship, which were inspired by the power industry primarily, and fostered by the satellite lobbies and congressional errand boys of the reactionary interests. That these will be a directing source of future efforts to break down the present restrictions on the use of atomic energy seems obvious.

promoter, and coordinator" of scientific research in atomic energy and "all its applications." We probably will have to wait until the threat of war has passed to see atomic power at work for the benefit of mankind. The clear intent of the act was to insure that the nation, through its agent, the Atomic Energy Commission, should plan research in such a way as to promote the development of atomic energy in the interest of the public welfare — to increase the standard of living and strengthen free competition in private enterprise. No layman can say how far these objectives have been pursued, but that it is in this field that private enterprise will attempt to break down the act no layman can afford to disbelieve. Private enterprise has always fought state intervention as a sort of unfair competition in any field it feels is best left to its profitable initiative, and that it will continue to do so through its Washington lobbies needs no arguing here.

The McMahon-Douglas Act makes specific the range of powers to be controlled by the commission. It is because of this that the act deeply invades that area which in the past has always been reserved for private property and free enterprise. This situation has led the act's historians to declare that it "does nothing less than establish in the midst of our privately controlled economy a socialist island with undefined and possibly expanding frontiers." [5]

If this is true we need only glance back at the recent chapters of this book to understand with what frenzy certain lobbies will attack this act as soon as the lessening of military controls and secrecy are possible. Had the business interests of this country fully appreciated the significance of the provisions for the control of private activity in the field of atomic energy they would undoubtedly have mobilized all their strength in 1946 to prevent their enactment. The act makes the production of atomic energy a government monopoly, it provides for direct governmental controls through licensing and the granting of the use of fissionable materials, and it provides for indirect controls of those parts of the national economy not directly in the field of atomic energy but likely to be affected by the exercise of the commission's monopoly activities or control functions. The AEC exclusively owns all fissionable material, which some day soon may be more important to the national economy than coal or oil or hydro-electric power.*

The AEC has the power to regulate any transaction involving source material of atomic energy, and any industrial or commercial application of atomic energy. It can eliminate patent rights if it finds they interfere with carrying out the purposes of the act. It can extend its control to any substance it finds essential to the production of fissionable material, regardless of its apparent remoteness to the field of atomic energy. The policies of the commission not only will affect through the years our military security and our foreign policy, but also the value of existing capital investments, the structure of industry, the level of prices and employment, and, it is quite probable, even "the structure of society itself." When Congress in its wisdom passed the Atomic Energy Act it "announced the end of the institution of the sovereign national state based on the system of capitalistic free enterprise." [6] We may think that an extreme statement, but the act has been on the books for only five years and that peaceful era which the act envisions is yet to come. When it does, private industry will not accept this conclusion without the greatest struggle in the history of Congress.

In November, 1948, *Fortune* told the dramatic story of Kellex and revealed in part the tremendous interest private enterprise has in the industrial future of atomic energy.[7] In 1942 the M. W. Kellogg Company, which had many interests but which had

* "Five big public utilities applied to the Securities and Exchange Commission last week for permission to raise $65 million in new capital. Their reason: A new atomic energy project will be built 'somewhere in the U. S.' at a site where power is unavailable. The applicants: Central Illinois Public Service Co., of Springfield, Ill.; Illinois Power Co., of Decatur; Kentucky Utilities Co., of Lexington; Middle South Utilities, Inc., of New York; and Union Electric Co., of St. Louis." *New York Herald Tribune*, Sec. 4, p. 1, December 17, 1950.

long specialized in the inventing, designing, and building of continuous fluid-cracking plants for the oil industry, was engaged to design and construct the "famous, gigantic, U-shaped K–25 plant at Oak Ridge for gaseous separation of Uranium 235 from the more plentiful and dormant U–238." Energy, power, and its actual development is the keynote of Kellogg's activity, although *Fortune* maintains that M. W. Kellogg himself asserts "that he was not in the pipe or oil-refinery business but the profit-making business." In 1944 Pullman, Inc., "which had just been divested of its sleeping-car business by anti-trust action," completed purchase of Kellogg's entire capital stock for $18,250,000.*

To carry on the building of the great K–25 plant Kellogg organized Kellex, probably the "oddest corporate formation in U. S. business history." It was capitalized on ten shares of $100 par stock, all owned personally by Morris Kellogg. By the time it had finished the Oak Ridge project it had "responsibilities running upward of $500,000,000." It drew its staff from such organizations as Standard Oil of Indiana, General Electric, Union Carbide and Carbon Chemical (which "ran" K–25). At the end of the war it was not dissolved. Instead it became occupied principally with atomic energy, but it also became interested in rockets and guided missiles (with which another Kellogg subsidiary, Special Projects, was also involved) because these may one day be powered by atomic fuel. It also was engaged to design for the Atomic Energy Commission and General Electric Corporation the big extension to the Hanford plutonium plant at Richland, Washington.

"But its prime contract calls for work on atomic energy for industrial applications," *Fortune* revealed. "That is Kellex's main interest. Kellex has plans, process designs, and the consuming urge to apply continuous-flow principles to an atomic power

---

* Pullman, Inc., is one of the corporations which defied the House Select Committee on Lobbying Activities by refusing to answer the questionnaire on its contributions to lobbies. *Expenditures by Corporations*, p. 423.

plant: 'burning' atomic fuel in a power pile, which by the . . . 'breeding' principle will make more of its own fuel in the form of plutonium; employing the heat for power; taking off useful by-products and processing them for a continuous, automatic, and economical cycle of operations. . . . Eventually Kellex is bound to make heavy contributions, and thus open for Kellogg a new industry. Kellogg has two standby corporations — Atomic Energy Corporation and Nuclear Energy Corporation — awaiting developments."

By this one instance we can see further evidence of the future hope of private industry to turn atomic energy to its own profitable use — a hope that is perfectly natural and perfectly legal, but which, if the history of big business versus government means anything, suggests a coming gigantic struggle for private power through legislation. Equally great — if not greater — stakes are held by such enterprises as Du Pont, Allis-Chalmers, Union Carbide and Carbon, General Electric, Monsanto Chemical, and many other great corporations.

The point of the Kellex story, the point in mentioning Du Pont and the rest, is obvious. Big business spends hundreds of millions annually to influence legislation in its behalf. Unless the people of America are eternally vigilant many of these millions will go to abrogate the Atomic Energy Act, which was lobbied through Congress for the people and by the people to prevent forever the private control of atomic energy, which is of the people. The lobbies, now and in the future, are *your* business.

Appendix A

THE REGULATION OF LOBBYING ACT
Title III of the Legislative Reorganization Act of 1946

SHORT TITLE

SEC. 301. This title may be cited as the "Federal Regulation of Lobbying Act."

DEFINITIONS

SEC. 302. When used in this title —

(a) The term "contribution" includes a gift, subscription, loan, advance, or deposit of money or anything of value and includes a contract, promise, or agreement, whether or not legally enforceable, to make a contribution.

(b) The term "expenditure" includes a payment, distribution, loan, advance, deposit, or gift of money or anything of value, and includes a contract, promise, or agreement, whether or not legally enforceable, to make an expenditure.

(c) The term "person" includes an individual, partnership, committee, association, corporation, and any other organization or group of persons.

(d) The term "Clerk" means the Clerk of the House of Representatives of the United States.

(e) The term "legislation" means bills, resolutions, amendments, nominations and other matters pending or proposed in either House of Congress, and includes any other matter which may be the subject of action by either House.

DETAILED ACCOUNTS OF CONTRIBUTIONS

SEC. 303. (a) It shall be the duty of every person who shall in any manner solicit or receive a contribution to any organization or fund for the purposes hereinafter designated to keep a detailed and exact account of —

(1) all contributions of any amount or of any value whatsoever;

(2) the name and address of every person making any such contribution of $500 or more and the date thereof;

(3) all expenditures made by or on behalf of such organization or fund; and

(4) the name and address of every person to whom any such expenditure is made and the date thereof.

(b) It shall be the duty of such person to obtain and keep a receipted bill, stating the particulars, for every expenditure of such funds exceeding $10 in amount, and to preserve all receipted bills and accounts required to be kept by this section for a period of at least two years from the date of the filing of the statement containing such items.

RECEIPTS FOR CONTRIBUTIONS

SEC. 304. Every individual who receives a contribution of $500 or more for any of the purposes hereinafter designated shall within 5 days after receipt thereof render to the person or organization for which such contribution was received a detailed account thereof, including the name and address of the person making such contribution and the date on which received.

STATEMENTS TO BE FILED WITH CLERK OF HOUSE

SEC. 305. (a) Every person receiving any contributions or expending any money for the purposes designated in subparagraph (a) or (b) of section 307 shall file with the Clerk, between the first and tenth day of each calendar quarter, a statement containing complete as of the day next preceding the date of filing —

(1) the name and address of each person who has made a contribution of $500 or more not mentioned in the preceding report; except that the first report filed pursuant to this title shall contain the name and address of each person who has made any contribution of $500 or more to such person since the effective date of this title;

(2) the total sum of the contributions made to or for such

person during the calendar year and not stated under paragraph (1);

(3) the total sum of all contributions made to or for such person during the calendar year;

(4) the name and address of each person to whom an expenditure in one or more items of the aggregate amount or value, within the calendar year, of $10 or more has been made by or on behalf of such person, and the amount, date, and purpose of such expenditure;

(5) the total sum of all expenditures made by or on behalf of such person during the calendar year and not stated under paragraph (4);

(6) the total sum of expenditures made by or on behalf of such person during the calendar year.

(b) The statements required to be filed by subsection (a) shall be cumulative during the calendar year to which they relate, but where there has been no change in an item reported in a previous statement only the amount need be carried forward.

STATEMENT PRESERVED FOR TWO YEARS

SEC. 306. A statement required by this title to be filed with the Clerk —

(a) shall be deemed properly filed when deposited in an established post office within the prescribed time, duly stamped, registered, and directed to the Clerk of the House of Representatives of the United States, Washington, District of Columbia, but in the event it is not received, a duplicate of such statement shall be promptly filed upon notice by the Clerk of its nonreceipt;

(b) shall be preserved by the Clerk for a period of two years from the date of filing, shall constitute part of the public records of his office, and shall be open to public inspection.

PERSONS TO WHOM APPLICABLE

SEC. 307. The provisions of this title shall apply to any person (except a political committee as defined in the Federal Corrupt Practices Act, and duly organized state or local committees of a political party), who by himself, or through any agent or employee or other persons in any manner whatsoever, directly or indirectly, solicits, collects, or receives money or any other thing of value to be used principally to aid, or the principal purpose of which person is to aid, in the accomplishment of any of the following purposes:

(a) The passage or defeat of any legislation by the Congress of the United States.

(b) To influence, directly or indirectly, the passage or defeat of any legislation by the Congress of the United States.

REGISTRATION WITH SECRETARY OF THE SENATE AND CLERK OF THE HOUSE

SEC. 308. (a) Any person who shall engage himself for pay or for any consideration for the purpose of attempting to influence the passage or defeat of any legislation by the Congress of the United States shall, before doing anything in furtherance of such object, register with the Clerk of the House of Representatives and the Secretary of the Senate and shall give to those officers in writing and under oath, his name and business address, the name and address of the person by whom he is employed, and in whose interest he appears or works, the duration of such employment, how much he is paid and is to receive, by whom he is paid or is to be paid, how much he is to be paid for expenses, and what expenses are to be included. Each such person so registering shall, between the first and tenth day of each calendar quarter, so long as his activity continues, file with the Clerk and Secretary a detailed report under oath of all money received and expended by him during the preceding calendar quarter in carrying on his work; to whom paid; for what purposes; and the names of any papers, periodicals, magazines, or other publications in which he has caused to be published any articles or editorials, and the proposed legislation he is employed to support or oppose. The provisions of this section shall not apply to any person who merely appears before a committee of the Congress of the United States in support or opposition to legislation; nor to any public official acting in his official capacity; nor in the case of any newspaper or other regularly published periodical (including any individual who owns, publishes, or is employed by any such newspaper or periodical) which in the ordinary course of business publishes news items, editorials, or other comments, or paid advertisements, which directly or indirectly urge the passage or defeat of legislation, if such newspaper, periodical, or individual, engages in no further or other activities in connection with the passage or defeat of such legislation, other than to appear before a committee of the Congress of the United States in support of or in opposition to such legislation.

(b) All information required to be filed under the provisions of this section with the Clerk of the House of Representatives and the Secretary of the Senate shall be compiled by said Clerk and Secretary, acting jointly, as soon as practicable after the close of the calendar quarter with respect to which such information is filed and shall be printed in the Congressional Record.

REPORTS AND STATEMENTS TO BE MADE UNDER OATH

SEC. 309. All reports and statements required under this title shall be made under oath, before an officer authorized by law to administer oaths.

PENALTIES

SEC. 310. (a) Any person who violates any of the provisions of this title, shall, upon conviction, be guilty of a misdemeanor, and shall be punished by a fine of not more than $5,000 or imprisonment for not more than twelve months, or by both such fine and imprisonment.

(b) In addition to the penalties provided for in subsection (a), any person convicted of the misdemeanor specified therein is prohibited, for a period of three years from the date of such conviction, from attempting to influence, directly or indirectly, the passage or defeat of any proposed legislation, or from appearing before a committee of the Congress in support of or opposition to proposed legislation; and any person who violates any provision of this subsection shall, upon conviction thereof, be guilty of a felony, and shall be punished by a fine of not more than $10,000, or imprisonment for not more than five years, or by both such fine and imprisonment.

EXEMPTION

SEC. 311. The provisions of this title shall not apply to practices or activities regulated by the Federal Corrupt Practices Act nor be construed as repealing any portion of said Federal Corrupt Practices Act.

Appendix B

LOBBYING BEFORE STATE LEGISLATURES

Lobbying is not now nor has it ever been an activity confined to the Federal Congress. It has always existed in state legislatures, often more corruptly and brazenly than in Washington. Long before Congress enacted the Regulation of Lobbying Act certain state legislatures took official notice of this problem. As we have noted elsewhere the state of Georgia, in 1877, wrote into its constitution the axiom, still retained, that "lobbying is a crime." We have referred to the Massachusetts act of 1890, the Wisconsin acts of 1899 and 1905, and referred to the disclosures of the Armstrong investigation in New York in the latter year which led to the passage of the New York lobby regulation act. Today thirty-eight states and Alaska regulate lobbies by law other than those laws forbidding bribery.

The practices of lobbies and lobbyists before state legislatures do not differ from those before the Federal Congress. It is generally agreed by political scientists that state legislatures are more likely to be swayed by lobbying than the national Congress. The attempt of the real estate lobby to force Congress to turn over rent control to individual state legislatures is a case proving the point. Each state, of course, has its own peculiar problems because of its own local political and economic situations which create local pressures — such as the mining interests in Montana and the steel industry in Minnesota.

To examine lobbying in each state would be an interesting and rewarding task. John Gunther explored the power of state and city pressure groups in most of the states he visited while gathering material for *Inside U.S.A.* Valuable information about lobbying is contained in *Our Fair City*, edited by Robert Allen, and in *Politics of New York State*, by Warren Moscow. But the most carefully documented research into this problem has been done by Miss Belle Zeller, professor of political science at Brooklyn College. Miss Zeller's *Pressure Politics in New York* is a pioneer study in this field and an enduring classic. Her chapter "State Regulation of Lobbying" in *The Book of the States* describes state regulatory laws up to 1949. This, however, should be supplemented with a reading of Miss Zeller's statement and testimony before the House Select Committee on Lobbying Activities, which can be found in *Hearings*, Part 1. Her testimony before the Committee on the Organization of Congress and her valuable article in the *American Political Science Review*, April, 1948, should also be consulted.

In 1946, during the first administration of Governor Thomas E. Dewey, a joint committee inquiring into the New York State lobby act recommended that "all representatives of groups interested in legislation" be required to register "whether or not they are compensated for legislative appearances" and urged that lists of lobbyists and their sponsors be "posted conspicuously" and that detailed information regarding expenditures and their sources and purposes be made in monthly reports during the legislative session. "It is generally recognized," says the report, "that special interest groups will exist as long as citizens have the right to petition. . . . In our complex society it is perhaps inevitable that most recommendations for legislation should be channeled through assorted private organizations. In New York such groups compete with each other on equal terms. Experience is the great school in which legislators learn to identify special interests and to assess their strength and the size of their following. It is recognized, too, that the mere enactment of a law will not eliminate the occasional abuse that may arise in law-making. The law has yet to be enacted which will necessarily eliminate human ingenuity."

As is the case in many states the New York law fails to give any public official the specific police power of enforcing the registration act.

The joint committee's frank admission of the important part played in New York State by private pressure groups in the enactment of legislation — an admission which says, in effect, that the legislature would not know how to act if the lobbyists were not on hand to tell them — is explored in an interesting article by Judge Charles D. Breitel, former legislative counsel to Governor Dewey, who takes the stand that "it is not the institution of the lobbyist or the pressure group that is evil" and states: "The imperfections of man reflected in the legislative process yield deficiencies ranging from corruption to the abuses of pressure groups; from the uninhibited expression of popular will to the restrictive practices of an all-powerful rules committee." See New York *Legislative Document* (1946), no. 31, p. 27; "A Commentary on the Legislative Process," by Charles D. Breitel. *Syracuse Law Journal*, vol. 1, no. 1; also, E. B. Logan, editor, "Lobbying," *Supplement* of the *Annals of the American Academy of Political and Social Sciences*, July, 1929.

An interesting account of the relationship between state lobbying and the national scene can be found in *Dry Messiah*, by Virginius Dabney, where the methods employed by Bishop Cannon and others to force local prohibition laws through the Virginia legislature before moving on to greater national victories are described in all their grim details.

Notes

CHAPTER II

1. *Report of the Joint Committee of the Senate and the Assembly of the State of New York Appointed to Investigate the Affairs of Life Insurance Companies*, Albany, 1906. Vol. 10, pp. 398–402.
2. A brilliant study of Lester Ward, many of whose theories became realities under the New Deal, may be found in Henry Steele Commager's exciting and stimulating book, *The American Mind: An Interpretation of American Thought and Character Since the 1880's*. New Haven, 1950. See especially chapters X, XV, and XVI. The quotation is on p. 210.
3. R. M. MacIver, *The Web of Government*, New York, 1947, p. 220.
4. MacIver, *op. cit.*, p. 220.

CHAPTER III

1. Woodrow Wilson, *The New Freedom*, edited by W. B. Hale. New York, 1913.
2. Josephus Daniels, *The Wilson Era, 1917–1923*. Chapel Hill, 1944–1946, pp. 7–8.
3. Cordell Hull, assisted by Andrew Berding, *Memoirs*. New York, 1948, pp. 71–72.
4. Oswald Garrison Villard, *Free Trade — Free World*. New York, 1947, pp. 40–41.
5. Ray Allen Billington, *et al.*, *The United States: American Democracy in World Perspective*. New York, 1947, p. 253.
6. Kenneth G. Crawford, *The Pressure Boys*. New York, 1939, p. 47.
7. *House Report No. 113, 63rd Congress, 2nd Session*. A report of the Select Committee of the House of Representatives, under H. Res. 198, on Charges Against Members of the House and

Lobbying Activities of the National Association of Manufacturers of the United States, and Others. Washington, 1913.

8. *Hearings* before the Select Committee of the House of Representatives, appointed under H. Res. 198, Sixty-third Congress, first session, Part 24, p. 2129.

9. *House Report No. 113*, Sixty-third Congress, second session, p. 5.

10. *Ibid.*, p. 15.

11. Billington, *et al.*, *op. cit.*, p. 631.

12. Virginius Dabney, *Dry Messiah: The Life of Bishop Cannon.* New York, 1949, pp. 117–118.

13. Quoted by Charles W. Smith, Jr., *Public Opinion in a Democracy.* New York, 1939, p. 245.

14. Peter Odegard, *Pressure Politics.* New York, 1928, pp. 127–128.

CHAPTER IV

1. Crawford, *op. cit.*, p. 3.

2. *Congressional Record*, Sixty-eighth Congress, first session, p. 5798.

3. Marcus Duffield, *King Legion.* New York, 1931, p. 48. Mr. Taylor was still going strong in 1948. He was registered as a lobbyist for the American Legion. *Congressional Record*, vol. 93, no. 148 (I), p. 10746.

4. Duffield, *op. cit.*, pp. 48–49.

5. Cited, Duffield, *op. cit.*, p. 49. (Italics added.)

6. Roger Burlingame, "The Embattled Veterans," *Atlantic Monthly*, vol. clii, 1933, p. 393.

7. The Caraway Bill was S. 1095, Seventieth Congress, first session. December 5, 1927 – May 29, 1928. His definition leaned heavily on the Wisconsin statute.

8. *Senate Report 342*, Seventieth Congress, first session. Washington, 1928, pp. 2, 3.

9. Charles A. Beard and Mary R. Beard, *America in Midpassage.* New York, 1939, p. 51.

10. See throughout *Hearings Before the Special Committee Investigating the Munitions Industry*, United States Senate, Seventy-fourth Congress, first session. Washington, 1936.

11. *Investigation of Concentration of Economic Power.* Temporary National Economic Committee, Monograph No. 26, *Economic*

Power and Political Pressures, by Donald C. Blaisdell, assisted by Jane Greverus. Seventy-fifth Congress. Washington, 1941. Senator Clapper's quotation is cited from *America in Midpassage*, by Charles A. Beard and Mary R. Beard, New York, 1939, p. 392.

12. *New York Times*, January 1, 1950. Sec. 6, p. 29.

13. *Congressional Record*, Seventieth Congress, first session, pp. 2893–2894. Cited, TNEC, 26, pp. 156–157.

14. Federal Trade Commission, *Summary Report*. Doc. 92, Part 71A, Seventieth Congress, first session, p. 18.

CHAPTER V

1. Beards, *op. cit.*, p. 293.

2. *The Public Papers and Addresses of Franklin Delano Roosevelt*. New York, 1938, vol. IV, pp. 98–103.

3. TNEC, 26. See Note 11, Chapter IV. The monograph urged the "securing, and periodic publications, of data on lobbyists — names, sponsors, and principal sources of funds, receipts and disbursements, purposes of expenditures, especially for public relations services, advertising, radio, etc." It also thought private radio chains should be "required . . . as a condition of retaining their licenses and as a public service" to "publicize the activities of lobbyists in Washington and elsewhere." If this could not be done it suggested the establishment of a government-owned and -operated station for "the dissemination, among other things, of such information." P. 194.

CHAPTER VI

1. See: *Senate Report of Special Committee to Investigate the National Defense Program*. No. 480, Seventy-seventh Congress, second session; and No. 10, Seventy-eighth Congress, first session.

2. *The Reorganization of Congress*. A report of the Committee on Congress of the American Political Science Association, 1945, p. 80.

3. *Organization of Congress*. Report of Joint Committee on the Organization of Congress, pursuant to H. Con. Res. 18, Seventy-ninth Congress, second session. House Report No. 1675, and Senate Report No. 1400. Washington, 1946, p. 80. See also: *Organization of Congress*. Summary of Hearings Before the Joint Committee on the Organization of Congress. March 13 —

June 29, 1945. Seventh-ninth Congress, second session. Washington, 1945, throughout. Also, George B. Galloway, *Congress at the Crossroads*. New York, 1946, pp. 302–307.

4. *Organization of Congress*. Joint Report, p. 26.

5. *Ibid.*, p. 27.

6. *Legislative Reorganization Act of 1946*. Seventy-ninth Congress, second session. Senate Report No. 1400, pp. 4–5.

7. *Ibid.*, p. 27.

8. Harold J. Laski, *Parliamentary Government in England*. New York, 1938, p. 57. For an exciting discussion of congressional provincialism and the power of local pressure groups see James MacGregor Burns, *Congress on Trial*. New York, 1949.

9. *Newsweek*, July 8, 1946.

CHAPTER VII

1. *Senate Report No. 1400*, Seventy-ninth Congress, second session, p. 27.

2. *Congressional Record*, vol. 93, no. 148, pp. 10725–10726, 10727, 10746.

3. Ruth Finney, "Washington Lobbies," *American Mercury*, February, 1948.

4. *The Truman Program: Addresses and Messages by President Harry S. Truman*. Ed. by M. B. Schnapper. Washington, 1949.

5. Elmo Roper, "Public Found to Know Little of Pressure Groups," *New York Herald Tribune*, March 18, 1948; also *Fortune Magazine*, February, 1948.

6. *Congressional Record*, vol. 93, no. 70, pp. 3530–3531. Statement by Representative Arthur G. Klein of New York.

7. *Washington Star*, June 12, 1948.

8. *New York Herald Tribune*, February 17, 1948. (My italics.)

9. *Hearings Before the Committee on Expenditures in Executive Departments on Evaluation of Legislative Organization Act of 1946*. Eightieth Congress, second session. February, 1948, p. 116.

10. *Ibid.*, p. 94.

11. *New York Herald Tribune*, January 29, 1948.

CHAPTER VIII

1. *New York Herald Tribune*, November 24, 1948; *New York Times*, same date; *Congressional Quarterly Log*, April 14, 1950, pp. 439–442.

2. *Congressional Quarterly Log*, April 14, 1950, p. 439; *Report and Recommendations on Federal Lobbying Act* (H. Report No. 3239), pp. 22–23.
3. Schnapper, ed., *op. cit.*, p. 196.
4. *New York Times*, December 1, 1949.

CHAPTER IX

1. *Congressional Record*, vol. 95, no. 88, May 18, 1949, pp. 6547–6553; vol. 95, no. 147, August 12, 1949, pp. 11614–11618. All quotations in this section are from the above sources.
2. Eighty-first Congress, first session, H.R. 5784: A Bill to require legislative representatives to register and report. . . . Introduced July 27, 1949, and referred to the Judiciary Committee.
3. *Congressional Quarterly*, August 18, 1950, p. 929.
4. *Congressional Quarterly*, August 11, 1950, p. 887; August 25, 1950, p. 956.
5. *Congressional Quarterly*, September 15, 1950, p. 1035.
6. *Congressional Quarterly*, July 21, 1950, p. 823.
7. Lindsay Rogers, "When Congress Fumbles for Facts." *New York Herald Tribune*, March 29, 30, 31, 1950.
8. See *The Outlook*, November 27, 1929.

CHAPTER X

1. *General Interim Report of the House Select Committee on Lobbying Activities*, House of Representatives, Eighty-first Congress, second session. Washington, 1950, p. 4.
2. *Ibid.*, p. 5.
3. *Ibid.*, pp. 5–6.
4. *Ibid.*, p. 6.
5. *The Role of Lobbying in Representative Self-Government.* Part 1 of Hearings Before the House Select Committee on Lobbying Activities. House of Representatives. Eighty-first Congress, second session. Pursuant to H. Res. 298. Washington, 1950. Hereafter the documents of the committee will be referred to merely as *Hearings*. The full list of printings for the committee will be found in the Bibliography.
6. *Hearings*, Part 1, pp. 58–79. This is discussed in a later chapter.
7. *Ibid.*, pp. 132 ff. and pp. 151 ff. These are discussed in a later chapter. The hearings on specific lobbies are given separate chapters.

8. *Ibid.*, Part 3, p. 2.
9. Cited in *ibid.*, p. 4.
10. *Ibid.*, p. 39; *Yale Law Journal*, January, 1947, vol. 56, no. 2.
11. *Hearings*, Part 2, p. 5.
12. *Ibid.*, pp. 25–26; 45–46.
13. *Ibid.*, Part 4, pp. 98–99.
14. *Ibid.*, Part 7, p. 56.
15. *Interim Report*, p. 62.   All quotations to the end of this chapter are from pp. 62–67.

CHAPTER XI

1. June 12, 1950.
2. *New York Herald Tribune*, June 13, 1950.
3. *Hearings*, Part 4, pp. 9–10.
4. *Ibid.*, pp. 68–70, 155–161, 196–200.
5. *Interim Report*, table, p. 9.
6. *New York Times*, October 23, 1950.
7. *Washington Post*, October 27, 1950.
8. *Congressional Quarterly*, June 16, 1950, pp. 675–682.
9. *Interim Report*, p. 22; *Hearings*, Part 8, pp. 114–115.
10. *Hearings*, Part 2, p. 530.
11. *Interim Report*, p. 10.
12. Read's salary from *New York Post*, March 4, 1949; CCG spending figure from *Congressional Quarterly*, February 24, 1950; Hart salary from *Hearings*, Part 4, p. 69.
13. *Interim Report*, pp. 10–11.
14. *Hearings*, Part 4, p. 69.
15. *Interim Report*, p. 10.
16. *Hearings*, Part 4, p. 76.
17. *Ibid.*, pp. 60–61.
18. *Ibid.*, p. 78.
19. *Interim Report*, pp. 11, 20.
20. *Hearings*, Part 5, pp. 143 f.; *Interim Report*, p. 12.
21. *New York Times*, June 28, 1950.
22. *Interim Report*, pp. 32–33.
23. "Statement by Representative Clyde Doyle, of California, Member, House Select Committee on Lobbying Activities. Subject: The Facts Concerning 'Educator-Publisher' Edward A. Rumely." Issued, mimeographed, June 29, 1950, Washington. Cited, *Report and Recommendations*, p. 24, fn. 71.

24. *Hearings*, Part 1, p. 35.
25. *Ibid.*, pp. 36, 39.
26. Compiled from *Congressional Quarterly Reports*. See especially February 24, 1950, p. 209, and September 15, 1950, pp. 1035–1036.

CHAPTER XII

1. *Hearings*, Part 8, pp. 119, 169.
2. *Ibid.*, Part 7, p. 7; Part 8, p. 97.
3. *Hearings*, Part 8, pp. 22–23. Certificate of incorporation, Foundation for Economic Education. This, it is only fair to point out, was signed by the incorporators on March 7, 1946, five months before the Registration of Lobbying Act of 1946 became law on August 2, 1946.
4. *Hearings*, Part 7, p. 9.
5. *Labor*, March 26, 1949, p. 2.
6. *Congressional Quarterly*, February 24, 1950, p. 290.
7. *Hearings*, Part 1, pp. 34–35; Part 8, pp. 57–58.
8. *New York Post*, March 4, 1949.
9. *Hearings*, Part 8, pp. 12–20, p. 52; also *Interim Report*, table, p. 13.
10. *Hearings*, Part 8, p. 4.
11. *Interim Report*, pp. 22–23.
12. *Hearings*, Part 8, pp. 114–115.
13. *Interim Report*, p. 33.
14. *Ibid.*, p. 34.
15. *Hearings*, Part 8, p. 113.
16. *Ibid.*, p. 9.
17. *Ibid.*, p. 82.
18. *Interim Report*, p. 35.
19. *Hearings*, Part 8, pp. 119–120.
20. *Ibid.*, Part 2, p. 5.
21. *Ibid.*, Part 8, p. 179.
22. *Ibid.*, pp. 134–138.
23. *Ibid.*, Part 7, p. 46.
24. *Ibid.*, pp. 4, 5.
25. Compiled from *ibid.*, pp. 62–65.
26. *Ibid.*, pp. 65–69.
27. *Ibid.*, p. 72; the list of sixty-five is on *ibid.*, p. 42.
28. *Ibid.*, p. 25.
29. *Ibid.*, pp. 48–49, 52.

CHAPTER XIII

1. *FDR: His Personal Letters. 1928–1945,* edited by Elliott Roosevelt and Joseph P. Lash. New York, 1950, vol. 1, pp. 94–95.
2. *Hearings,* Part 5, p. 442.
3. *Interim Report,* p. 31.
4. *Ibid.,* p. 2, n. 1; p. 36. *Hearings,* Part 7, p. 59.
5. Quoted from *Congressional Record* in *New York Post,* November 3, 1950.

CHAPTER XIV

1. *Interim Report,* p. 23.
2. *Hearings,* Part 2, p. 964.
3. *Ibid.,* pp. 1097–1098.
4. *Ibid.,* p. 958.
5. *Ibid.,* Appendix, exhibits 262–303, 350–457, pp. 822–860, 954–1083.
6. *Ibid.,* p. 958.
7. *Ibid.,* p. 1341. The local lobbyist was Earle M. Willis of the Housing Authority of the City of Lakeland, Florida, and the congressman was J. Hardin Peterson of the First Florida District.
8. *Ibid.,* pp. 543–544.
9. *New York Times,* November 4, 1950.
10. *Ibid.*
11. *Interim Report,* p. 44.
12. *Hearings,* Part 2, p. 879.
13. From a release by the National Association of Home Builders. *Hearings,* Part 2, p. 531.
14. *Interim Report,* p. 38.
15. *Ibid.,* p. 42.

CHAPTER XV

1. *Interim Report,* p. 65; *Report and Recommendations,* pp. 1–2.
2. *Interim Report,* pp. 65–67.
3. See *The Theory and Practice of Modern Government,* by Herman Finer, rev. ed., New York, 1949. Pages 463–470 describe and discuss lobbying techniques in Great Britain, Germany and France.
4. *Interim Report,* p. 66.
5. *Toward a More Responsible Two-Party System. A Report of the Committee on Political Parties.* American Political Science Association. New York, 1950.

6. *Interim Report,* p. 66.
7. *Ibid.,* pp. 66–67.
8. *New York Journal American,* July 13, 1950; cited, *Report and Recommendations,* p. 4, fn. 11; pp. 43–44.
9. *Report and Recommendations,* p. 4.

CHAPTER XVI

1. James R. Newman and Byron S. Miller, *The Control of Atomic Energy. A study of Its Social, Economic and Political Implications.* New York, 1948, pp. 3–4.
2. John A. Simpson, "The Scientists as Public Educators: A Two-Year Summary," *Bulletin of Atomic Scientists,* vol. 3, no. 6, September, 1947.
3. Newman and Miller, *op. cit.,* p. 9.
4. Newman and Miller, *op. cit.,* pp. 16–17, 173, 176. The registered lobbyists for the National Association of Manufacturers list "subsidization of research" among legislation to which they are opposed. See 1947–1949 quarterly reports in the *Congressional Record.*
5. Newman and Miller, *op. cit.,* pp. 19–20.
6. Newman and Miller, *op. cit.,* p. 23.
7. *Fortune,* vol. xxxviii, no. 5, November, 1948, pp. 107–112, 192 f.

A Selected Bibliography

The literature on lobbying is extensive and varied. I have made use in some way of all the books, newspaper and magazine articles, government reports and publications, and other works listed below. To some of the listings I have added comment that may possibly be of interest to the general reader or of help to the student of this subject. In the footnotes I have indicated the source of quotations in the text. To those authors from whose work I have borrowed brief quotations I herewith give due acknowledgment and my thanks.

A. Congress of the United States

I. PUBLIC DOCUMENTS RELATING TO THE REGULATION OF LOBBYING ACT OF 1946

Organization of Congress. Report of the Joint Committee on the Organization of Congress, pursuant to *H. Res. 18,* Seventy-ninth Congress, second session. *House Report No. 1675* and *Senate Report No. 1400.* Washington, 1946. *Summary of Hearings, March 13 — June 29, 1945.* Washington, 1945.

Congressional Record, passim, index under Lobbying, and related titles.

Public Law 601, Seventy-ninth Congress, Second Session, Ch. 753 (S. 2177), Title III, *The Federal Regulation of Lobbying Act of 1946.*

Hearings Before the Committee on Expenditures in the Executive Departments on Evaluations of the Legislative Reorganization Act of 1946, Eightieth Congress, second session, February 2, 17, 18, 23, and 25, 1948. Washington, 1948.

II. PUBLIC DOCUMENTS RELATING TO THE INVESTIGATION IN 1950 BY THE HOUSE SELECT COMMITTEE ON LOBBYING ACTIVITIES

H. Con. Res. 62, May 18, 1949, Eighty-first Congress, first session.
S. Con. Res. 41, May 26, 1949, Eighty-first Congress, first session.

H.R. 5784, July 27, 1949, Eighty-first Congress, first session (the so-called Buchanan bill, not reported out of committee).

H. Res. 297 and *H. Res. 298,* July 27, 1949, Eighty-first Congress, first session (the resolutions setting up the House Select Committee on Lobbying Activities).

Congressional Record, vol. 95, no. 88, pp. 6547–6553; vol. 95, no. 157, pp. 11614–11618 (debate on the joint resolution and the House resolution (*H. Res. 298,* above).

Select Committee on Lobbying Activities of the House of Representatives, Eighty-first Congress, second session, *Administration of the Lobby Registration Provision of the Legislative Reorganization Act of 1946,* by W. Brooke Graves; *The Role of Lobbying in Representative Self-Government,* Hearings, Part 1; *Lobbying Direct and Indirect:* Hearings, Part 2, Housing Lobby; Hearings, Part 3, Contingent Fee Lobbying; Hearings, Part 4, National Economic Council, Inc.; Hearings, Part 5, Committee for Constitutional Government; Hearings, Part 6, Americans for Democratic Action; Hearings, Part 7, Public Affairs Institute; Hearings, Part 8, Foundation for Economic Education, Inc.; Hearings, Part 9, Civil Rights Congress; Hearings, Part 10, Legislative Activities of Executive Agencies. *Expenditures by Corporations to Influence Legislation* (H. Report No. 3137). *General Interim Report* (H. Report No. 3138); *United States Savings and Loan League* (H. Report No. 3139); *Conference of Small Business Organizations* (H. Report No. 3232); *Expenditures by Farm and Labor Organizations to Influence Legislation and Supplement to Expenditures by Corporations* (H. Report No. 3238); *Report and Recommendations on Federal Lobbying Act* (H. Report No. 3239); *Report and Recommendations on Federal Lobbying Act, Minority Views* (H. Report No. 3239, Part 2). Washington, 1950.

III. OTHER PUBLIC DOCUMENTS OF INTEREST IN CONNECTION WITH LOBBYING ACTIVITIES

House Report No. 113, 63rd Congress, 2nd Session, Select Committee of the House on Charges against Members of the House and Lobbying Activities of the National Association of Manufacturers of the United States and Others. Washington, 1913.

Summary Report, Federal Trade Commission, Doc. 92, Part 71A, Seventieth Congress, first session. Washington, 1928.

Senate Report No. 342 and S. 1905, Caraway Bill, Seventieth Congress, first session. Washington, 1928.

Senate Report No. 3, Utilities Corporations, Doc. 92, Part 3, Seventieth Congress, first session. Washington, 1928.

Hearings Before the Special Committee Investigating the Munitions Industry, United States Senate, Seventy-fourth Congress, first session. Washington, 1936.

Violation of Free Speech and Rights of Labor, Report of the Committee on Labor and Education pursuant to S. Res. 266, Seventy-fourth Congress Report No. 6, Part 6: Labor Policies of Employers' Associations, Part III, the National Association of Manufacturers. Washington, 1939.

Temporary National Economic Committee, Seventy-sixth Congress, first session: *Hearings*, Part 10, Life Insurance: Intercompany Agreements, Terminations, Savings Bank, Insurance, Legislative Activities; *Final Report of the Executive Secretary*; Monograph No. 26, *Economic Power and Political Pressures*, by Donald C. Blaisdell and Jane Greverus. Washington, 1940.

Atomic Energy Act of 1946, *Hearings*, Seventy-ninth Congress, first session, 5 parts. Washington, 1945, 1946.

Administrative Procedure Act, *Legislative History, 1944–1946*. Washington, 1947.

Labor-Management Relations Act of 1947, *Legislative History*, 2 vols. Washington, 1948.

B. Other Material

Aikman, Duncan, "Lobbyist — 1936 Model," *New York Times Magazine*, March 13, 1936.

Allen, Robert, syndicated Washington column, *passim*.

American Political Science Association, *Towards a More Responsible Two-Party System. A Report of the Committee on Political Parties*. New York, 1950.

—— *American Political Science Review, passim*.

Annals of the American Academy of Political and Social Sciences, especially: "Lobbying," July, 1929; "Pressure Groups and Propaganda," edited by H. L. Childs, May, 1935; "Pressure Groups and Foreign Policy," by H. H. Sprout, May, 1935; "Lobbies and Pressure Groups," by B. Zeller, G. L. Schermerhorn, H. Parkman, Jr., January, 1938; "Pressure Groups and Administrative Agencies," by

H. S. Foster, May, 1942; "Administrative Regulation of Private Enterprise," March, 1947; "Pressure Groups vs. Political Parties," by E. E. Schattschneider, September, 1948.

Bailey, Stephen K., *Congress Makes a Law*. New York, 1950.

Brown, Nona Baldwin, "Long Distance Lobby," *New York Times Magazine*, September 25, 1949.

Beard, Charles A., "Whom Does Congress Represent?" *Harpers*, January, 1930.

— and Mary R. Beard, *America in Midpassage*. New York, 1939.

Bentley, A. F., *The Process of Government*. Chicago, 1908.

Billington, Ray Allen, James Loewenberg and Samuel Hugh Brockunier, *The United States: American Democracy in World Perspective*. New York, 1947. The best one-volume history of the United States I have recently encountered. It pays attention throughout to the part played in our history by pressure groups. It is intelligently informative, and deserves to be read.

Binkley, Wilfred E., *President and Congress*. New York, 1947.

— and Malcolm C. Moos, *A Grammar of Politics: The National Government*. New York, 1949. This is an excellent book about our form of government, which treats adequately the part played by lobbies and lobbyists.

Brogan, Denis W., *The Era of Franklin D. Roosevelt*. Chronicles of America Series, vol. 52. New Haven, 1950. The student of government who has not read as much of Mr. Brogan as he can get his hands upon is missing an intellectual treat. No Britisher and few Americans understand the United States better.

Breitel, Charles D., "A Commentary on the Legislative Process," *Syracuse Law Journal*, vol. 1, no. 1, Spring, 1949.

Buck, S. J., *The Granger Movement*, Cambridge, Massachusetts, 1913.

Burlingame, Roger, "The Embattled Veterans," *Atlantic Monthly*, vol. clii, 1933.

Burns, James MacGregor, *Congress on Trial*. New York, 1949. One of the best and brightest dissertations on how Congress and its members work, with some intelligent recommendations towards improving the democratic legislative process.

Carlson, John Roy, *The Plotters*. New York, 1946.

Caton, Bruce, *The War Lords of Washington*. New York, 1949.

Chamber of Commerce of the United States, *Policies Supported As In The Public Interest*. Washington, 1936. *Policies Advocated by the Chamber of Commerce of the United States*. Washington, 1940.

Chase, Stuart, *Democracy Under Pressure*. New York, 1945.

Cleveland, Alfred S., "NAM: Spokesman for Industry," *Harvard Business Review*, vol. xxvi, no. 3, May, 1948. A brief but cogent study of the National Association of Manufacturers. It contains an interesting summary of the NAM's legislative stands in recent years.

Comer, J. P., *Legislative Functions of National Administrative Authorities*. New York, 1927.

Commager, Henry Steele, *The American Mind: An Interpretation of American Thought and Character Since the 1880's*. New Haven, 1950. Informative for its animadversions on Bentley, Ward, and other thinkers about democracy.

Congressional Quarterly News Reports: Weekly Log: Annual Almanac. Washington, 1947–1950. Since the passage of the Regulation of Lobbying Act of 1946 this factual and complete report of the day-by-day doings of Congress has maintained a virtual monopoly on the coverage of the reporting and filing of information required by the act and it has consistently reported all identifiable lobbying activity in connection with pending legislation. Without bias or editorial slant, the CQ *Reports* have filled a hitherto lamentable gap in Washington news coverage. I believe it no exaggeration to say that 80 per cent of the news and editorial articles that have appeared in the national press about Washington lobbying have stemmed from these unique weekly reports. The CQ *Log* is sold on a pro rata basis to newspapers, magazines, individual writers, columnists and radio commentators. The annual *Almanac* is (or should be) available in all well-equipped libraries. It is excellently indexed. By means of it one can trace back the source of pressures for or against almost any piece of legislation before Congress. Wise editors have made excellent use of the CQ lobby reports, thus keeping their readers well informed of an aspect of the democratic legislative process too often neglected by the daily press coverage of the national capital.

Crawford, Kenneth G., *The Pressure Boys*. New York, 1939.

Dabney, Virginius, *The Dry Messiah*. New York, 1949.

—— "Prohibition's Ghost Walks Again," *Collier's*, November 6, 1949.

Dahl, Robert A., *Congress and Foreign Policy*. New York, 1950.

Daniels, Josephus, *The Wilson Era, 1917–1923*. Chapel Hill, 1944–1946.

de Roos, Robert, *The Thirsty Land*. Stanford, 1948.

de Roos, Robert, and Arthur A. Maass, "The Lobby That Can't Be Licked: Congress and the Army Engineers," *Harper's*, August, 1949.

Detzer, Dorothy, *Appointment on the Hill*. New York, 1948. An honest lobbyist for peace tells of her experiences on Capitol Hill with humor and insight. A good account of how lobbyists actually work for their causes.

Dillon, Mary E., "Pressure Groups," *American Political Science Review*, vol. 36, 1942.

Dorfman, Joseph, *The Economic Mind in America, 1606–1918*. 3 vols. New York, 1946 and 1949.

Douglas, Paul H., with James G. Derieux, "Big Grab at Washington," *Collier's*, vol. 125, no. 6, February 11, 1950.

Duffield, Marcus, *King Legion*. New York, 1931.

Finer, Herman, *The Theory and Practice of Modern Governments*, revised edition. New York, 1949. Dr. Finer's information about lobbying in European nations, especially by big business interests, is extremely valuable. He contrasts various systems with our own.

Finney, Ruth, "Washington Lobbies," *American Mercury*, February, 1948.

Flynn, John T., *The Road Ahead*. New York, 1949.

Galloway, George B., *Congress at the Crossroads*. New York, 1946.

Gray, Justin, *The Story of the Legion*. New York, 1948. Although *King Legion* by Marcus Duffield is an older book, it is a far better study than Mr. Gray's, and gives a clear if dated picture of the Legion as a lobby.

Gunther, John, *Inside U.S.A.* New York, 1947. Valuable for first-hand accounts of lobbying in the various states visited.

Hartley, Fred A., Jr., *Our New National Labor Policy*. New York, 1948.

Herring, E. Pendleton, *Group Representation Before Congress*. Washington, 1949.

—— *Public Administration and the Public Interest*. New York, 1936.

Holcombe, A. N., *The Political Parties of Today*. New York, 1924.

Hull, Cordell, *The Memoirs of Cordell Hull*. New York, 1948.

Johnson, Gerald, *Incredible Tale*. New York, 1950.

Kefauver, Estes, "Democracy's Bottleneck," *New York Herald Tribune*, May 9, 1948.

—— and Jack Levin, *A 20th Century Congress*. New York, 1947.

Kent, Frank R., *The Great Game of Politics*. New York, 1924.

Key, V. O., *Politics, Parties, and Pressure Groups*, second edition. New York, 1948. This is exactly what its title says; a study (perhaps the best) of politics, parties, and pressure groups and their relationships to each other, that is basic to any considered study of the subject of lobbies and lobbyists.

La Follette, Robert M., Jr., "Some Lobbies Are Good," *New York Times Magazine*, May 16, 1948.

Laski, Harold J., *Parliamentary Government In England*. New York, 1938. *The American Democracy*, New York, 1948.

Lasswell, H. D., *Politics — Who Gets What, When, How?* New York, 1926.

Liebling, A. J., "The Press," *Holiday*, vol. 7, no. 2, February, 1950.

Lipsett, Alexander S., "Congressional Lobbyists," *New York Times*, August 26, 1948.

Long, Stuart, "Thunder on the Right," *The Reporter*, June 6, 1950.

Lynch, David, *The Concentration of Economic Power*. New York, 1936.

McBain, H. L., "Does a Minority Rule America?" *New York Times*, June 7, 1931.

MacIver, R. M., *The Web of Government*. New York, 1947.

—— "Pressure Groups," *Encyclopaedia of Social Sciences*.

Markel, Lester, *et al.*, *Public Opinion and Foreign Policy*. New York, 1949.

Meigs, Cornelia, *The Violent Men*. New York, 1949.

Mencken, H. L., *The American Language*, fourth edition. New York, 1936.

Merrian, C. E., and H. F. Gosnell, *The American Party System*. New York, 1929.

Munro, W. B., *The Invisible Government*. New York, 1928.

National Association of Manufacturers, *The American Individual Enterprise System*, 2 vols. New York, 1946.

—— *Fact and Fancy in TNEC Monographs*, John Scoville and Noel Sargent, compilers. New York, 1942.

National Resources Committee, *Structure of the American Economy*. New York, 1946.

Nevins, Allan, *Ordeal of the Union*, 2 vols. New York, 1949.

Newman, James R., and Byron S. Miller, *The Control of Atomic Energy: A Study of its Social, Economic and Political Implications*.

New York, 1948. For the legislative history of the Atomic Energy Act of 1946 and an on-the-scene interpretation of the legislative intent of the authors of the act this book is essential.

Nichols, Roy, *The Disruption of the American Democracy*. New York, 1948.

Nicolson, Harold, *The Congress of Vienna*. New York, 1946.

Odegard, Peter, *Pressure Politics*. New York, 1928. Still the best story of how prohibition was foisted on the country by the Anti-Saloon League lobby.

Othman, Frederick C., "Wild Lobbyists I have Known," *Saturday Evening Post*, March 6, 1948.

Payne, Robert, *Report on America*. New York, 1949.

Phillipps, Cabell, "200,000 Lobbies," *New York Times*, March 27, 1949.

Rogers, Lindsay, *The Pollsters*. New York, 1949. This wholly delightful examination of polls contains much of value from a long-time student of pressure politics.

—— "When Congress Fumbles for Facts," *New York Herald Tribune*, March 29, 30, 31, 1950. A serious study of congressional investigating committees and why they don't always work well, with recommendations for their betterment.

Roosevelt, Elliott, and Joseph P. Lash, editors, *FDR: His Personal Letters, 1928–1945*, vol. 1. New York, 1947.

Rosen, S. McKee, *The Political Process*. New York, 1925.

Rosenman, Samuel, *The Public Papers and Addresses of Franklin Delano Roosevelt*, 4 vols. New York, 1950.

Samuels, Ernest, *The Young Henry Adams*. Cambridge, Massachusetts, 1948.

Schattschneider, E. E., *Politics, Pressures, and the Tariff*. New York, 1935.

Schlesinger, Arthur M., Jr., *The Vital Center*, New York, 1949.

Schnapper, M. B., editor, *The Truman Program. Addresses and Messages of President Harry S. Truman*. Washington, 1949.

Simpson, John A., "The Scientists As Public Educators: A Two-Year Summary," *Bulletin of the Atomic Scientists*, vol. 3, no. 9, September, 1947.

Smith, Charles W., Jr., *Public Opinion in a Democracy*. New York, 1939.

Spargo, Mary, series on lobbying, *Washington Post*, October 9, 1949, *et seq*.

Spitz, David, *Patterns of Anti-Democratic Thought*. New York, 1949.

State of New York, *Report of the Joint Committee of the Senate and Assembly of the State of New York Appointed to Investigate the Affairs of Life Insurance Companies*, vol. 10. Albany, 1906.

Stokes, Thomas, syndicated Washington column, *passim*.

Toulmin, Henry A., Jr., *Diary of Democracy: The Senate War Investigating Committee*. New York, 1947.

Trott, Harlan, "Lobbyists Really Swarm," *Christian Science Monitor*, May 26, 1948.

United Press, lobbying roundup by Washington staff, *Kansas City Star*, January 11, 1949.

U. S. News and World Report, "About Controls on Lobbyists," December 17, 1948.

Van Deusen, Glyndon G., *Thurlow Weed: Wizard of the Lobby*. Boston, 1947.

Villard, Oswald Garrison, *Free Trade — Free World*. New York, 1947.

Von Mises, Ludwig, *Human Action*. New Haven, 1949.

Voorhis, Jerry, *Confessions of a Congressman*. New York, 1948.

Welles, Sumner, "Pressure Groups and Foreign Policy," *Atlantic Monthly*, November, 1947.

Walker, Harvey, *Law-Making in the United States*. New York, 1934.

White, L. D., *Public Administration*. New York, 1926.

Willoughby, W. W., and Lindsay Rogers, *An Introduction to the Problem of Government*. New York, 1921.

Wilson, Woodrow, *The New Freedom*, edited by W. B. Hale. New York, 1913.

—— *Congressional Government*. Boston, 1895.

—— *Constitutional Government in the United States*. New York, 1908.

Yale Law Journal, unsigned article on the Lobby Act of 1946, vol. 56, no. 2, January, 1947.

Zegoria, Sam, "Advertising: New Lobbying Technique," *Guild Reporter*, June 11, 1948.

Zeller, Belle, *Pressure Politics in New York*. New York, 1937.

—— "The Federal Regulation of Lobbying Act," *American Political Science Review*, vol. xlii, no. 2, April, 1948.

—— "State Regulation of Lobbying Act," *The Book of the States*, *1948–1949*. Chicago, 1949.

Acknowledgments

My thanks go to all those scholars and journalists of whose labors I have made generous use. And I should like to thank Stanley Salmen and Dudley and Jeannette Cloud for many kindnesses and much patience, and Clayton H. Knowles and Samuel Shaffer of the Washington press corps, who were always willing to help.

Index

Index